BRAZIL, 1964–1985

THE YALE-HOOVER SERIES ON AUTHORITARIAN REGIMES

BRAZIL, 1964–1985

THE MILITARY REGIMES OF

LATIN AMERICA IN THE COLD WAR

HERBERT S. KLEIN AND
FRANCISCO VIDAL LUNA

HOOVER INSTITUTION
STANFORD UNIVERSITY
STANFORD, CALIFORNIA

Yale UNIVERSITY PRESS
New Haven and London

Yale University Press books may be purchased in quantity for educational, business,
or promotional use. For information, please e-mail sales.press@yale.edu (U.S. office) or
sales@yaleup.co.uk (U.K. office).

Set in Sabon type by Newgen North America.
Printed in the United States of America.

ISBN 978-0-300-22331-6
Library of Congress Control Number: 2016951587
A catalogue record for this book is available from the British Library.

This paper meets the requirements of ANSI/NISO z39.48-1992 (Permanence of Paper).

10 9 8 7 6 5 4 3 2 1

Contents

Introduction

THE TWENTY YEARS from the 1960s to the 1980s were among the most bitter and difficult periods in Latin American history. The progressive overthrow of one democratic regime after another by national military establishments led to the collapse of democratic rule throughout much of the hemisphere. Previously long-term stable democratic societies succumbed to authoritarian military regimes, which often used violence against their citizens on an unprecedented scale. Thought was controlled, opponents were killed or exiled, and fear became the cement that kept most of these regimes in power. All of this occurred in the context of the Cold War, the long postwar international conflict between the United States and the Soviet Union, which led the United States, especially after the Cuban Revolution of 1959, to support many of these authoritarian governments.

But just as there were different preexisting democratic states, there were different styles of military regimes that emerged in this period. Some led to dictatorships of one-man rule, as in the case of Chile, and others guaranteed that such a dictatorship would not be the norm, either because of institutional instability in the army or because the army itself was powerful enough to maintain the institution above the demands of any particular individual. In the first case, typified by the Bolivian experience, this led to constant regime change under competing military officers. In the second, as in Brazil, Uruguay, and Peru, it led to orderly transitions that mimicked democratic presidential terms.

Moreover, not all regimes had the same ideology. Some, like Argentina, were primarily repressive states with little interest in promoting an economic or social agenda, while others were bent on restructuring their societies in a profoundly new way, as was the case with Peru, Brazil, and Chile. For all their hostility to previous democratic governments, some of these regimes continued to develop earlier institutions and programs of the overthrown democratic states and can be seen as a continuum of previous eras. Although anticommunism and fear of popular mobilization were common motivations in all these regimes, how to deal with demands for social and economic change differed among Latin American authoritarian governments. Some were totally repressive and hoped that the opposition could be simply liquidated and never return. Others tried divide and rule, as in Bolivia, whose military used peasant unions to put down miner unions and the urban Marxist parties. Others, such as leaders in the military government in Peru and Brazil, tried to modernize their societies and resolve social, economic, and class conflicts by forcing through basic reforms from above. They in essence tried to anticipate potential radical movements by providing land reform, or creating a modern social welfare system, or even by completely reorganizing the state and the economy in the name of a new definition of the state and the economy. But even in these reformist states there were major differences among the types of regimes that adopted authoritarian "developmentalist" models. Some primarily emphasized the takeover by the state of the economy; others applied a mix of private and public capital; while still others adopted radical neoliberal models and rejected the role of the state in education and the economy and even in the provision of social welfare.

In the case of the Peruvian, Brazilian, and Chilean military governments, many of the programs and reforms initiated by these regimes would survive and become part of the basic post-military democratic governmental structure. On the other hand, the overthrow of the Argentine and Uruguayan military regimes left few positive changes that the post-military democratic governments could adopt. But the state violence unleashed by the military in this period also had important unintended consequences that would lead to profound changes in the post-military era. Except for the Peruvians, all of these military regimes used state terror to control their populations, which resulted in a long and bloody history of torture and killings. It was this extraordinary violence of the military era and the bitter defeat of armed revolutionary movements of the period that profoundly changed the entire ideology of the democratic political world in Latin America after 1990. For the parties of the center and the left, human rights became a fundamental part of democratic politics. In many post-military regimes, this led to multiparty coalitions of the center-left, which eventually brought the left back to power in most of these countries, sometimes even with the old guerrilla leaders becoming president. It also convinced the civilian right-wing parties that calling in the military for support could only lead to disaster. Thus, in virtually all of the major South American states that experienced military regimes, one of the most important results of the military era was the emergence of a renewed and more powerful democratic state in the region, something most of these regimes did not anticipate or wish to occur.

In this volume we both survey and compare the experience of the major military regimes of South America in the period of the Cold War, from their origins and evolution to their final conclusions. We have selected these regimes because they were more independent of North American influence than the states of the Caribbean and Central America, which experienced a nonending North American influence that rendered their regimes far less stable both before and after the military era of the 1960s to the 1980s. In fact, for all their violence and constant cross-border invasions of dissidents and rebels, with the exception of Guatemala, they offer no real comparison to the experience of the significant South American countries.

How all these major regimes evolved is best seen from the experience of one such state. For this we have selected for more detailed study the Brazilian military governments of the period 1964–85. In this in-depth analysis we concentrate on the political, economic, and social evolution of this regime, which had a profound impact on modern Brazilian developments. We also try to situate this Brazilian experience in the context of the other South American countries that passed through this extraordinary period in the history of the continent.

This work is a synthesis of our own monographic studies published in Portuguese, English, and Spanish, as well a large number of contemporaneous and more recent studies that have dealt with this period.[1] Given the extensive literature on revolutionary protest and democratic opposition against the regime, we have concentrated more on the economic and social changes that have received less attention. There is also a vast literature on the return to democratic rule, which occurred after our period of analysis. Our survey of Chile, Uruguay, Argentina, and Bolivia is based on ongoing extensive research on the regimes in these countries; this has not been the case for the Velasco period in Peru, however, which was well studied at the time it was in power. In the case of Brazil, the fiftieth anniversary of the founding of the military regime is now producing an impressive rethinking of all aspects of its time in power, and we hope this study will contribute to this basic reanalysis of the Brazilian experience.

*

We would especially like to thank Sonia Rocha, Antonio Zapata, Ivan Jaksic, and Alexander Galetovic for their help with our research on the different regimes discussed in this study, and Matiko Vidal Kume for her editorial assistance. We would also like to acknowledge the support provided by Eric Waikin, director of the Hoover Archives and Library, and the editors of the Yale-Hoover Series on Authoritarian Regimes.

Abbreviations

ABI	Associação Brasileira de Imprensa
ADN	Acción Democrática Nacionalista
AGF	Aquisições do Governo Federal
AI to AI8	Atos Institucionais
APRA	Alianza Popular Revolucionaria Americana
ARENA	Aliança Renovadora Nacional
BNDE	Banco Nacional de Desenvolvimento Econômico
BNDES	Banco Nacional de Desenvolvimento Econômico e Social
BNH	Banco Nacional da Habitação
BPC	Benefício de Prestação Continuada
CAEM	Centro de Altos Estudios Militares
CAP	Caixa de Aposentadoria e Pensões
CAPES	Coordenação de Aperfeiçoamento de Pessoal de Nível Superior
CELADE	Centro Latinoamericano y Caribeño de Demografía
CENIMAR	Centro de Informações da Marinha
CEPAL	Comisión Económica para América Latina y el Caribe
CLT	Consolidação das Leis do Trabalho
CNBB	Confederação Nacional dos Bispos do Brasil

CNPq	Conselho Nacional de Desenvolvimento Científico e Tecnológico
CNT	Confederación Nacional de Trabajo
COB	Confederación de Obreros Bolivianos
COMIBOL	Corporación Minera de Bolivia
CONTAG	Confederação Nacional dos Trabalhadores na Agricultura
CVM	Comissão de Valores Mobiliários
DASP	Departamento Administrativo do Serviço Público
DNS	Departamento Nacional de Saúde
DNSAMS	Diretoria Nacional de Saúde e Assistência Médico-Social
DNSP	Departamento Nacional de Saúde Pública
DOI-CODI	Departamento de Operações de Informações–Centro de Operações de Defesa Interna
DOPS	Departamento de Ordem Politica e Social
EAPPs	Entidades Aberta de Previdência Privada
ECLA	Economic Commission for Latin American and the Caribbean
EFPPs	Entidades Fechada de Previdência Privada
EGF	Empréstimos do Governo Federal
EMBRAER	Empresa Brasileira de Aeronáutica
EMBRAPA	Empresa Brasileira de Pesquisa Agropecuária
EMG	Estado Maior Geral
ESG	Escola Superior de Guerra
FGTS	Fundo de Garantia por Tempo de Serviço
FIESP	Federação das Indústrias do Estado de São Paulo
FSTMB	Federación Sindical de Trabajadores Mineros de Bolivia
FUNRURAL	Fundo de Assistência ao Trabalhador Rural
GDP	Gross Domestic Product
GRFA	Gobierno Revolucionario de la Fuerza Armada
IAP	Instituto de Aposentadorias e Pensões
IAPAS	Instituto de Administração Financeira da Previdência e Assistência Social
IAPS	Institutos de Aposentadoria e Pensões
IBAD	Instituto Brasileiro de Ação Democratica
IBC	Instituto Brasileiro do Café

IBGE	Instituto Brasileiro de Geografia e Estatística
IMF	International Monetary Fund
INAMPS	Instituto Nacional de Assistência Médica e Previdência Social
INPS	Instituto Nacional de Previdência Social
INSS	Instituto Nacional de Seguro Social
IPEA	Instituto de Pesquisa Econômica Aplicadas
IPES	Instituto de Pesquisa e Estudos Sociais
IPM	Inquérito Policial Militar
LOAS	Lei Orgânica da Assistência Social
LTN	Letras do Tesouro Nacional
MDB	Movimento Democrático Brasileiro
MIR	Movimiento de Izquierda Revolucionaria
MNL-T	Movimiento Liberación Nacional
MNR	Movimiento Nacionalista Revolucionario
OAB	Ordem dos Advogados do Brasil
OBAN	Operação Bandeirantes
ORTN	Obrigações Reajustáveis do Tesouro Nacional
PAEG	Programa de Ação Econômica do Governo
PASEP	Programa de Formação do Patrimônio do Servidor Público
PCB	Partido Comunista Brasileiro
PDS	Partido Democrático Social
Petrobrás	Petróleo Brasileiro S.A
PGPM	Programa de Garantia de Preços Mínimos
PIB	Produto Interno Bruto
PIR	Partido de Izquierda Revolucionaria
PIS	Programa de Integração Social
Plano de Metas	"Goals Plan"
PMDB	Partido do Movimento Democrático Brasileiro
PNAD	Pesquisa Nacional por Amostra de Domicílios
PND (II)	Segundo Plano Nacional de Desenvolvimento
PRI	Partido Revolucionario Institucional
PRORURAL	Programa de Assistência ao Trabalhador Rural
PT	Partido dos Trabalhadores
RMV	Renda Mensal Vitalícia
SENAC	Serviço Nacional de Aprendizagem Comercial
SENAI	Serviço Nacional de Aprendizagem Industrial

SINAMOS	Sistema Nacional de Apoyo a la Movilización Social
SINPAS	Sistema Nacional de Previdência e Assistência Social
SNCR	Sistema Nacional de Crédito Rural
SNI	Serviço Nacional de Informações
STF	Supremo Tribunal Federal
UDN	União Democrática Nacional
UNICAMP	Universidade Estadual de Campinas
UNIMED	Generic name for all medical cooperatives in Brazil, called Sociedades Cooperativas de Trabajo Médico
UDP	Unidad Democrática y Popular

BRAZIL, 1964–1985

1 National Security and the Destruction of Democratic Regimes in Latin America

NO SOONER HAD the Second World War ended than the Cold War began. Although the prime concern of the United States was "containing" Russian expansion in Eastern Europe, it was also committed to eliminating the communist parties in the Mediterranean and western European countries. Already in 1948 the U.S. State Department was warning that communism could spread from France and Italy to Latin America.[1] In 1949 came the overthrow of the nationalist government in China and the establishment of a communist state in the world's most populous country. By early 1950 the United States was in the throes of a red scare unleashed by Senator Joseph McCarthy and others, with witch-hunting campaigns against left-wing intellectuals and political activists in government, universities, unions, and the media. Liberals in the State Department were removed, and United States diplomats became more sensitized to the "Bolshevik" threat everywhere in the world.

It was in this context that the United States abandoned the non-interventionist position of the Franklin D. Roosevelt period, with its "Good Neighbor Policy," and returned to systematic and often violent intervention in almost every country in Latin America for the next four decades. All that the U.S. diplomats could see were communists everywhere, and they were especially to be found in thriving democratic regimes. By 1947 the U.S. embassy in Guatemala had turned on the reformist Juan José Arévalo's government (1945–51), which had been passing laws establishing land reform and supporting unionization, all of which affected the operations of the United Fruit Company in that country. Local embassy officials declared that communists were actively involved in these reforms and that "a suspiciously large portion of the reforms advanced by the present revolutionary Government seem motivated in part by a calculated effort to further class warfare."[2]

Thus, early on, social and economic reform in postwar Latin America, especially as it affected U.S. companies—whether communist party members were present or not—would lead to a definition of communist penetration. By the time of the election of Dwight D. Eisenhower in late 1952, whatever moderating impulses may have existed under Harry S. Truman were totally abandoned. The Republican administration of Eisenhower charged the Democrats with "losing China" and coddling communists everywhere. The new president sent his brother Milton Eisenhower on a fact-finding mission to Latin America in 1953, and he concluded that Guatemala, now under the reformist and democratically elected Jacobo Árbenz (1951–54), had in fact "succumbed to communist infiltration."[3] Very quickly both Republican and Democratic politicians demanded the overthrow the newly elected Árbenz regime, and Adolf Berle, a leading Democratic adviser to Roosevelt and soon to be ambassador to Brazil, told a U.S. congressional committee that the response to the Guatemala "threat" was not direct intervention, but should rather be in "organizing a counter-movement capable of using force if necessary, based in a cooperative neighboring republic."[4] This in fact became one the major policies of the Central Intelligence Agency in subsequent interventions in Central America over the next three decades. Another strategy was to get control over the local military establishment through cooperative training programs at U.S. bases in the Panama Canal Zone and in the United States, and encourage them, with financial support, to overthrow their own democratic governments.[5] But if all of these programs failed, then direct military invasion would occur, though this was mostly confined to the Caribbean and Central American republics.

In March 1954 the United States prepared for the coming forceful overthrow of the legally elected Guatemalan government by having seventeen of the twenty-one American republics sign a "Declaration of Solidarity for the Preservation of the American States Against . . . Communism," which supposedly gave official sanction for the coming invasion.[6] The U.S. government could offer no proof of any communist penetration in Guatemala, but it simply would not tolerate a reformist government, using as justification its idea of the domino theory: if any one government went reformist in these poor countries, then all would follow and eventually all would fall into the Soviet sphere of influence. Moreover, to guarantee that no communist parties could function in the Americas, the United States encouraged the other American republics to declare these parties illegal and remove any of their members from government positions. By the mid-1950s the United States had succeeded in having fourteen of the American countries outlaw the party.[7]

But the removal of the formal communist party was just the first in a long series of antireformist acts. There was also direct and indirect intervention to guarantee "stability" and a pro-U.S. government. Direct intervention included the landing of marines if no other option was available, or the arming of insurgents who could overcome a government that was still protected by its own military. In June 1954 this second option was carried out in the case of Guatemala. In that month a CIA-organized army invaded Guatemala from friendly Honduras and overthrew the government, creating a classic authoritarian regime that was immediately recognized by the United States.[8] This was the first act in what became the long-term U.S. policy of promoting dictatorships to replace reformist governments throughout Latin America in the Cold War period, a policy that differed little whether the president was Republican or Democratic, except during the administration of Jimmy Carter (1977–81), which only temporarily reduced the unquestioned support for authoritarian rulers with a campaign to protect human rights.[9] This pause led to a period of fostering democratic options over authoritarian solutions. But the arrival of Henry Kissinger to power under Presidents Richard Nixon and Gerald Ford, and Jeane Kirkpatrick under President Ronald Reagan, led to an even more crude form of intervention in the following years. Even with the end of the Cold War, the United States could not refrain from its policy of intervention, as the case of Panama was to prove. It was only the distraction of active wars in the Middle East and the return of powerful democratic governments in the Americas in the past few decades that has prevented an even more activist Latin American policy of the United States government.

Typical of what was to follow, the Eisenhower administration actively supported the dictatorships of Fulgencio Batista in Cuba, Rafael Trujillo in the Dominican Republic, Carlos Castillo Armas in Guatemala, and Anastasio Somoza in Nicaragua. But each of these regimes was attacked or overthrown in the coming years, and in 1959 Fidel Castro came to power in Cuba. In March 1960, Eisenhower approved the application of a Guatemalan solution to Cuba. This policy was even more forcefully pursued by the new Democratic administration of John F. Kennedy, which had the CIA equip an exile army in now friendly Guatemala, which led to the failed Bay of Pigs invasion in 1961.

Nor was this the only area of concern. It was in this decade that the CIA and the military systematically intervened in South America. In 1961 British Guiana was preparing for independence, and Cheddi Jagan came to power. Although the British were often opposed to Jagan in the 1950s, by the 1960s they accepted his legitimacy and allowed his government to rule. But the United States refused to accept this decision and in 1963 paid for a massive national strike against the government. Kennedy eventually persuaded the British to intervene again and rig new elections, which ended with the fall of the government.[10]

Although a concomitant commitment to major foreign aid for Latin America was also proposed in 1961, with the Alliance for Progress, it was assumed that this would end the appeal of communism in poorer nations in the hemisphere and create stability, rather than lead to more democratic participation.[11] In fact this aid was often tied to military and police assistance to regimes, which often used the aid to suppress their own populations, or found other ways of negating its effectiveness.

These developments set the stage for the biggest intervention to date: the overthrow of the democratic government of Brazil in 1964 by the Johnson administration and its Cold War liberal advisers. Already by July 1962 the U.S. ambassador to Brazil, Lincoln Gordon, a liberal Harvard economics professor, declared to President Kennedy: "I think one of our important jobs is to strengthen the spine of the [Brazilian] military. To make clear, discreetly, that we are not necessarily hostile to any kind of military action."[12] In December 1962, Robert F. Kennedy was sent to Brazil to talk with President João Goulart. He stressed that the United States had "the gravest doubts" about Brazil, given the "signs of Communist or extreme left-wing nationalists infiltration into civilian government positions" and Goulart's opposition to "American policies and interests as a regular rule."[13] So extreme became the opposition to Goulart and fear of a failed right-wing coup attempt that Ambassador Gordon proposed a contingency plan suggesting "heavy emphasis on U.S. armed intervention." This was on the very day in November 1963 that John F. Kennedy was assassinated in Dallas.[14] For the moment, National Security Adviser McGeorge Bundy and the new Johnson administration continued to emphasize an internal military coup as the best solution. But the hostility of the Kennedy and Johnson administrations was so virulent that if the coup failed, they were willing to contemplate outright military intervention, which would have been the largest invasion ever carried out by the United States in the Western hemisphere.[15] The intense negotiations with the generals continued, and by early 1964 it was clear that a coherent group of pro-U.S. officers had been conscripted into the conspiracy.[16] On March 27, 1964, the National Security Council received a memo from Ambassador Gordon calling for covert delivery of armaments and gasoline, as well as the positioning of a U.S. naval task force off the coast of Brazil in support of a planned coup.[17] Before the actual *golpe* (coup) occurred, the U.S. military attaché to the U.S. Embassy in Brazil, Vernon Walters, reported on March 30 to the Joint Chiefs of Staff that "it had been decided to take action this week" after meeting with the leading coup-plotting generals.[18]

After the success of the coup in Brazil, the largest country in Latin America and one of the largest in the world, the United States was emboldened to try other large state interventions in the name of anti-communism along with its traditional automatic interventions in Central America and the Caribbean. Johnson sent the marines to the Dominican Republic to prevent the return of the democratically elected Juan Bosch to power just a year after the Brazilian coup. Then came the CIA-sponsored overthrow of Salvador Allende of Chile in 1970.[19] With Chile and Brazil in the hands of military regimes, democratic governments in the region became ever more fragile. In June 1966 the Argentine military ousted the democratic government of Arturo Illia and began what would become, with a short pause for the return of Juan Domingo Perón and his followers to power, almost two decades of military rule, which involved mass killing and came to be called the "Dirty War." In 1970 the Bolivian government was overthrown by the military under Hugo Banzer, and then in 1973 an elected conservative government in Uruguay turned the country over to a military junta and abandoned all democratic institutions. The only exception to this pattern of conservative military regimes was the establishment in 1968 of a left-wing military government under Juan Velasco Alvarado in Peru.

What is impressive about this particular period of authoritarian rule in the Southern Cone region was its unusually high level of killings, torture, and violence in the name of state security, its intimate cooperation between all the national militaries, which led to cross-border assassinations, and the close ties with the United States. Civilian political leaders of the center and left were systematically gagged, exiled, or assassinated. Free elections were eliminated, and the press was censured and controlled. This type of systematic state violence was the norm for Central America from the overthrow of Jacobo Árbenz in 1953 until very recently. The Guatemalan military attacked Mayan peasant groups even during democratic periods; from its takeover in 1972 the Salvadoran military also engaged in a massive killing campaign, which reached its peak in the early 1980s. The collapse of the Somoza regime in Nicaragua in 1979 brought the Sandinistas to power, which led in turn to the creation of the U.S.-backed contra army, a major factor in sustaining violence and destroying the Nicaraguan economy until 1987.[20] This type of systematic violence pursued by the state against its citizens was unusual in the more advanced and less peasant-based societies of South America, but that changed with the new-style military governments that were established in the Southern hemisphere in the 1960s and 1970s.

This military interregnum lasted for two decades or more in Central American and South American nations and led to a massive outflow of political refugees. By 1977 there were only three democratic governments left in Latin America—Costa Rica, Venezuela, and Colombia.[21] In most cases the authoritarian regimes did not come to an end until the 1980s (Peru, Brazil, Argentina, and Uruguay), and not until 1990 in Chile. This was also a period when the fear of a Cuban-style revolutionary movement or of class warfare, or even of moderate social and economic change, led governments to levels of state-sponsored killings of civilians that were unique for Latin America. These killings did not stop with peasants and workers, but included students and intellectuals of the middle and upper classes, groups formerly isolated from these state-sponsored campaigns of terror. In fact so violent were these regimes that they forced a profound rethinking of the progressive and radical parties in Latin America. Previously derided as bourgeois values, human rights now became a profound binding ideology that could unite the left-wing and center parties.[22] This rethinking of basic relations of citizens to the state throughout Latin America led to new powerful and previously unthinkable coalitions of communists, socialists, and Christian democratic parties. When these coalitions won the elections and plebiscites of the late 1980s, they finally brought about the demise of the military regimes and generated surprisingly powerful democratic movements that have solidified democratic rule in Latin America until today.

Although the military regimes of the 1960s to the 1980s were antidemocratic and violent, they were not all of the same mold. The two extreme cases in terms of violence were Argentina and Chile. In Argentina, the military deliberately carried out the so-called Dirty War to eliminate all possible liberal or left-wing groups in the country. Starting with the first military government of Juan Carlos Onganía, the public universities were destroyed. Then under the military regimes of 1976–83 democratic parties and institutions were suppressed, and an estimated thirty thousand persons were killed.[23] A highly organized system of state terror completely controlled by the junta generals became the norm as the military adopted indiscriminate torture, killings, and kidnappings to silence all liberal and progressive political expression.[24] Moreover, the military leaders were quite deliberate in their language about the declared need to "cleanse" Argentine society.[25] Any serious guerrilla movements had been eliminated by 1976, but it was in this year that the true Dirty War began, lasting until 1982. Although national security doctrine had promoted the idea of economic development as well as the elimination of potential left-wing movements, such social and economic development was not a serious concern of the Argentine military. The right wing of the Catholic Church supported the revolt, and it became a staunch ally of the regime. Violence for its own sake became the norm, and the economy was left to the traditional classes to run as they saw fit with no effort to modernize the economy in any serious way. Nor was any systematic effort made to resolve growing social conflict by instituting any new developments such as land reform or the creation of a modern welfare state. In short, this was a violent retrograde regime, hostile to modern life, totally dominated by conservative Catholic ideologues, anti-Semitic, and xenophobic. In the very first days of the Onganía military period in 1966, the army destroyed the distinguished Faculty of Sciences of the University of Buenos Aires to show its unequivocal hostility to science and Enlightenment thought in general.[26]

The long-term military phase can be said to have begun with General Onganía in 1966–70, with a pause for the revival of Peronism, and then returned in full force from 1976 until 1983. The violent and extremely reactionary nature of the Onganía regime marked the beginnings of an ever more violent and reactionary military government over the next two decades. All of this occurred in a country where no serious radical forces existed to threaten the establishment or where there was any social conflict that could not have been easily resolved by the military, despite the late Peronist conflicts and terrorist movements. In fact the army remained relatively passive during the Perón interregnum and developed its own right-wing militias, which it immediately subordinated to the state system once it came to power. But aside from setting up a highly unified killing machine to cleanse the country of leftist and progressive elements in its own population, the army had no new economic or social plan to propose, and its various finance ministers were faced with a constant threat of hyperinflation, stagnant public enterprises, and low capital investment. They were forced several times to freeze prices or devalue the currency, or both. Of course the military also squeezed wages, since the unions had been muzzled, but this had little effect in promoting economic development. The foreign debt went from 14 percent of GDP in 1977 to 26 percent of GDP in 1981. By the final three years of the regime, there was a banking crisis, and from 1980 to 1983 there was a consistent decline in total GDP. By the end of the military era, there were few results to show for this violent regime except thousands of deaths and an economy in shambles, which the first democratic government inherited and which soon forced the early retirement of its president.[27] So out of touch with reality were the Argentine generals that they started a war against England to distract the nation from a failing economy and increasing demands for democratic government. The resulting Falklands War, disastrous for Argentina, finally bought an end to the violence.[28]

At the other extreme was the straightforward dictatorship established by the military under Augusto Pinochet in Chile. This regime, equally supported by the upper class and parts of the Catholic Church, was also given massive U.S. support and finances and eventually killed an estimated three thousand or more persons, with thousands more being forced into exile. Half of those killed were assassinated in the first few years of the regime, but killings, torture, and imprisonment continued until the end of the Pinochet government, and repression actually increased during the economic crisis years of 1982–83.[29] It was estimated that eventually sixty thousand people were imprisoned in Chile, compared with thirty thousand in Argentina and twenty-five thousand in Brazil.[30] Moreover, as an active member of the Condor "plan," the Chilean regime was ruthless in its prosecution of left-wing leaders, which led to a break in diplomatic relations with countries as distinct as Mexico, Colombia, and Great Britain. Even the United States, the regime's ally, was shocked when the Chilean secret service arranged the killing of an opposition leader in Washington, D.C., in 1976.[31]

Whereas the military intervened in Argentina for no discernable reason, since the democratic government was only moderately reformist and the serious guerrilla movements had been mostly repressed at that time, this was not the case in Chile. In Chile the army, with very active support from the United States, allied itself with the conservative elements of the upper classes and the business elite to overthrow a socialist administration led by Salvador Allende, which was actively pursuing a nationalization of industry and a major redistribution of income. Although these leftist policies were being carried out by a democratically elected regime, they created deep class divisions that were very systematically exploited by the military elite.[32] The resulting dictatorship thus had a solid civilian base of active supporters. Instead of experiencing the shifting alliances among various military factions common to the Argentine regime, which would lead to constant presidential changes, the government in Chile was dominated by one man throughout the seventeen years of military rule and even afterward, as Pinochet remained chief of the army until 1998, eight years after the return of democracy. Although the military had no coherent social plan other than eliminating all left-wing and liberal opposition, Pinochet decided to support a radical neoliberal reorganization of the national economy based on the ideas of the so-called Chicago School of Economics.[33] It was in fact an elite group of young Catholic University graduates, all of whom obtained their doctorates in economics at the University of Chicago, who carried out this program under his administration.[34] Not only was this regime totally committed to market solutions and a deregulated economy, which would be carried out at the cost of worker income, but its ideas related to privatization of education and social welfare became the model for what was later called the Washington Consensus. But such a shock treatment for the Chilean economy could be carried out only by an authoritarian regime, and it occurred with a cost in repression, torture, death, and exile for thousands of Chileans.

As Alejandro Foxley has noted, this was a radical economic program in two fundamental respects. First, it applied the usual orthodox "shock treatment" to the economy to stop inflation, which forced a recession, high unemployment, and increasing inequality. But, second, it proposed basic structural changes that included privatization of economic activities; "a withdrawal of the state from its regulatory and development functions; opening the national economy to international markets and capital; and freeing prices and promoting a capital market."[35] While many military regimes applied orthodox shocks to cut inflation at the cost of welfare and wages, the structural changes enacted by the Pinochet regime were unique to Chile, and not adopted by any other developing nation in this period. Most Latin American states did not open their markets to foreign capital and free trade until a few decades later, and few carried out the extremes of privatization of social welfare and education that were undertaken in Chile even after their promotion by the World Bank and the United States.

There were, according to Ricardo Ffrench-Davis, two distinct policy periods during the Pinochet years: the aggressive pure monetarist neoliberal Chicago-style policies that lasted from 1973 to 1981, and what he calls a more pragmatic and more traditional period from 1982 to 1990. In the first, the national economy was opened up with an across-the-board reduction of all tariffs to 10 percent, all expropriated companies were returned to their owners, a free exchange rate was established, and the capital market was totally liberalized. The virtual abandonment of government regulation led to high levels of monopolization of industry and corruption, as officers and elite individuals were favored in the new authoritarian economy, and consumers were left to fend for themselves. But inflation remained stubbornly high, in the 300 percent per annum range for most of the period, and was only brought down to moderate levels in 1982 after the application of orthodox shocks with a reduction in government spending, wage freezes, and devaluations of the national currency. Given the petroleum crises of 1973 and 1979 and the rather wild swings in world copper prices, the economy experienced abrupt periods of growth and severe declines, with an especially acute depression in 1982–83. Because the neoclassical shock treatment and the opening up of the economy to international competition badly affected national industry, the economic elite forced the military to adopt a more pragmatic economic policy from 1982 to 1990. This led the government to temporarily raise its average tariff wall from 10 percent under the Chicago plan to 35 percent in the early 1980s, to create price support programs for agriculture, to provide major subsidies to nontraditional exporters, to create more strict regulation of the market, and finally to have the state help in renegotiating private foreign and domestic debt. Overall, for all the supposed positive impact, the economy grew at only 2.9 percent in the Pinochet period, compared with an explosive growth of 7.7 percent under the first post-Pinochet democratic government of Patricio Aylwin (1990–93). Of course, real wages dropped significantly in the military era and did not recover to their 1970 level until 1994. Unemployment reached 18 percent under Pinochet, compared with 4.6 percent under Allende and 7.3 percent under the first post-military government. Thus the neoliberal experiment, greatly heralded abroad, especially in the United States, was not an unalloyed success.

That some of the reforms clearly aided the modernization of the Chilean economy is without question, but the real economic growth along with increased well-being of the population came in the post-military era, when the government again took a far more active role in the economy. Under the military the distribution of income was increasingly distorted and the internal market was severely limited by a brutal policy of wage suppression and union destruction. Also, deregulation not only led to the abandonment of environmental protection, but as could be expected, it led to much speculation and accentuated the periodic economic crises.[36] Moreover, for all the free-market ideology, an authoritarian dictatorship by its very nature creates crony capitalism, as supporters are favored over other economic actors and crucial information is provided to a select few, also leading to systematic corruption. As the wealth accumulated by General Pinochet proved, the military officers were not above taking advantage of their new power to enrich themselves.[37] As Carlos Huneeus has noted, the Chicago boys were so antistatist that they not only failed to create regulatory bodies to control the market, but "public administration was not modernized, so a solid institutional structure to support the reforms and prevent possible problems did not emerge." These privatizations totally lacked transparency, "which allowed top executives of public firms to take over controlling interest as they were privatized."[38] These executives were all loyal right-wing supporters appointed by Pinochet and in turn were given state loans and other government subsidies to purchase their companies. The payoff to the new industrial owners helps explain the extraordinary hostility of the business elite to the democratic governments of the post-Pinochet era. Finally, it should be recalled that for all the Chicago-style changes, the army never permitted the privatization of Chile's single most important enterprise, the crucial copper mining industry, which accounted for the bulk of Chile's exports.[39]

Thus while many of the liberalization policies applied to the economy were modified from their more extreme Chicago model, both at the end of the military period and under post-military democratic governments, this was not the case with the social reforms, especially in terms of the replacement of the standard social security model and the privatization of education. In these areas Chile went beyond any other nation in the world in eliminating the state's role in the protection of its citizens against risk and in providing education for its children. Chile in fact was defined by the United States and the World Bank as the model state in the period of the "Washington Consensuses." President George W. Bush even suggested that Chile should serve as a model for the United States in his campaign to eliminate Social Security and replace it with private "defined benefit" plans. In a famous and influential report on pensions, the World Bank in 1994 noted that "Chile was the only country that had fully replaced an existing public pay-as-you-go pension scheme with a mandatory saving scheme. Chile was also the only country whose mandatory saving program is privately and competitively managed."[40] The United States and the World Bank in this famous report recommended the adoption of Chilean reforms for all the other nations of the world. Although some aspects of Chile's privatization of pensions have been adopted even in Europe, few states have gone to the extreme of privatization as did Chile.[41] Even post-Pinochet regimes in Chile were forced to modify a pension system designed for highly capitalized countries, which proved difficult to implement in Chile with its limited capital market. The high costs and low savings of the private plan, along with its limited national coverage, compelled the democratic governments to create a mixed system. In fact, several countries adopted the model only to abandon it after the 2008 world economic crisis, and those programs that have survived are hybrid systems that usually include mixed pay-as-you-go pension plans or simple cash transfers from the state treasury to those outside the plans—which was the Chilean solution. Even the privatization of public education is no longer acceptable, and it became such a major political issue in Chile in the past decade that it brought down several ministries and led the second government of Michelle Bachelet to promise to abandon it altogether.

Along with its unusual economic and social reforms, the Chilean dictatorship was markedly different from other military regimes in its political base. In Argentina the military ruled over a passive population that was accustomed since the 1930s to periodic military interventions. Although the Dirty War generated a lot of enthusiasm on the far right, for the overwhelming majority there was resigned acceptance. In the case of Brazil, there was a constant shift of supporting and opposing groups, such that the military was forced to design policies that could capture more popular support beyond its original elite and right-wing base. In the Chilean case the support given to Pinochet was unconditional on the part of almost half the population. This support of the upper and middle classes for Pinochet lasted well into the twenty-first century and formed the basis for a very powerful and cohesive regime, which even at the end garnered 43 percent of the popular vote in the referendum called in 1988 to give Pinochet another presidential term.[42] But this was definitely not a populist regime in the style of Perón in Argentina or Velasco in Peru, and the Pinochet government made no appeal for popular support, content with the minority of the population that actively sustained it.

But the Pinochet regime shared a great deal with the post-1976 military regimes in Argentina. Like them its aim was to destroy or greatly modify the standard democratic institutions. Parties were abolished in 1977, Congress was closed, and the government ruled by a state of siege for most of its period of governance. In this area the Brazilian

generals stand out as unusual, in that the traditional democratic institutions were maintained in Brazil, even if in a limited form. Pinochet
carried out a reorganization of the military command as well, abolishing the promotions and appeals board and placing all their powers in
his own hands. He then proceeded to violate traditional career promotional and retirement standards and appointed loyalists over more
senior officers and allowed others to keep their posts past the usual
retirement age. He thus completely controlled the army and made the
other service chiefs dependent on his good will. He also expanded the
number of generals from twenty-four at the time of the coup to fifty-
three by the late 1980s, and he greatly expanded the middle-rank officer corps as well, all the while remaining head of the army, head of the
military junta's governing council, and president of the republic.[43] This
was in stark contrast to the military regimes in Brazil, Argentina, and
Uruguay, which kept retirement in place, rotated officers in and out of
power on a well-defined schedule, and otherwise guaranteed that there
would be no dictatorial rule as occurred in Chile. Brazil went to the extreme of having fixed "presidential" terms, and the Uruguayan generals
never appointed one of their own as president.

By the late 1970s Pinochet began to talk of a very slow return to a
democratic government. But like the generals of Brazil, he was determined to create only limited "democratic" institutions. In both Brazil
and Argentina the electoral rules were manipulated and future parlia-
ments were reorganized to give more weight to conservative rural areas
over large urban centers. The Chileans, however, went even further in
their desire, as Pinochet declared, to create a "protected and authoritarian democracy" with the appointment of non-elected senators and
other institutional restrictions to reduce popular influence on government.[44] Determined to create a political system that favored the most
conservative government possible, Pinochet prepared a constitution
in 1980 that remains in force today. The aim of the constitution was
to reduce popular participation as much as possible. He immediately
called a plebiscite that "approved" the constitution and then proceeded
to move quickly to the far right, expelling key opposition leaders and
even increasing the level of violence. But the further right he moved, the
greater was the organizing of the opposition and the fracturing of his
traditional civilian supporters.

All these plans for a slow "opening" (*apertura*) toward a democratic government to be guided by Pinochet himself until the end of the century were dashed by the severe economic crisis of 1982–83 and the increasing power of the opposition, despite all the violent repression that had been carried out. In fact, the mid- to late 1980s turned into a particularly violent period, as the Pinochet administration became more isolated and opposition to the regime became stronger and more public. Nevertheless, Pinochet thought he still had the support of the majority of the population, and he finally agreed to hold a plebiscite in 1988 for an eight-year presidential term, for which he alone would be the candidate. For this election, the government finally recognized political parties, allowed for voter registration lists and a semi-independent electoral commission, and permitted a less-controlled press to participate, on the assumption that this would totally legitimate the regime.

In fact, it gave opposition forces the space needed to organize and propagate their ideas. Moreover, the center and leftist parties allied for the first time to present a united front. Although he lost the vote and was forced to call real elections, Pinochet in his last years in government further bound the incoming administration by packing the Supreme Court, freezing administration appointments, and further protecting the autonomy and independence of the army. But the coalition of parties known as the Concentración de Partidos por la Democracia, which was led by the Christian Democratic leader Patricio Aylwin, was able to negotiate a series of amendments to the undemocratic constitution of 1980, which at least allowed the new democratic government to function in a more or less normal and independent way. Nevertheless, compared with all the other transitions to democratic rule, the post-Pinochet democratic governments have had as their task the slow and progressive dismantling of the Pinochet constitution, which is still in effect today.[45] It was not until Pinochet was arrested in London in 1998 for war crimes that the powerful civilian right and military support for him was finally broken—some eight years after the return of democracy. It was only then that the military finally backed down from its constant confrontations with the civilian government, and only then that one wing of the civilian right finally accepted the need to talk about the disappeared prisoners, the torture, and the deaths of the Pinochet years.[46]

The second of the major 1960s military governments established in South America was that of General Juan Velasco Alvarado in Peru in October 1968. In contrast to all the other military interventions in South America, the Peruvian military initiated the overthrow of an elected government on its own initiative and continued to rule without United States intervention. There were other distinguishing features as well. It was essentially a colonel's revolution led by one radical general; it made no effort to destroy the unions or imprison anyone; and although it hated the important political party known as APRA (American Popular Revolutionary Alliance) and was officially anticommunist, it declared that it would not use this as a tool to reject social and economic change.[47] Despite carrying out a major land reform, systematically promoting political mobilization of peasants and workers, joining third-world coalitions in the era of the Cold War, and confiscating U.S. property, the regime was officially anticommunist amid more radical regimes in the region, so it was ignored by Washington.[48]

The Velasco experience did, however, have much in common with the Chilean and even more with the Brazilian regimes in that the military was concerned with establishing an authoritarian developmental model. Peruvian historians agree that this was a government that profoundly transformed and modernized the nation. Although it muzzled the press and repressed the political parties, in one aspect it was significantly different from all the other authoritarian governments of the period. Unlike the other military governments during the Cold War, it did not engage in state-led violence against the population. There were no systematic killings, disappearances, incarcerations, or other typical aspects of the repressive regimes of the region in this military interregnum period. Also, with the exception of the Bolivian military regimes, it was the only military government to carry out a massive and fundamental land reform, one that fundamentally reshaped the national economy and society.

In the election of 1962 the army had intervened among the competing candidates to force the election of Fernando Belaúnde Terry, the leader of Acción Popular, fearing the potential election of the hated Víctor Raúl Haya de la Torre and his APRA party. But the army became frustrated with the reformist Belaúnde government. It had to fight an increasingly mobilized peasantry and various Che Guevara–inspired guerrilla movements in the 1960s and was eventually convinced that serious social and economic reforms had to be undertaken to prevent further social conflict. But Belaúnde faced a hostile APRA-dominated Congress that frustrated most of his reforms, resulting in a timid agrarian reform decree. A blocked government, conflicts with the Standard Oil subsidiary, the International Petroleum Company, and a major depression in 1967 finally brought the army back to power.[49] The leading generals were now sure that the oligarchic structure of the nation could only be broken with an authoritarian modern reformist government rather than by a pluralistic democratic one.[50] There was much talk of breaking the control of the oligarchy and permitting the middle class and industrial elite to modernize the country. As Julio Cotler has noted, all of these ideas were part of the general programs of all the parties of the left before the army took over, and especially of the APRA, which in its earlier radical days thought the society and economy could be modernized and developed under a pluralistic and democratic state.[51] Although APRA lost its radical drive by midcentury, it was soon replaced in the center and far left by such parties as Acción Popular, Movimiento Social Progresista, Democracia Cristiana, and the Movimiento de Izquierda Revolucionaria (MIR, Leftist Revolutionary Movement), all of which stressed basic reform.

The ideas circulating in these various progressive political movements were absorbed by the officer class at the end of the decade. Probably as important was their education in the Center for Higher Military Studies (CAEM). Founded in 1950, the CAEM offered a one-year course for elite senior officers on social, economic, and political problems. Unlike the comparable Escola Superior de Guerra (ESG) in Brazil, it sent its students to study economics at a United Nations agency, the Economic Commission for Latin American and the Caribbean (ECLA) in Chile, and at other overseas training programs. As could be expected, there was much research and discussion at the school on national security, but also on the basic problems facing Peruvian society. That this school was the incubator for many of the ideas of the military regime can be seen in the fact that two-thirds of the ministers of the first military revolutionary regime were graduates of CAEM, including the head of the armed forces. As in Brazil's ESG, civilians also attended, accounting for 29 percent of the 367 students enrolled between 1951 and 1968.[52] Even national security was defined at CAEM in the broadest terms, as "the need to ensure an order conducive to national well-being, that is to say, the well-being of all Peruvians, not just of the dominant social classes."[53] In fact, its curriculum has been called "a military approach to social science."[54] As early as 1958 CAEM published a detailed economic study proposing development of the agricultural and industrial sectors of the Central Selva region, suggesting that it should be put under military control as an experiment.[55] Equally, the leading military journals of the period also stressed the need for "preventive" social change to both improve society and the economy and reduce any potential communist mobilization.[56] Along with promoting modern economic and social ideas, the school also declared that "so long as Peru does not have programmatic and well-organized political parties, the country will continue to be ungovernable."[57]

The shock for the army was the guerrilla campaigns of 1965–66, which it easily suppressed. But from this experience, influential members of the army became convinced that only basic reform could prevent more rural rebellions from occurring. They believed Peru had entered a period of what Luigi R. Einaudi called "latent insurgency"; from the experience of the defeat of France in Indochina and the United States in Vietnam, they realized that Peru would have to solve its own problems. The dilemma of how to control these developments led the military to commit itself to agrarian reform and industrialization to resolve what it saw as the weakness of Peru, which opened the country up to communist subversion. While their attack on the traditional oligarchy was an obvious issue, given the extraordinarily backward land tenure in Peru, military leaders were surprisingly hostile as well to foreign capital, especially from the United States, despite their previously close ties to the U.S. military. In fact, it was the local oil contract with Standard Oil in 1968 that enraged the military, which was one of the participating factors causing the revolt.[58] This also led to the expulsion of the U.S. military mission to Peru in 1969, even though Peru had been the second largest Latin American recipient of U.S. military aid, after Brazil, in the 1950s and 1960s.[59]

But the Peruvian army officers shared one basic belief common to all the regimes of the era, and probably inherent in any military government of the right or left. Like all the radical or conservative social engineering attempted in this era of military regimes, it was to be a top-down "mobilization" designed to anticipate and reduce conflict. Even in the Peruvian military's radical attempt to mobilize peasants and workers, there was a basic "refusal to recognize the legitimacy of social conflict, and a desire to impose a kind of authoritarian collectivism under which conflict would no longer occur."[60] Also, the officers made it clear that, however radical these necessary policies were, they would be carried out within a "western and Christian" model.[61]

To the surprise of many, the army was serious about its desire to reform Peru, and it announced itself as "the Revolutionary Government of the Armed Forces" (GRFA) when it seized power in October 1968. The regime declared as its model "autonomous development" that was "neither capitalist nor communist"—a theme much espoused by Perón in Argentina—and that it would establish a "society of solidarity."[62] This latter theme was unique to the Velasco regime. Not only would the new government nationalize significant parts of the economy and carry out a major reform of land tenure, but it would also implant cooperatives in farms and factories and promote worker participation and other social groupings more like a corporative state. It proposed creating a "new Peruvian" and reorganizing the society in self-governing communities and enterprises, all in the name of eliminating class conflict, unions, and formal civilian parties. It would also turn the state into a major force in the economy.[63]

In the first week of his administration, Velasco announced the nationalization of the International Petroleum Company (IPC), a U.S. subsidiary of Standard Oil, and by the end of its first year it proclaimed a new and very effective agrarian reform. The nationalization of IPC, and of the U.S.-owned Cerro de Pasco copper mines in 1974, along with a foreign policy that sought to associate Peru with the nonaligned third world, caused immediate friction with the United States. But with Allende's government still functioning in Chile and a radical leftist military regime that had just come to power in Bolivia under General Juan José Torres (1970–71), the U.S. government was more concerned with preventing the regime from becoming another Cuba than with trying to overthrow it. By 1974 the U.S. government even gave Peru a major loan, which was used to pay off the expropriated American companies.

The Peruvian military, like its counterpart in Brazil, turned the state into a major participant in the national economy. In fact, the Peruvians went well beyond the Brazilians in the financial sector. The banks were nationalized in 1970, and the state began to establish heavy industries and to take over mines and factories and large parts of the export economy. The formerly liberal state became the single most important participant in the economy. It nationalized foreign-owned mines, oil fields, telecommunications, and railroads and placed them in large state enterprises. A national airline and a shipping company were created, and even a state-owned hotel chain was established. By 1975 more than fifty state enterprises accounted for half of mine production, a fifth of industrial output, and two-thirds of banking. The military also invested in capital goods industries and provided subsidies to private capital for the creation of import substitution industries. By 1974 central government expenditures accounted for 39 percent of Peruvian GDP. This state industrial activity continued to expand even after the fall of Velasco. By the first industrial census of 1977, there were 174 state enterprises listed, and by the early 1980s, state expenditures accounted for over half of GDP. The government also increased its administrative control over the economy. In 1969 a Ministry of Industries was established, and the strengthened state planning commission provided multiyear development plans. As many authors have noted, at this point "state capitalism" became the dominant model of the national economy and lasted long after the fall of the military regime.[64] It was only in 1990, with the accession of Alberto Fujimori to the presidency, that this state capitalist model was finally and totally abandoned and replaced by a neoliberal economic regime.[65]

Along with establishing a state presence throughout the economy, the Velasco government even announced in the Industrial Law of 1970 co-government for workers in state and private enterprises as well as profit-sharing schemes. These industrial and commercial "communities" were the urban counterpart of the cooperatives and mobilized communities being granted land in the interior.[66] In terms of social health and education, the military regime continued earlier government investments in education and health, and essentially left the previous structures intact, but heavily invested in these areas. The results can be seen in the number of children of primary school age attending public schools, which went from 70 percent in 1960 to 85 percent by 1971.[67]

In the rural area, change was profound. In addition to arranging for massive land distribution, the government created the National System of Support for Social Mobilization (SINAMOS) to promote peasant and worker cooperatives and other self-governing base organizations. All the haciendas confiscated were turned into self-governing cooperatives, and the regime established a national agrarian trade union confederation designed to take control of the mobilized peasants and rural workers who had so agitated the national scene in the previous years.[68] But many of these rural cooperatives and self-governing "communities" of urban workers did not long survive the fall of the military regime. If there is an ongoing debate about the effects of the state industrialization policies of the military or the nature of its attempts to create a citizens' participatory state, there is really no question that the agrarian reform profoundly reorganized rural land tenure and was successful.[69] One of Latin America's most sweeping land reforms was promulgated under the Velasco regime. By the end of 1979, some 16,000 properties, consisting of almost 9 million hectares, had been expropriated, and some 369,000 peasants had been given lands.[70] Almost as important, considering Peru's ecology, was the Water Law (Ley General de Aguas) of 1969, which not only guaranteed the traditional state ownership of all water, but also elaborated a complex administrative structure for each water district, with the state administering and granting water rights. This law denied private ownership of water rights, which had been an important tool of oligarchic domination. The Water Law lasted until 2009, when a new decree gave more power to the users of water to administer their own regional consumption.[71]

By 1975, Velasco was ill, and his regime was under great pressure to modify its reformist policies. This led to the regime being replaced by the more conservative wing of the military, which moderated the more radical aspects of the officer-led reforms and also moved to return the government to civilians. In short order, the new regime called for a constitutional assembly and allowed both the traditional and new left-wing parties to participate in the coming elections. The elections of 1980 brought Belaúnde back into the government—the very leader the military had initially overthrown.

Except for its lack of systematic state violence, the Velasco experiment was closest to the Brazilian military experience, in that a part of the officer class believed social and economic reform were essential for the modernization of their country. By contrast, in Chile, it was civilian advisers rather than the military that effected social and economic

change, and in fact only one single figure in the military was willing
to commit to this reform—and that was the dictator. It should also be
stressed that all of the Peruvian military reforms had as one of their
basic aims an attempt to anticipate and essentially neutralize popular
protest and anticipate any potential reform from below.

The civil-military regime in Uruguay that lasted from 1973 to 1985
was a strange alternative to the other authoritarian regimes of this
period. Like Peru, Argentina, and Brazil, Uruguay had experienced
a significant guerrilla movement in the 1960s and early 1970s. The
Uruguayan version was known as the Tupamaros, or the Movimiento
Liberación Nacional (MLN-T). Founded in 1960, the Tupamaros proposed armed urban struggle as the only way to achieve a socialist revolution.[72] In fact, it was estimated in 1969 that more armed violence
was directed at the Uruguayan government than at any other in Latin
America that year. Initially, the Tupamaros had a great deal of popular support—at least until the assassination of the U.S. police adviser
Dan Mitrone in August 1970, which led many Uruguayans to reject
armed violence. Although the police mostly dealt with the Tupamaros
until 1971, in that year the army took over.[73] Within a few months the
movement was destroyed, and by early 1972 the army declared that the
guerrilla movement had been eliminated.[74]

But the officer class, having tasted increased power in the conflict
with the Tupamaros, decided to seize control of the government the
next year.[75] In April 1972, Congress declared a permanent state of
emergency revoking all civil liberties; then in February 1973 the army
led an open rebellion against the new minister of defense and forced his
withdrawal. Unable to mount any serious opposition, President Juan
María Bordaberry then agreed to have the military officers become directly involved in the national government. At the same time radical
military officers issued two communiqués proposing basic reforms for
the country that included many of the demands of the left, such as
agrarian reform. Initially, some on the left looked with favor on what
they thought was a progressive or "peruvianista" section of the officer
class, and it appeared for a time as if this group would come to power
in the military establishment.

A profound change in Uruguayan political organization also occurred during this period. In addition to the traditional Colorado and
Blanco parties, in 1971 the Frente Amplio (Broad Front) was formed,

a coalition of leftist parties from the communists to the Christian democrats and even including dissidents from the two established parties. In that year the Frente Amplio participated in the presidential and congressional elections of 1971, receiving a significant 18 percent of the presidential vote and electing five senators and eighteen deputies to Congress.[76] But in June the president and the military called for the expulsion from the Senate of one of the new party's elected members, which Congress refused to act on. The result was that Bordaberry dissolved Congress on June 27, and thus formally began some eleven years of civil-military authoritarian government. The national confederation of workers (CNT) called a general strike to protest the closing of Congress, but the army broke the strike and the CNT was dissolved. The government then proceeded to outlaw the Frente Amplio, the communist party, and other leftist parties and to suspend the traditional parties as well. Severe censorship was imposed and numerous periodicals closed, and finally a systematic and continued use of torture and massive imprisonment occurred.

Given the hostility of the traditional parties to the Frente Amplio, a united opposition to the new authoritarian government proved difficult to establish, and the regime settled in for a long period of rule with a State Council (Consejo del Estado) composed of selected civilians and top military officers replacing Congress. The government began its most violent period and abandoned any serious reformist stance or any vestiges of democratic rule. In 1986 the officers decided to replace Bordaberry with another passive civilian president. The principal reason for his ouster was his proposal to abolish the two traditional political parties (which had been suspended) and run a straightforward authoritarian regime. But the officer class refused to take such a move and remained committed to a guardianship role, to prepare for the eventual redemocratization of the country, though with the usual expected constraints and long years of preparation.[77] At the same time the Argentine golpe of that year allowed Uruguay to create a united front of military regimes, with Argentina, Chile, Brazil, Paraguay, and Bolivia, in the systematic cross-border hunt for exiled radicals and progressive leaders in what became known as Plan Condor.[78] Although the Uruguayan regime did not systematically adopt death squads as in Argentina and Chile, by 1976 it had the highest per capita prison population in South America.[79]

But if the number of people killed was modest, the regime's massive attack on the employment of center and leftist workers in the government was even more extreme than in most of the other authoritarian regimes. Adopting the Brazilian military norms of government, the generals issued many so-called Institutional Acts that revised the basic constitution of the country. In 1977 came the Institutional Act decree AI-7, which ranked all Uruguayan citizens in three classes depending on their past politics. All B- and C-ranked persons were henceforth prevented from holding any government office, which resulted in the firing of ten thousand state workers. Whatever "peruvianista" progressive tendencies still existed in the military command were eliminated with the new Organic Military Act of the same year, whereby the conservative generals adopted a Pinochet-style retirement plan allowing them to obviate the usual career requirements. This resulted in 450 more liberal officers and subalterns being forced to retire. Finally, in the Institutional Act AI-8, the army destroyed the independence of the judiciary.[80]

As for economic policies, the officers had little preparation and less fixed positions. The progressive intake of businessmen and technical personnel in the successive military administrations resulted in a push for a more neoliberal policy. For the officers in Uruguay, as in many of the other authoritarian regimes of the period, "economic growth became identified as a surrogate for legitimacy." But they "were torn between nationalist and neoliberal visions of the country's reconstruction," as Charles Guy Gillespie has noted. "In Uruguay as in Argentina, privatization was blocked by the nationalist sectors of the armed forces, who often saw state industries as geopolitical resources," even though they eventually supported some opening.[81] The regime did promote industry and supported new exports, and in fact there was considerable economic growth until the Mexican debt crisis of 1982. But the economy grew with increased debt, significant and uncontrolled inflation, and declining real wages in an evolution not that different from the other regional authoritarian economies in this period.[82]

But, as in Chile and Brazil, the army thought its ferocious anticommunist and antiguerrilla campaign was popular and began to talk about a slow "apertura," or moving toward a limited and controlled democratic regime. In 1980 a new, highly restrictive constitution was proposed by the military and a plebiscite organized to approve it. But to the military's surprise, 58 percent of the electorate voted no. Although

the army next proposed an even slower "opening," it allowed the traditional parties to reorganize and elect new directors in 1982, which
resulted in opposition leaders gaining control. By the next year there
were well-organized popular protests and the beginnings of a significant coalition of legal and illegal opposition parties against the regime,
which in turn slowly abandoned its campaign of violence and began to
permit a limited return of exiles and the release of political prisoners.
Finally in 1984 came another plebiscite and then formal presidential
elections, with Julio María Sanguinetti of the conservative Colorado
Party winning and taking office in early 1985, though with the army
command still intact and threatening to carry out another golpe if the
political situation returned to 1973 conditions.[83] But, as in the other
post-military transitions, even in Chile and Brazil, once the democratic
transition occurred, it was impossible to stop. With each election the
nation has moved further to the left, finally voting the Frente Amplio
into the presidency in 2005 and electing a former leader of the Tupamaros as president in 2010. The violence of the military era, here as in
all the republics, has forced the parties of the left and right to finally
accommodate one another, abandoning both the armed struggle and
the willingness to call on the military when conservative parties lose
power.

The case of the military regime in Bolivia reflected many of the developments in Chile and Argentina, but evolved in far different ways
because of both the previous evolution of Bolivian politics and society
and the nature of the military establishment, which was far less hierarchical and organized than the other national militaries. To begin with,
the social and economic revolution that Bolivia experienced in 1952
brought in a powerful political party that actually defeated the army
in the revolution and reconstructed it under the tutelage of the victori-
ous Movimiento Nacionalista Revolucionario (MNR). That party was
committed to a state-controlled economy and agrarian reform. It created a state mining company called COMIBOL (Corporación Minera
de Bolivia), which took over all of the major mines and proceeded to
effectively break up the latifundia of the highland region and distribute
these lands to the Indian communities, known as *ayllus*. It gave universal suffrage to all citizens, including illiterates, and armed the peasant *sindicatos,* or unions. Because the U.S. government believed that
Víctor Paz Estenssoro, the head of the party and leader of the so-called

National Revolution of 1952, was both a fascist and a Peronist ideo-logue and because U.S. investments in the country were minimal, the regime escaped being labeled a communist threat to the United States. As nationalization and land reform unleashed an economic crisis, Paz Estenssoro quickly became pro–United States in his foreign policy, re-ceiving vital food and economic support in return.[84]

During most of the period from 1952 to the 1960s, Bolivia was dominated by Paz Estenssoro, who after serving as president for four years beginning in 1960 was reelected in 1964, with, however, the left and center of his old MNR in opposition and the Falange Party, the leading party of opposition, still an implacable enemy of Paz Estens-soro. Given these conditions, it was inevitable that the army would be encouraged to return to power. In November 1964, a few short months after the presidential elections, the army ousted the president in a rela-tively bloodless coup and put the government in the hands of a junta headed by the vice president, General René Barrientos. Thus the army was back in national politics, and it remained the dominant force in the national government from 1964 until 1982. The revolutionary phase of the National Revolution came to an end, and a long Thermidorian reaction was to ensue.

For these eighteen years, various groups and institutions within the national society would struggle to dominate the forces that had been unleashed in the period of the National Revolution. The army, the peasants, organized labor, and both traditional and new political par-ties all sought power. Though leaders of the MNR opposition assumed that the overthrow of Paz Estenssoro was a temporary transition, the reality was that a new political era began in 1964. Younger military officers who had come to power under the MNR were to create a com-plex alliance with the peasants and were hostile to democratic politics and organized labor. These officers justified the legitimacy of military authoritarian governments as the only solution to modernization—an ideology prevalent throughout the Americas in this period. Many of these regimes would also find support among the newer elements of the wealthiest classes and powerful regional elites, which saw the military as more likely to favor their interests than political organizations like the old MNR.

But the Bolivian military institution itself was rather fluid. The lead-ing officers often violated the rules of advancement and were themselves more riven by ideological conflict than most of the other regional armies due to their recent rebirth and the strong influence of the reforms that had already been carried out by the MNR governments. In contrast to more traditional and firmly hierarchical military organizations in Chile, Argentina, Uruguay, and Brazil, the Bolivian officer class was far more unpredictable than most others in Latin America. Thus the era of military regimes was one of radical shifts of viewpoint, abrupt changes of regime, and the constant emergence of new and unexpected personalities. But despite all the very rapid and often seemingly random changes, there existed a series of basic arrangements that were only rarely modified. These coalitions were based on the army's acceptance of the fundamental social and economic reforms of the National Revolution and above all a firm commitment to agrarian reform and mobilization of the peasantry. Even the regime of Velasco in Peru was not as tied to a peasant base as were the Bolivian officers. It was their recognition and active acceptance of the peasantry that would mark these new military regimes as semi-populist ones essentially founded on an often unexpressed, but nevertheless fully functioning, alliance of peasants and the military. All these features were clearly expressed in the first of these military regimes, that of René Barrientos, which established most of the basic norms that would dominate these military governments in the years to come.[85]

The Barrientos regime quickly showed its implacable hostility to organized labor and the left. It sought its urban support in a new governmental party coalition from among the Christian Democrats and elements of the Falange. But from the beginning it gave unstinting support to the revolutionary reforms that affected the peasants, such as agrarian reform and universal suffrage. One of the first acts of the new regime—one supported by every subsequent military regime of the left and right—was to declare its unswerving support for agrarian reform by increasing the distribution of land titles. Full assistance was also given for welfare programs, rural education, and the peasant unions, which both retained their arms and received protection. In fact, in the countryside the Barrientos regime became the most popular one after that of Víctor Paz Estenssoro. A native speaker of Quechua, Barrientos dominated the peasant unions and was known for his largess in buying individual aid and peasant support. The result was an urban anti-labor and conservative populist military regime allied with the Indian peasantry. It was, in short, a powerful coalition, eventually rendered unworkable only by the rampant corruption and instability of the army itself.

The Barrientos regime succeeded in dismantling the mine union (FSTMB), discharged some six thousand miners from the state mining company COMIBOL, and even massacred striking miners on the night of San Juan in June 1967 at the Catavi-Siglo XX mines. Barrientos was temporarily able to decapitate the union movement, but he did not eradicate its potential power. Bolivian labor had become radicalized in the 1940s and successfully resisted the repeated interventions and suppressions that a succession of military regimes attempted after 1964. Nevertheless, the almost constant use of troops at the mines served to isolate and temporarily control the once-all-powerful labor movement for the first time since 1952. In 1965 a liberalized investment code for foreign capital was issued: United States Steel was allowed to rent the Matilda zinc mine from COMIBOL, and Gulf Oil was given further concessions. All of these economic developments aided Barrientos in his political positions. In the 1966 presidential election, he was able to put together a powerful coalition party of peasants, the new wealthy groups, the conservative Falange politicians, and members of the government bureaucracy. Despite his landslide victory and the seeming disintegration of the formal leftist opposition, however, worker hostility toward the regime did not abate, and for the first time since 1952, the government in La Paz began to experience a problem with armed rebellion.

While many small, largely urban intellectual-based guerrilla groups began to operate during the Barrientos period, the most important instance of rebellion came from a source totally external to the national scene. In March 1966, the Argentine revolutionary Che Guevara arrived in Bolivia. Establishing a base camp in the province of Santa Cruz, Che was apparently more interested in setting up a central guerrilla headquarters for operations in Argentina and Brazil than in Bolivia itself. Although he was in touch with the Bolivian Communist Party, he made no attempt to contact or work with the miners. Yet at this very moment the mining camps were under siege by the army, and violence and conflict were an almost daily occurrence. Che seemed intent on quietly establishing an extremely isolated training center for his small band in preparation for other adventures. But in March 1967, a year after his arrival, Che and his group at Nancahuazu had their first clash with the Bolivian army. With strong support from the United States, Barrientos and his chief of staff, General Alfredo Ovando, crushed the rebels. By April, Régis Debray, the French journalist accompanying Che, had been captured, and by October the rebels had been taken and Che was executed. Thus Barrientos was able to survive the armed opposition of the left and yet retain vast popular support among the peasantry and the middle class. There is little question that when he died in an air accident in April 1969 he was still in full control of the nation. Despite the corruption of the regime, Barrientos proved to be such a consummate politician that he could surely have won a second term in open elections.

The military caste that supported Barrientos was incapable of maintaining his ideological and political position. Its members remained divided and corrupt. Despite their common background and experience, their political tastes differed widely, so there was no guarantee that their past histories would prove any guide to their future political positions. All of this became evident in the regimes that replaced Barrientos. From 1969 until 1982, one military regime after another would emerge, with their politics stretching all the way from extreme left through reformist to reactionary right. Government policies depended completely on the personalities and ideas of the individual officers who seized power and in no way reflected a coherent position of the army itself. Whereas in most of the major states of South America in this period the army was presenting a corporate personality and common policy toward the civilian world, in Bolivia this did not occur.

General Alfredo Ovando eventually seized power in September 1969. He was of the moderate reformist MNR tradition and, in fact, tried slowly to push the regime toward a modus vivendi with the left. In October 1969 he nationalized the Gulf Oil Company of Bolivia, and by early 1970 had once again legalized the national Confederation of Bolivian Workers (COB) and the miners union (FSTMB) and permitted the head of the union, Juan Lechín, to return to power; troops were withdrawn from the mines for the first time since 1964. Ovando also tried to mobilize the old left in a newly revitalized MNR. In the end, however, he could neither generate the popular support that Barrientos had achieved nor organize a coherent political party system to support his regime. At the same time, the army became unhappy with Ovando, who had been in power as chief of the general staff or as president for some eight years. Frustrated ambitions of the military thus played their part. The result was the decision in October 1970 to replace Ovando with General Juan José Torres, his former chief of staff.

Thus began one of the most extraordinary governments in Bolivian history. From October 1970 to August 1971, when he was overthrown, Torres would prove to be the most radical and left-leaning general ever to have governed Bolivia. Although he had been a Falangista in his youth, active in the campaign against Che, and supported the army's actions in the period up to his own takeover, Torres emerged as an idealistic leftist politician who wanted to extend Ovando's "democratic opening" to include an even more radical mobilization of workers and leftist politicians. One of his first acts upon taking office was to accept Russian and Eastern European financial aid for COMIBOL. Such support had been offered several times in the past, but the MNR and previous military governments had procrastinated in accepting it under pressure from the United States. Torres also signed contracts for the construction of a tin smelter, thereby liberating Bolivia for the first time from its dependence on European and North American smelters to process its ores. In the end the Russians were to provide almost as much financial assistance to COMIBOL as the United States, each giving in the neighborhood of a quarter billion dollars. Torres also annulled a special COMIBOL contract with a U.S. mining company for extracting tin from Catavi wastes and rescinded the contract with U.S. Steel for running the Matilda Zinc mine. While this type of anti-U.S. company sentiment was not without its precedents, Torres went one step further and expelled the Peace Corps on the grounds that it was fomenting abortion policies among the peasantry.

Although these anti–North American actions were popularly supported, they produced a strong reaction from the United States, which found itself almost totally estranged from Bolivia for the first time since 1952. Torres's efforts to create a united left on the national front were less effective. Torn by the divisions of the Communist Party into Muscovite and Chinese wings, and the subdivision of the new left-wing party the MIR into numerous factions, the COB, Lechín, and their supporters failed to unite on policies and actually feared the increasing radicalization of their erstwhile middle-class radical allies. At the same time, their experiences under Barrientos made them wary of allying with the powerful peasant sindicatos. But in early 1970 the COB did establish a political assembly, which sought to bring some unity to the old MNR left. This formed the basis for a so-called Popular Assembly organized in June 1970 for the purpose of replacing Congress. But this assembly obtained neither the legitimacy of a popular vote nor the powers of a Bolivian legislature. Moreover, the radical left and the labor unions were unable to secure the full cooperation of the relatively unstable Torres or gain major support among the peasant unions. Although the Popular Assembly frightened the right and the center with symbolic acts of defiance, it enacted no significant legislation.

There thus emerged a consensus of the center and right on the need for a new regime. In January 1970 Colonel Hugo Banzer, then head of the Colegio Militar, attempted an overthrow, but the army remained loyal. The subsequent radicalization of the Torres regime, however, meant that when Banzer attempted a second coup in August 1971, the left was unable to stop him. The overthrow of Torres was not without resistance. Though Torres refused to open up the arsenals to the workers, students and workers did oppose the military, while loyalist troops attempted to defend the president. The result was that the Banzer coup of 1971 was the bloodiest overthrow since the April 1952 rebellion.

Banzer himself, while conservative and pro-privatization, was nevertheless relatively moderate. The rise of international mineral prices and the development of modern commercial agricultural in the Santa Cruz region brought an unprecedented boom to the Bolivian economy, and the government itself was modernized with a more technocratic elite. The Banzer regime was consistent with its predecessors in pushing agrarian reform and encouraging active lowland colonization. It granted more land and benefited more peasant families than any previous regime, military or civilian. Thus of the 31 million hectares granted to the 434,000 landless peasant families between 1953 and 1980, some 81 percent of the land went to 62 percent of all families in the military interregnum period from 1964 to 1980, with the Banzer regime alone granting over half the total lands and benefiting half of all the landless families.

But despite this strengthening of a fundamental aspect of the military-peasant pact, Banzer was the first of the generals to reduce the importance of the peasants in national political life largely because of changing demands coming from the peasant sector. The growth of population in the rural areas and the consequent fragmentation of holdings, plus the emergence of a new consciousness of peasants as farm producers for urban markets, were beginning to have an effect on the rural populations. No longer content with land titles, they now wanted credit and price supports and other government assistance in improving their leverage in the marketplace. Thus it was no accident that the first peasant-military confrontation and massacre since 1952, which occurred in the Cochabamba Valley in January 1974, concerned peasant protests over government-maintained food prices.

The Banzer administration also adopted the antidemocratic ideas then dominating the continent. The Brazilian model became an example to the Bolivian military. It was held that democratic rule ultimately led to social chaos, and only through "depoliticizing" the masses could economic development proceed in a rational manner. Through careful tutelage and "controlled" participation, rapid "modernization" could occur. Military intervention was no longer seen as a temporary affair, but rather as a long-term alternative to democratic politics. Almost immediately upon taking office, Banzer declared the COB and the FSTMB illegal, and all of the parties to the left of the traditional MNR were formally denied recognition. This resulted in the jailing or exiling of most of the opposition political and union leaders. He also resolved the tensions with the U.S. government by enacting a more liberalized investment code, and considerable U.S. aid was again sought, and obtained, for the building of army matériel and personnel. But the new relationship with the USSR and Eastern Europe had become too important for even the Banzer regime to reject, so the socialist states continued to provide long-term aid for the development of smelters for processing tin and other metals. The Banzer government also made an abrupt shift from the traditional alliance with Argentina to a new, close relationship with Brazil. Reflecting long-term Santa Cruz interests in opening up their economy and products to Brazilian markets, the Banzer regime signed an important series of international economic pacts that favored Brazilian participation over Argentina in the development of Bolivia's natural resources, above all with the natural gas resources of the southern and eastern lowland regions.

Banzer attempted to create a national political party and forced his two allies, the Falange and the Paz Estenssoro wing of the MNR, to ally themselves with his "Frente" before participating in the government.

This attempt at creating a populist right-wing military government would ultimately prove uninviting to Banzer, and, by late 1974, he announced an abrupt shift in his entire regime by carrying out an *auto-golpe,* as it was called, and establishing an all-military non-party government based on support of the technocrats and nonaligned ex-politicians. Dismissing the MNR from his regime and then exiling Paz Estenssoro, Banzer announced that all parties, even those of the center and the right, were henceforth abolished and that the army would now rule without any democratic concessions whatsoever.

The decision to break sharply with tradition was clearly based on two important developments, one international and the other local. The first and most important factor was the overthrow of the Allende administration in Chile in September 1973 and the coming to power of the Pinochet regime. It was clear to Banzer that the model of a non-democratic authoritarian regime was becoming the norm in the region. The second factor was the extraordinary growth affecting the national economy, which now included commercial agriculture, oil, and—for the first time—natural gas exports. All this created popular support for the regime despite its antidemocratic activities.

But the boom faded as world prices declined, and Banzer could not control the profoundly mobilized Bolivian society. Overspending on national budgets and rising corruption forced him to devalue the national currency by 40 percent, the first devaluation since the 1956 stabilization act. The resulting inflation created unrest, and the clampdown on wages proved to be only a stopgap measure. Despite the maintenance of troops at the mineheads and the supposed liquidation of the FSTMB and COB, strike activity and worker violence continued. By early 1976 there were national strikes, and Banzer had to close the universities. Not only was the regime unable to suppress the unions, but it also lost most of the middle-class nationalist vote when it admitted defeat on the negotiations with Chile for an outlet to the sea. Finally, the middle and upper classes, which provided the civilian base of support for such military regimes in the rest of Latin America, were far more willing in Bolivia to trust their interests to a democratic party system than to an unknown military regime. Given the corruption and indiscipline of the officer corps, the civilian elite could not trust the outcome of an anti-Banzer coup, since there was no way of knowing if the next leader would be a Torres, a Barrientos, or a Banzer.

By early 1977 Banzer promised presidential elections in 1980, and by November, just three years after their promulgation, all the authoritarian decrees were removed. But so hostile had the army become that Banzer was forced to announce that he would not become a candidate, and by the end of the year he announced that elections would be held in 1978. But even this was not enough, for demands were soon made for a total amnesty for the 348 syndical and political leaders in exile. When Banzer refused, wives of mine union leaders began to conduct, in late December 1977, a hunger strike in the Cathedral of La Paz. The Church fully supported the move, and by early January more than a thousand people from all over the country had joined the hunger strike. The strikers demanded total amnesty and syndical freedom as well. So overwhelming was the strike that Banzer was forced to capitulate and was even made to sign a formal agreement with the human rights groups supporting the movement.

The returning exiles seized the unions from the government interventors, and within days the FSTMB and the COB were re-created with the same leadership that had existed prior to the 1971 coup. Strikes, labor agitation, and feverish political activity led Banzer to give up any pretense of attempting to maintain himself in office. He announced that General Juan Pereda Asbún would be his successor and that the new regime would reestablish democracy. Opposing the army candidate was Hernán Siles Zuazo and a new grouping of left and center political parties. To the shock of the military, the election showed that the peasants were no longer voting as a bloc. So many peasants supported the popular Siles slate that the regime found the election going against them, and the military decided to undertake a coup.

But the resulting Pereda government lasted only a few months, and in November came a new junta under General David Padilla, which not only proposed free elections but also announced that the government would not present a formal candidate or support any of the civilian contenders. Both Víctor Paz Estenssoro and his revived MNR, as well as Hernán Siles Zuazo and his Unidad Democrática y Popular (or UDP) alliance of left-wing parties, found support among the peasants and the workers. Moreover, the new professional classes established new parties and alliances to express their particular needs. Suddenly, the new and older parties found themselves in a balanced series of groupings on the right, the center, and the left. Even the formerly despised Banzer succeeded in organizing his own party, with some important regional support, and eventually converted himself into one of the leading national civilian politicians, a rare case of a transition in Latin American politics in any country. The election of 1979 was extraordinary. One of the most honest elections in national history, it brought more than 1.6 million Bolivians to the polls, with most of the alliances and parties showing strengths in all regions.

No candidate won a majority for the presidency, however, and the parties could not agree to a compromise solution, especially as Banzer and his new party were still considered unacceptable partners by the other groups. To forestall a bitter fight, Congress eventually decided to rerun the election the following year and appointed Walter Guevara Arze, president of the Senate and an old friend of both Siles and Paz Estenssoro, as the caretaker president until the new elections. The first civilian regime since 1964, the Guevara administration lasted only a few months and then was temporarily overthrown by a military junta in November 1979. But the political opposition in the nation was so intense, inciting violence and general strikes, that the military was forced out within a few weeks. A compromise civilian, Lydia Gueiler Tejada, was put into office. She was the first woman president in national history. The selection of Gueiler also demonstrated the tremendous popular support for the return of a civilian regime. No party in November 1979 supported the coup, and accusations that Paz Estenssoro had been in favor of it were sufficient to break the electoral deadlock that had prevailed in the previous two elections. In a third national election in as many years, Hernán Siles Zuazo and the UDP achieved a plurality victory in June 1980.

The temporary return to civilian rule under Gueiler, however, cost the hard-line military officers led by General Luis García Meza too many concessions. In July 1980, refusing to allow Siles to assume office, the army seized the government, despite opposition from all civilian parties and groups. But the return to an early Banzer-style authoritarian military regime had destroyed neither the powerful unions nor the civilian party system. Though declared illegal as in times past, these organizations continued to maintain a powerful following among the civilian population. Throughout the two years of junta domination, there was massive civil opposition, which included everything from illegal strikes and marches to hunger demonstrations, which destroyed any possible civilian base for the military regimes. The level of corruption in the army achieved new heights with its direct involvement in the newly emerging international cocaine trade. Finally, the authoritarianism of the officer class reached the point where it carried out the assassination of nine leaders of the MIR in La Paz in January 1981 and organized paramilitary death squads along the lines of the contemporary Argentine model. So extreme was the government of García Meza, which lasted until August 1981, and the ensuing temporary juntas that they employed internationally known fascists such as the Italian Pier Luigi Pagliai and the German Klaus Barbie of World War II infamy and worked closely with the regimes in Brazil, Chile, and Argentina.

Unrelenting civilian opposition, the highly publicized corruption of the army, and the unresolved economic problems of the late 1970s came to haunt the junta governments and finally destroyed even their support among the officer corps. Bolivia was entering into one of its longest depressions in national history, a crisis that would last into the decade of the 1990s. In the context of this political and economic crisis, the violent and exploitative military regimes became an anachronism the country could ill afford. Nor could a violent military, however repressive, control so mobilized a society. The forced resignation of the last military junta in September 1982 and the decision to recall the Congress that was elected in 1980 finally brought an end to the era of authoritarian military regimes. The reconstituted Congress immediately elected Hernán Siles Zuazo to the presidency in August 1982. In one stroke the democratic political system was revived. On the left was Siles Zuazo, the leader of the reconstituted progressive wing of the MNR, who was allied with traditional labor leaders of the central labor confederation, the COB, newer peasant leaders, various parties of the left, and the important MIR group of radical intellectuals led by Jaime Paz Zamora, who became his vice president. To the right and center were the parties that had run in the original 1979 and 1980 elections, all now well-developed political forces that would dominate the national political scene for the next decade. In the center was the historic MNR—led by Víctor Paz Estenssoro—which incorporated both the older center and right of the party, and a group of older Indian leaders who, though now independent of the MNR, still gave strong support to Paz Estenssoro. Finally there was the ADN (Acción

Democrática Nacionalista), the party that Banzer founded at the end of his military rule, which he then expanded in April 1979 to include elements of the old Falange as well as the reconstituted Party of the Revolutionary Left, or PIR. To the surprise of many, the ADN proved more forceful than was thought possible and legitimated Hugo Banzer as a powerful civilian leader. Banzer managed to distance himself from the military juntas of the 1979–82 period, and consistently threw his support behind the democratic process, becoming a pillar of the civilian political system.

*

Thus there was a commonality to most of the Latin American military regimes of this period, with their suppression of congresses, parties, and the media, and their application of state violence to demobilize their societies. These regimes all were an authoritarian response to the new demands and power of landless farmers and peasants, the new industrial labor force and the expanding urban middle classes. They, like the United States, assumed that these demands would inevitably lead to socialist or communist regimes, and they were supported in this by the traditional upper classes, which no longer accepted the democratic system and were willing to call on the military to protect their own economic interests.

Although the perceived "threat" was more or less immediate or more or less intense in the differing countries in the years preceding the military takeovers, once the militaries were in power, they had a commonality of responses. Almost all responded with ruthless violence that often had no relationship to the original "threat." No matter how professional the officers were, "as soon as the military defined fellow countrymen as enemies against whom all-out war had to be waged, every conceivable repressive measure became justifiable."[86] With the exception of Peru, each of these regimes at one time or another carried out periods of uncontrolled state-sponsored violence against its own citizens, with assassinations, torture, imprisonment, and exile as tools of the government. In contrast to the pre-1960s Latin American "theater" of protests and conflict, no class or group was exempt from this violence, and the usual mitigating institutions of family, friendships, and class were useless against state-sponsored terror that often knew no limits, as the Argentine killing of expectant mothers and the forced adoption of their children showed.

But these authoritarian governments differed in how to respond to the new social and economic demands for change. Some simply repressed all organizations and parties that espoused reform and tried to turn back the clock, destroying the associations, parties, and institutions of civil society and killing or imprisoning any liberal or progressive persons within their societies who might promote change. This was best exemplified by the Argentine and Uruguayan experience. Others thought that only the military itself could modernize and develop their own societies and thus eventually negate the need for serious social reform, because it was supposed that the populations would be richer and better educated and would no longer accept radical solutions. The classic cases of this alternative were Brazil and Peru, whose officer class had a long history of studying these issues and offering ideas about what the military should do in promoting such change. And then there was the Chilean experience, with an attempt to modernize the society in a neoliberal reform that was carried out under a dictator allied with conservative civilian technocrats in which the officer class provided little serious input. The case of Bolivia, though sharing the ferocious antidemocratic aspects, was also a case apart. It had a newer officer class with fewer traditions and humbler origins than the militaries in the other states. Moreover it was still committed to agrarian reform and based its support, uniquely, not on an upper class and the Catholic Church, but on a newly enfranchised and landed Amerindian peasantry organized in powerful rural unions and ayllus, or community governments. Moreover, its officer class reflected the ideologies of the political movements of the nation, and the military governments ran from populist and radical left to hard-line authoritarian administrations. In many ways the Bolivian army well reflected the special nature of its post-1952 society than the more highly structured armies in the more economically advanced countries of the region.

Finally, it is worth noting that however the political parties of the center, left, and right were divided before the authoritarian regimes came to power, the historically unusual and new levels of state violence that the regimes promoted finally forced a basic reevaluation of the commitment by all parties to a democratic process of negotiation.

On the left, the issue of human rights now became a serious concern, and armed struggle was rejected as a failed experiment. For the center parties, neutrality no longer remained a possibility when regimes killed members of the middle and upper class. In turn, the parties of the right realized that they ultimately could not trust the military to protect their interests. Such regimes divided the elite into supporters and non-supporters and encouraged crony capitalism and non-transparent economies with non-level playing fields. Thus the ultimate impact of all of these military regimes was a major strengthening of the democratic process in Latin America. It is no accident that by the second decade of the twenty-first century, two guerrilla leaders became president in Brazil and Uruguay and a socialist tortured by the Pinochet regime was elected president of Chile for two terms.

2 The Brazilian Military Interregnum
The Politics

WHEREAS PREVIOUS MILITARY interventions in Brazil had been largely of domestic interest, the military revolt in April 1964 was of major concern internationally to at least one of the players in the Cold War. For the United States, this revolt was an essential part of its Latin American policy. João Goulart, to the United States, was another Jacobo Árbenz—a populist leader promoting social and economic reform and therefore "class warfare." That such reformers in poor countries could only lead to communist regimes was the standard position of the Democratic and Republican administrations of the United States. U.S. State Department planners believed that poverty and backwardness in the third world, and especially in Latin America, could be resolved only by authoritarian governments in alliance with private capital.[1]

This well-known U.S. policy was not lost on the Brazilian military leaders. It strengthened their own position that this intervention should be a major departure from previous ones. The army no longer would act as an arbiter to balance democratic forces and control "excesses," but instead would take over the government in order to "modernize" the country and destroy communist penetration by demobilizing the left-wing parties and unions. Accepting the Vargas development model as a viable objective, it nevertheless saw the democratic process as a threatening and unnecessary impediment to this developmental policy.

Although the United States was also interested in pushing for open markets, it was willing to subordinate that demand in return for an authoritarian regime that was pro-Western. It thus offered powerful political and economic support for the generals even as they further nationalized and closed the economy. Moreover, the United States actively supported the police agencies of all the regional authoritarian regimes in their hunt for "subversives." In turn, as more and more Latin American governments were becoming authoritarian, the generals saw no need to conform to any democratic norms then prevalent in the region. Finally, like all of these military-dominated regimes, the Brazilian officers would often lose control over their more reactionary colleagues, which would lead to periods of extreme violence against the citizenship, including torture, disappearances, and assassinations.[2] Censorship, repression, imprisonments, torture, and murder became generalized practices. Some twenty-five thousand persons were arrested, including dissident military officers and labor leaders. The northeastern peasant leagues and the national student unions were disbanded and the labor unions put under tight military supervision. Finally, almost all of the older and newer radical, liberal, or progressive political leaders were officially denied their political rights (making them *cassados*), and many of them were forced into exile.

Brazilian military intervention in national politics has a long history that went back to fundamental changes in the military establishment from the end of the empire until 1964. As José Murilo de Carvalho has noted, the Brazilian military establishment initially differed from most of its Latin American counterparts in the preservation of its class origins and stratification in the nineteenth century. Its officer class produced no caudillos and was far less democratic in terms of social origins. It inherited its aristocratic culture from the Portuguese models, with nobles being the officer class and the mostly illiterate peasants or urban poor being the common troops and sailors. Although the Brazilian monarchy had to expand the conception of nobility to include elite families of all kinds, the officer class was fully part of the national elite in origin and identity for most of the nineteenth century. This began to change at the end of the empire, when only half the generals were of noble status—even generously defined. By the time of the Old Republic (1889–1930), more and more officers were of middle-class origins. Bright students from the middle class often chose a military career to further their education, since they did not have the funds to do it on their own and the military academy was one of the few institutions of higher learning in the country. In fact, the military academy often taught as much liberal arts as the military ones for most of its earlier period.

By the end of the empire, the officer class consisted of veterans of the Paraguayan War and liberal arts graduates of the military academy. Deodoro da Fonseca, the first president of the Republic, was typical of the former, and Benjamin Constant and Euclides da Cunha were examples of the latter type of officers. But both were essentially authoritarian and corporatist. When a new military academy opened in 1917, it had both more military instruction and a strong current of conservative Catholic teaching added to the curriculum. Foreign training also had its influence in modernizing the army and making it more cohesive. From 1906 to 1910 three groups of Brazilian officers were sent to train in Germany for two years each, and in 1920 a French military mission was brought to Brazil, which led to the establishment of advanced specialized technical schools for the officer class. It also led to a reorganization of the army under the General Staff (Estado Maior) and a tighter control over junior officers, especially after the 1922 rebellion of the lieutenants, which had involved many of the recent graduates of the Military Academy. Finally in 1927 came a formal Council of National Defense within the Army High Command, whose job it was to plan for mobilization and for national defense, which was defined in the broadest possible terms.[3]

The failed revolt in 1922 of lieutenants in Rio de Janeiro was made in the name of officers who claimed they could direct the nation toward a more just society. The army was bottom heavy with these recent graduates who had little chance for advancement and pushed their revolutionary ideas of reform, which were rather incoherent.[4] Although the revolt was eventually put down, many of its leaders later joined the 1930 rebellion that brought Getúlio Vargas to power. Moreover, as Murilo de Carvalho has argued, it was the Vargas revolution of 1930 that combined the usually rebellious junior officers with an important group of senior officers for the first time in republican history. These officers had a much clearer sense that the army was above the state and had a moderating role to play in the new republic, much as the emperor had in the empire.[5] The Vargas government also gave many of the officers involved in the 1930 revolt high administrative positions either as state interventors (that is, governors) or as central government administrators in positions not associated with the army. Though the officers had been in civilian ministries before and even had senators and deputies elected to office, the Vargas period saw the most active intervention of the officer class in government administration. Thus the army was more and more brought into the civil part of the government just as it was developing and debating its role within the state. While there was always a group that held the army to be totally subordinate to civil power, whom Murilo de Carvalho calls "neutralists," there was also an important group going back to the positivists and the lieutenants revolt who believed in "reformist intervention." There also existed a small far-left group of officers who proposed a popular army-led revolution and who eventually joined the Communist Party. By the 1930s the two major currents of reformists and neutralists had finally combined to form what Murilo de Carvalho calls the "controlling interventionist" majority, which believed in an active role as moderator of the more extreme aspects of republican politics and with a possibility to propose its own ideas of development.[6]

There was also a progressive cleaning of the army. The Paulista revolt against Vargas in 1932 allowed the army to eliminate most of the senior officers still loyal to the old republic, and the military reforms in the 1930s and 1940s progressively isolated the officer corps from the society. Subalterns were denied access to officer positions, meaning only graduates of the preparatory schools and military academies could become officers, and admission to these educational institutions was limited to Catholics, older immigrant groups, and those who showed positive national values. Finally, officers on active duty were prohibited from voting or participating in civilian parties. All this was done to further isolate the military from active civilian politics—the norm in earlier periods—and to create a cohesive distinct ideology and culture well removed from civilian politics.[7]

Much of that ideology had its origins in the debates current in Brazil following World War I and the rise of an antiliberal ideology in Europe in the period after 1914.[8] Equally, the origins of the Vargas dictatorship and the 1964–85 authoritarian regimes have much to do with the specifics of the republican government established in Brazil in 1889. The Brazilian republic began as an oligarchic-controlled limited democratic regime with a decentralized federal system managed essentially by the elites of two states: Minas Gerais and São Paulo. The revolution led by Vargas in 1930 was a response to the excesses of that regime. It immediately pushed the balance of power away from the states and back to the central government as it had been under the empire. Vargas also found himself alienated from the planter elite of São Paulo, which even led an armed rebellion against his government in 1932. In this context the liberal state was rejected by the political leaders who supported Vargas. Moreover, since Vargas faced a hostile elite, it was essential for him to create new sources of power. He was the first major Brazilian leader to realize the potential of the urban working classes. They were an untapped power just beginning to find expression through strikes and incipient socialist, communist, and anarchist political movements and had the potential to be mobilized in support of the Vargas regime, which feared their radical orientation and hoped to control it.

The intellectuals who supported the Vargas revolution in turn were much influenced by the antiliberal ideology that became fashionable in Europe after the crisis of World War I. These antiliberal ideologies ran the spectrum from *hispanidad* and corporativism through fascism and reactionary Catholicism and found a ready response in the 1920s and 1930s among a group of Brazilian intellectuals opposed to the liberal elites who had ruled under the Republic. Though a few became fascists,[9] and others turned to conservative Catholic ideologies,[10] the dominant group that would emerge with the most political power promoted a combination of nationalist, authoritarian, and racist ideologies.[11] Though flirting with corporate and fascist models, especially after the arrival in power of fascism in Italy in the 1920s and the evolution of the fascist state there in the 1930s,[12] they primarily promoted the idea of a charismatic authoritarian leader as the best solution to the "crisis" of the Brazilian republic.

In the 1920s ferment of new ideas in Brazil from the modernists in São Paulo to the fascists and conservatives in other Brazilian states, the antiliberal and antidemocratic ideologues that had the most political influence in the era of Vargas and military regimes were those whom Boris Fausto and others have called "authoritarian nationalists." These ideologues believed that only a nonliberal response could resolve the growing tensions of the increasingly serious "social question"—that is, issues raised by class conflict in the new age of industrialization. Only an authoritarian regime could control the excesses of capitalism, repress the left-wing movements, and create harmony. But even more important, they argued that a coherent development toward a modern industrial society could come only through a powerful centralized state directed by an all-powerful executive uncontrolled by local elites and unfettered by democratic constraints. It was this ideology that emerged as the dominant one both for Vargas and for the generals who governed after 1964. That some of these same intellectuals and their ideas were present in both periods can be seen in the figure of the jurist Francisco Campos (1891–1968) from Minas Gerais, one of the leading ideologues of this school who helped write both the authoritarian 1937 charter of the Estado Novo and the first Institutional Acts or governing decrees of the military regime in 1964. He was minister of education and health and later of justice under Vargas, and then worked closely with the civilian supporters of the 1964 military revolt. Under the Estado Novo dictatorship established by Vargas, the rule was government by decree. In turn, Campos used decrees to model the "constitutional" Institutional Acts (Atos Institucionais, or AI) written for the post-1964 military regimes. The preamble to the first of these famous AI decrees, which gave unlimited power to the executive, stressed that their legitimacy came from the revolutionary act itself, which Campos held was as valid for justifying the government as a popular vote.[13]

Thus the entire process of creating a modern state would be a top-down development as a way to generate support from the working class, prevent it from spontaneous organizing, and convert it into a new potential political power in Brazil.[14] For the authoritarian nationalists, far less interested in the potential support that this class might generate for the government, these reforms were a way to move the working classes away from the left-wing parties and movements that were thought to be "exotic" ideologies preventing the natural evolution of the Brazilian people.[15] It was also thought that modern welfare institutions could be used, as Vargas declared, to "invigorate the race," and more specifically to "eugenically improve the race."[16] This was a clear reference to the racist and eugenics ideas then much prevalent among the authoritarian ideologues.[17] To this ideology was added the older one of the military as the defenders of the state and the "moderating power" in Brazilian politics—there to keep the country on the road to development and to prevent the excesses of democratic politics from derailing this process of modernization.[18]

The period from the overthrow of Vargas to 1964 showed a new power of the military to act as an independent and autonomous institution. While supporting the authoritarian aspects of the regime, the pro-labor program of Vargas particularly upset the military officers, for they feared it was an indication of a drift toward a left-wing populist government and the possibility that Vargas would turn himself into a version of Perón. In 1945 the majority of the generals turned on Vargas and with civilian support were able to bring an end to his authoritarian state. This was the first republican golpe that saw a united front of the army, the navy and the air force together against the government. Thus began their constant intervention and formal "tutelage" of all the regimes that followed.

Moreover, dissident generals and junior officers, who supported Vargas, were quickly brought in line after the golpe and none were removed from the army. There was no cleansing as occurred in the 1930s as the army now maintained a united front. The return of Vargas as an elected president in 1951 created another episode of direct military intervention. Although the generals fully supported the economic nationalism and the pro-industrial policies of Vargas, they opposed his labor and social policies. These they felt were counter to the needs of the modernization process and could potentially lead to a pro-communist regime under populist leaders. More and more, the admirals and generals found themselves in agreement with the far-right politician Carlos Lacerda and his UDN (União Democrática Nacional) party. In 1953 Admiral Carlos Pena Boto even founded a movement called the Brazilian Anticommunist Crusade with the support of the Church, ex-fascists, and even some labor unions.[19]

Fearful of the populist tendencies of Vargas, the military in August 1954 demanded that he resign as president, which led to his suicide.[20] In the ensuing twenty years the military constantly acted as arbiter and controller of the political scene, under conservative, center-left, and left-leaning democratic regimes. As political mobilization increased in this highly democratic period, the role of the army in "arbitrating" the political system also increased. The army in this period was the single most important political party in the country, and once agreement had been reached among the generals, it would find itself capable of over-throwing the entire democratic system in 1964. But this time it came to rule in its own name, no longer acting as a moderator or protector of constitutional democratic institutions.[21]

The origin of this shift has much to do with the changing ideology and education of the officer class in the period following World War II. Aside from the officers' increasing anticommunism, fostered by close ties with the U.S. military in these years, there was also another part of the new ideology of the army that came out of their older "developmental" ideas. This newly expanded "developmental" ideology had a great deal to do with the establishment in 1948 of the Escola Superior de Guerra (ESG, Superior School of War). Modeled along the lines of the U.S. National War College, which had been created two years earlier, and the older French Institut des Hautes Études de Défense Nationale founded in 1936, its aim was to gather officers from all three services along with selected civilian experts to discuss national and strategic issues and propose solutions. Unlike the National War College, its primary interest was to be national development rather than international relations. Moreover, its civilian participants were more numerous and included many more groups than just the government officials that formed part of the classes of the U.S. institution. To aid the school, Washington provided a U.S. advisory mission that remained in Brazil from 1948 until 1960.[22] In contrast, the similar and equally important institution founded in the same period by the Peruvian military, the Centro de Altos Estudios Militares (CAEM), did not have senior U.S. advisers and sent its officers to CELADE and other United Nations agencies in Chile for training. The ESG worked closely with American advisers, and its purpose was to open up a dialogue with leading Brazilian businessmen, judges, legislators, government officials, and educators. All participants were required to be university educated, which of course excluded labor leaders. The idea was to create an interdisciplinary discussion between elite civilian leaders and officers in all principal areas of society and the economy, and prepare reports and analyses of the basic national issues of concern to both. By the late 1960s the school had more than twelve hundred graduates, half of whom were civilians. The course was a yearlong full-time activity, with field trips throughout Brazil and a visit to the United States. An active alumni association (ADESG) of some twenty-five thousand carefully selected members held meetings throughout the country as well and disseminated the reports and ideas discussed in the Escola. The ESG was also closely associated with highly politicized "think tanks" of the era, such as the Brazilian Institute for Democratic Action (IBAD), a businessmen's group founded in the 1950s, and the Research Institute of Social Studies (IPES), a broader conservative group of businessmen, former government officials, and military officers like General Golbery do Couto e Silva, which was founded in 1961 and was essentially a political action group.[23]

The ESG's organizer and first director was General Osvaldo Cordeiro de Farias, one of the lieutenants in the rebellion of 1922 and one of the leaders of the Prestes Column, which grew out of the rebellion, and thus one of the earliest "developmentalist" officers in the army. He also served in the Brazilian Expeditionary Forces in Italy in World War II and participated in the overthrow of Vargas in 1945. One other founding member of the staff and a major military intellectual was the engineer Juarez Távora, an ardent Catholic and both a participant in and one of the key ideologues of the 1922 lieutenants (tenentes) rebellion as well. He was also one of the generals who demanded the resignation of Vargas in 1954 and was the candidate of the conservative UDN for the presidency in the election of 1955.[24] The other founding members of the school had all participated in the Vargas regime as interventors, administrators, or military educators. These included Ernesto Geisel, who later became one of the principals of the ESG, and the important theoretician Golbery do Couto e Silva, who was a firm Catholic, an anticommunist, and a supporter of the doctrine of national security, but also a major proponent of modernization and development.[25] Almost all of these leaders in the school had served on the general staff and had either fought in Italy or had extensive training in the United States. They were in essence an elite group of officers, well trained, long involved in national politics, and adherents of the same set of beliefs and ideologies.[26]

The school was famous for promoting the doctrine of National Security and National Development. The security of a developing country like Brazil was intimately tied to its economic development. As Alfred Stepan succinctly put it, this meant "maximizing the output of the economy and minimizing all sources of cleavage and disunity within the country."[27] In this second aspect was embedded a virulent anticommunism and a belief that only a powerful central government could control these cleavages and disunities. The stress was on the need for a hierarchical order directing and controlling change, rather than on any democratic process of negotiations, participation, and consensus. In essence, the ideology proposed was antithetical to the democratic process. The planning papers that were produced dealt with all aspects of the economy and national infrastructure, though all solutions were seen as technocratic and with little attention to the political realities of their implementation. This intense planning for change and modernization was seen as the best strategy to fight internal subversion. Moreover, by the 1960s more and more of the school's ideology was being taught in all the other military schools; that ideology now placed ever increasing emphasis on preparation for internal war, rather than on preparation for international conflict.[28]

In the end the staff and students at the ESG became the major focus for all the hostility toward the post-Vargas governments. As Ernesto Geisel, commandant of the school and one of the "presidents" of the post-1964 military regime, noted, the ESG's opposition to many of these governments of the period was fueled by their association with João Goulart, who "was in our understanding, a weak man dominated by the left. What we had against him was that he came from the tradition of the Vargas labor policy group. We thought that his government would be divisive, devoted entirely to the working class, at the expense of the development of the country—it was his tendency to move to the left. Since the revolution of 1935, the Armed Forces considered communism to be the principal problem of internal security."[29]

Conservative and anticommunist, the officers teaching at the school and those who graduated from its classes were the key figures in the 1964 golpe. In fact, the graduates of the ESG were overrepresented among the golpistas of 1964.[30] According to Stepan, 60 percent of the generals involved in the 1964 golpe attended the ESG.[31] These revolutionary generals had double the average years working in the Estado Maior Geral than non-golpe officers and in contrast only 8.9 years leading troops, compared with the non-golpe generals' average of 14.5 years as troop commanders. They were also more likely to be teachers in all the upper-division military schools. This was especially the case with Emilio Garrastazu Medici and Humberto Castelo Branco. Also most of them were more engaged in politics than most generals, some four of them having directly participated in the *tenentes* revolt of 1922, with many of them declaring sympathy with that movement and with most of them also involved in the 1930 Vargas rebellion.[32] This time around, there was no tolerance for dissent, and after 1964 the "legalists" who opposed the intervention were systematically eliminated. From 1964 to 1968 some 574 officers who did not support the golpe were expelled from the army.[33]

There is little question that the 1964 golpe was generated by a chaotic political environment, in no small part due to the unending hostility of the military to all the old Vargas labor politicians and to mistakes made in mobilizing popular protests by leading democratic politicians. It also occurred in a period of high inflation and economic stagnation. These problems might have been resolved by a democratic regime, but the unrelenting pressure from the military and business leaders and the ongoing anticommunist campaigns of the United States, which unceasingly viewed these Vargas leaders as socialists and potential communists, created a basic situation of instability. Even Juscelino Kubitschek, the most extraordinary president and political figure in this postwar period, was disliked by the military, and members of the right were upset by the actions of President Janio Quadros, whom they thought as one of their own. Would the golpe have occurred if the United States, the army, and the far right had been less hostile? The answer is probably not, as the democratic negotiations between classes and factions would probably have led to more solid civilian regimes. But Kubitschek and Goulart and the other civilian leaders faced such implacable hostility that it is difficult to see how they could have created solid coalitions in the style of Vargas to overcome this implacable resistance. Finally, there was the long tradition of authoritarian developmentalism in the army and among its conservative civilian allies, which went back to the early twentieth century. That tradition finally found full expression in the minority of politically impassioned generals who were desperate to prove that their authoritarian leadership could lead the country into the first world.

The military generals under Castelo Branco had a clear plan of action. For the majority of this group, an immediate return to another civilian government was out of the question. Stability and change had to be carried out. Inflation needed to be controlled by a classic orthodox shock, and some of the ideas for structural change developed by the

ESG group had to be implemented, which could not be easily done in a civilian regime. At the same time the majority of officers supporting the coup rejected the idea of a strongman government, and they were determined "to maintain some semblance of democratic legitimacy by obeying constitutional requirements of a fixed presidential mandate with no second term."[34]

Immediately after the expulsion of Goulart, the military dismantled the democratic institutions that might have impeded their activity. They agreed not to return to democratic rule until they felt all the subversive elements had been eliminated and some significant political, social, and economic change had been undertaken. Castelo Branco, the leader of the coup, organized a military junta of the three services.[35] On April 9, the new military regime decreed the first of a long list of institutional acts that moved the country away from a democratic position toward an authoritarian regime. The act was drafted by the jurist Milton Campos, who had also drafted the Vargas Estado Novo dictatorship constitution of 1937. Institutional Act 1 created a powerful autonomous presidency and a far more limited Congress in terms of budgets and legislation. Moreover, it allowed the president to suspend the political rights of any citizens "in the interest of peace and national harmony" and granted the president the right to cancel the mandates of any state or municipal legislative council.[36] It also transferred to Congress the power to elect the new president of the republic, and Congress then on April 11 elected General Castelo Branco as president. Instead of turning to their civilian allies in the UDN, the military leadership for the first time decided to develop its own political project without sharing control, and it remained in power for twenty-one years. This of course alienated all the centrist and right-wing politicians who had supported the coup against Goulart. As for the centrist and left-wing politicians, especially the old Vargas pro-labor group, many had their political rights canceled even though they had supported the coup and the appointment of Castelo Branco. Those expelled included the ex-president Juscelino Kubitschek.[37]

Although unqualifiedly authoritarian in nature and intent, the Brazilian military regime exhibited characteristics common to other regimes in the region and several that were unique to it. On one hand, it was typically repressive and ferociously anticommunist, siding with the United States as a staunch ally in the Cold War. It was also committed to a powerful centralized state dominated by the federal executive branch, limiting the power of other branches of the central government as well as the states and municipalities. At the same time, it tried to maintain elections and kept Congress functioning. The powers of Congress were, of course, much reduced, and its membership was controlled through expulsion of a large number of left-wing and centrist politicians, whose political rights were revoked. As Thomas Skidmore noted, the new military government "did not attempt to work through the rules of democratic politics as its predecessors had done. It unilaterally changed the rules."[38]

The military did not constitute a homogeneous group. There were divisions between nationalists and internationalists and between the so-called hard-liners (*linha duras*), who saw no need to return to democratic rule, and the legalist authoritarians, who eventually espoused the goal of a return to a controlled and modified civilian-led democracy. For some, repression, censorship, and torture were extreme means only to be used as a last resource, but for others those were fundamental instruments needed to destroy the left and all progressive elements. The government itself lost control of repression and torture, and both became a part of the system at the local level. The differences between the various officer groups showed up with greater intensity in the presidential succession process—another peculiar feature of the Brazilian dictatorship. Fearing the emergence of a powerful personalistic regime under a caudillo, which would lead to a Pinochet- or Franco-type system, the military establishment committed itself to fixed presidential terms and formal "elections." During the entire military period, the presidential terms were for limited periods and were formally "elected" first by the leading generals and then by a controlled Congress, which confirmed the prior selection of the military establishment. Internal conflicts in the choice of new presidents were kept under military control and out of public debate until the early 1980s. Different groups alternated in power but always needed a consensus in the military to maintain themselves in power.

There were also subtle differences in the phases of the military government. The leading chronicler of the military rule, Elio Gaspari, has argued that there was a first period from 1964 to 1977 in which the head of the army and the president were indistinguishable, with the president being either the representative of the army or its prisoner.

The second period began with the dismissal in 1977 of the minister of war, General Sylvio Frota, by President Ernesto Geisel (1974–79). From then on there was a clear differentiation between the war minister and the president, with an autonomous president now in control of the army. This control eventually permitted Geisel to begin the famous and slow decompression process of democratic *abertura,* or opening of the regime in 1975.[39] If this is the case, then the previous period (1964–77) can be considered a more typical type of Latin American dictatorship of the era, with the army fully in control of the executive branch. In turn Gaspari and some historians have divided this more authoritarian period of 1964–74 into another two parts, a period of more moderate and semi-constitutional rule from 1964 to 1969, and the period of repression, known as the "Lead Years" (*anos de chumbo*), from 1969 to 1974, during which the elite lost control to the violent elements in the military and censorship, repression, and violence for the sake of violence became the norm.

But it should be stressed that most of the instruments of repression were put in place from the very first years of the military regime, even if they became more intense in the period from 1969 to 1974. Thus opposition newspapers were attacked from the first days, and increasingly more rigid censorship became the norm as everything from radio to music and theater was strictly controlled.[40] Moreover, the state political police, the DOPS (Departamento de Ordem Politica e Social), which in the 1960s were centers of repression and torture, already had support from the military officers even before they were placed directly under the military command in the Medici period. In addition, the navy through its Naval Intelligence Center, CENIMAR, was from the beginning a center for torturers.[41]

Initially there was a debate in the military and its allies as to how long the military would rule. The overthrow had initially been a defensive act against the increasing radicalization of Goulart and his allies in the labor movement. The question was then, what should come next. The hard-liners wanted a long-term military rule to surgically excise communism and "varguisimo" from the body politic, with torture, assassinations, and repression as the means to do it. Another group, which Daniel Reis has called the "liberal-internationalist-modernizers" originating in the ESG, wanted to use army rule to carry out basic economic and social reform. In short, they wanted to achieve a "revolution" in the name of the people, but under control of the armed forces.[42] In the end both groups in the army would come to power. The liberal modernizers held sway until 1969, and the more violent and conservative group came to power in the Medici period, from 1969 to 1974. Nevertheless, with their strength in the garrisons and the organs of the secret police and intelligence service, the most conservative group would make important bids for power in all the periods of military rule until the very end, and even when the modernizers were in power their activities often could not be controlled.

Even in the relatively less violent early period of the military regime, imprisonment, explosions, and systematic violation of basic rights were the norm. Between 1964 and 1966, some 5,000 people were taken into custody; 2,000 public employees were dismissed or forced into retirement; some 500 political leaders were "cassado" and had their political rights withdrawn altogether or suspended for ten years;[43] 421 military officers were either forced to retire or were expelled, among whom were 24 of the 91 active generals; some 70 percent of the unions with more than 5,000 workers had their entire leadership removed—which involved the dismissal of some 10,000 union leaders. Many political leaders went into exile as the regime continued; former presidents were constantly brought in for interrogations; and in the first nine months of the regime there were 13 deaths at the hands of the military.[44] There was also the beginning of systematic torture used in some of the formal military investigations (Inquéritos policial-militares) into corruption and subversion led by regular army officers, which the older generals could not stop for fear of losing the support of these hard-line younger officers.[45] The army in its "Operation Cleanup" closed down everything from the regular Communist Party of Brazil to the Maoist Communist Party and from the Catholic Church's base educational and religious communities to peasant leagues.[46]

Contrary to how Pinochet would totally manipulate the army promotion and retirement system in Chile to appoint only personal loyalists, Castelo Blanco reformed the retirement rules for the army so as to guarantee both greater institutional autonomy and more rapid turnover at the top of the hierarchy. The rules of promotion through the ranks and retirement remained the same, but no general was allowed to serve in that rank for more than twelve years or beyond sixty-two years of age, and all three levels of generals had to have a quarter of their members changed every year. If none were eligible for retirement, then the oldest would be forced to retire. The rank above general, marshal, was eliminated. This guaranteed a constant renovation at the top and the removal of older officers from power. Finally, both to control potential corruption and to prevent military officers from isolating themselves from the army, no active serving officers could remain in civilian administration jobs for more than two years.[47] All of these reforms, in contrast to what Pinochet would do in Chile, prevented even a serving military president from controlling the army and its appointments.

It was also under a supposedly liberal military regime that a complex secret police and intelligence service was established, one that was typical of all authoritarian regimes. Under Golbery do Couto e Silva, a loyal ally of Castelo Branco and Ernesto Geisel, the National Service of Information, or SNI, was created as a superministry that reported only to the president. It was in essence a political police force designed primarily to spy on and root out "subversive" elements in the country and coordinate anti-left-wing activities with all the Cold War regimes in Europe and America, which often involved assassinations and kidnapping. The SNI was staffed by graduates of the ESG and by 1982 had 6,000 employees, most of whom were officers. It also housed the secret services of the three branches of the armed forces as well as that of the federal police. Organized like the CIA, its concern was strictly national rather than international, as in the case of the American service. It would eventually be led by two future presidents. The first was the hard-liner General Emilio Medici, and the second was General João Baptista de Oliveira Figueiredo, who like Golbery came from IPES to the SNI. The SNI worked closely with the CIA and all the intelligence services of the authoritarian governments of South America and Portugal as well as of Israel and the major European powers. Very well paid and equipped, it had little difficulty in quickly identifying and dismantling all of the small guerrilla movements that rose up in the late 1960s and early 1970s against the government. But as many scholars have pointed out, the SNI was more autonomous and independent than any other major secret service, even the KGB. With no transparency and little or no control, this "state within the state" was involved in everything from contraband, electoral manipulation, provocative acts of violence, and corruption to cross-border assassinations. The SNI itself seems to have lost control over its associated police and military action groups and of local army commanders who wished to actively engage in violence. But it remained firmly under the control of the military president, who sometimes used it to quash military revolts and keep himself informed of all the army plots.[48]

General Castelo Branco, who had studied in France and the United States and led the ESG, was considered a leader of the moderate military group that believed it would be possible to return power to civilians as soon as subversives were eliminated and populist politicians expelled from the political scene. It was the same vision of the civilian leaderships represented by the UDN, which had played an active role in the military coup and now represented its parliamentary base. Initially, Castelo Branco assumed power for the duration of the Goulart mandate, which would conclude at the end of 1965, but he finally agreed to extend his mandate until March 1967. He also changed the electoral laws to require a 50 percent–plus majority for election to the presidency, an issue much pushed by Carlos Lacerda and his conservative UDN party, which claimed all the previous elections had led to minority victories. Thus it appeared that the regime would eventually turn the government over to its conservative civilian ally in 1967. The provisions of AI-1 were allowed to expire, and Castelo Branco accepted the continuation of normal elections. Most of the "populist" leaders had been cassados, which left the field open to the right-of-center leaders. His government also clearly supported the UDN for the coming elections, though its leader Lacerda vociferously opposed the orthodox economic shock that the government was implanting at this time.

In November 1965, elections for state governors took place, still with the old political party structure intact. In two of the most important states, Minas Gerais and Guanabara (Rio de Janeiro), opposition politicians from the hated Partido Democrático Social (PDS) were elected. The government's reaction was to decree a new Institutional Act that modified the party system and the entire electoral process. In future elections for president and governors, the vote would be indirect, occurring in the respective national and state legislatures in open sessions. What is impressive about this military overreaction was that the governors elected were either moderates or political and union opponents who were willing to work within the political restraints proposed by the military regime.[49] But the military refused to deal with them. It decided that the old parties were to be abolished and a new system of only two legal parties (one for the government and another for the opposition) was created, eliminating the previous party structure that had survived for twenty years. ARENA (Aliança Renovadora Nacional) and the MDB (Movimento Democrático Brasileiro) were established, with the former being the government party that gathered together members of the old UDN and other conservative leaders, and the MDB representing the opposition. The government was again given the right to disqualify from political life any citizen for ten years and was again empowered to arbitrarily remove any legislator at any level—powers that had been allowed to lapse from the AI-1 decree. In an attack against all the habeas corpus decisions of the civilian judiciary against arbitrary arrest and torture, it transferred all political cases to the military courts. It also packed the Supreme Federal Court with five more judges sympathetic to its aims. The AI-2 act was a defeat of Castelo Branco by the hardliners and clearly showed the military's commitment to a long term in office. Some of the old UDN leaders such as Carlos Lacerda, who had taken part in all the rebellions to depose Vargas and Goulart and had even tried to depose Juscelino Kubitschek, joined the opposition. Even the justice minister of the government, Milton Campos, the author of the AI-1 decree and a leading UDN politician, refused to sign the AI-2 decree.[50] Finally, mayoral elections were abolished in a new AI-3 decree issued in February 1966, and henceforth all mayors of the capital cities would be appointed by governors.[51] In an attempt to control his more hard-line successors, Castelo Branco and his supporters issued a new constitution and a new national security law, which in effect locked in all the changes the government had made to that date. But this action was quite illusory, since the successive military administrations had no qualms about revising this ephemeral constitution with more institutional acts.[52]

In March 1967, General Artur da Costa e Silva assumed the presidency. A hard-line military officer and one of the leaders of the coup against Goulart, he had been minister of war during Castelo Branco's mandate and overcame the opposition of the moderates in Castelo's entourage. Although Costa e Silva proposed a liberalization of the regime, in fact this period led to increasing conflict between civil society and the military. There were increasing popular demonstrations of students and workers. Two strikes took place, one in Osasco (São Paulo) and another in Contagem (Minas Gerais) in early 1968, and both were

severely repressed, with the unions destroyed and their leaders imprisoned or exiled.[53] The military developed agents provocateurs, carried
out its own bombings, raided theaters, disrupted memorial masses,
arbitrarily kidnapped and tortured civilians, and entered a period of
anarchy whereby local officers could do whatever they wanted in the
name of anticommunism. It also began to work closely with the other
repressive regimes in the region.[54] It carried out a major program of
censoring books, plays, and movies, along with totally controlling the
media.

In turn, the opposition organized a Frente Amplio of all the leading
political parties and leaders, from Carlos Lacerda to Kubitschek, who
opposed the institutional acts. Students became more aggressive in demands for the return of democracy, and the hierarchy of the Church
slowly began to turn against the regime as some of its missionaries and
local priests were attacked by the military.[55] Even the severely controlled
Congress in late 1968 opposed the military government by protecting
one of its members, with even legislators of the ARENA government
party deserting the regime. The emergence of urban terrorist movements and rural guerrillas in the late 1960s was a consequence of this
repressive regime.[56] Despite the low risk of these guerrilla movements
to the regime, such acts further justified the repressive mechanism put
in place by the military. The increasing manifestations of opposition led
to an ever more truculent regime, which viewed all of these activities
by peaceful political alliances, marches, and masses for victims of the
regime as further indications of a country filled with communists and a
political system not yet cleansed of dissident elements.[57]

The military abandoned all efforts to preserve democratic norms
and, in supposed response to congressional independence, issued the
Institutional Act no. 5 in December 1968, thus consolidating the dictatorship and ushering in one of the most repressive and bitter periods in
Brazilian history. The military government could now close all federal,
state, and municipal legislatures at will and dismiss any elected official,
judge, or government employee it wanted to; it denied habeas corpus
to those accused of political crimes, who could be tried only in military courts, allowed the confiscation of property of subversives, and
otherwise created a total police state. Moreover, this law—unlike the
previous acts—had no time limitations and could be changed only by
the president. Congress was closed; some 349 government officials and

politicians were purged—the most in any military administration. In March 1969 a new, draconian censorship law covered all types of artistic expression, prohibited public notices of strikes or protests, and put the media under military law. It was illegal to defame the government or the armed forces. More officers and enlisted men were dismissed, and exile became the destiny of thousands of Brazilians. In April 1969 some sixty-five university professors were expelled, including the future president Fernando Henrique Cardoso, who was forced into exile. This expulsion even included the historian Eulália Maria Lahmeyer Lobo, the sister of the then minister of mines and energy. Finally in June 1969 came the joint police-army and businessmen-funded OBAN, or "Operation Bandeirantes," which involved dragnets detaining thousands of citizens in São Paulo and other cities.[58]

In September 1969, President Costa e Silva suffered a stroke and became incapacitated. In the midst of this crisis the U.S. ambassador was kidnapped by left-wing guerrillas, and the government had to exchange him for fifteen imprisoned militants who were sent to Mexico.[59] To add to its problems the military was about to violate its own constitution of 1967. Instead of permitting the civilian vice president Pedro Aleixo to take the presidency, the military changed the rules and in AI-12 announced that a military junta would rule until a president was selected. Several months of tough negotiations among the generals began. Finally the former head of SNI and a close friend of Costa e Silva, General Emílio Garrastazu Medici, was selected in October to rule for five years, with an admiral as his vice president. To give the election process more legitimacy and show this was not a dictatorship, they had to recall Congress, which had remained closed since the implementation of Institutional Act no. 5. Congress was presented with only one candidate and was forced to elect the president indicated by the *junta militar*.[60]

President Medici's term would be the most closed and repressive of the military regimes. He increased the power of SNI dramatically as an organ that vetted all appointments. He also controlled appointments to the Military Council and increased the power of the presidency. The government gave absolute control over the economy to Antônio Delfim Netto, who was maintained as economics minister from the previous government, using the AI-5 and supplementary acts as a basis for authority to change basic economic structures and even the way funds were distributed between the central government and the states without legislative approval. Medici was of the hard-line group who believed in a total cleansing of the society before Brazil could become a democracy again. He would thus continue with the torture and repression, and further erode what few civil liberties existed. In the ideologies then current in the Army High Command, he was labeled both a hard-liner in terms of hostility to an immediate return of democracy and an internationalist opposed to the extreme nationalism and populism promoted by some generals. He was also a manager who delegated others to run the army, the political arena, and the economy. In turn Delfim Netto "consolidated the rule of the technocrats, who were spread through the public banks, utilities, and state enterprises."[61] This was the most technocratic government of the early military regimes, and the results showed in major economic and social changes and annual growth rates of 10 percent per annum.

The Medici government lasted from October 1969 to March 1974. These would be the years of major economic euphoria, with high growth rates and increasing income concentration. The economic growth created a better standard of living for the middle class, and the creation of new jobs incorporated significant new contingents of the population into the formal labor market. In fact it was a unique period of extraordinary social mobility with sons of lower-class individuals rising to middle- and upper-class positions.[62] These results gave the government a relatively popular acceptance despite its ferocious censorship, repression, and constant violation of individual rights. Even the elimination of guerrilla movements as a serious threat by 1971 did not put a halt to torture, kidnapping, and assassinations. As Skidmore has remarked, "The defeat of the guerrillas did not end government torture. That should not be surprising, since the torturers had not waited for an armed threat to begin their work."[63] Moreover, the Medici government finally took full command of the violence by shifting all the police operations of the local state DOPS and police units to army control under General Orlando Geisel, brother of the future president. This now fully tied the army, navy, and air force directly to the tortures and killings.[64] Also, the fragile relations with the Church were broken in the Medici period as priests and nuns were expelled, imprisoned, and tortured.[65] In contrast to other military presidential periods, the Medici administration used mass communication intensively to sell the image that Brazil was a rapidly progressing country on the way to quickly becoming a world power.[66]

By the end the Medici period, it looked like the regime, despite its claims, seemed headed toward some form of an authoritarian regime, though without a caudillo. As Philip Schmitter observed at the time, the military up to the early 1970s had easily liquidated the populist vestiges of the old Vargas authoritarianism, which had made for a weak democratic system prior to 1964; its internal conflicts notwithstanding, the military appeared to be moving to consolidate a new, more conservative authoritarianism.[67] But it was also evident to Juan Linz at the time that despite successfully implementing major economic and social programs, the military regime had come to no consensus on political institutionalization, as its constant changes of law and of institutions and the conflicts among the generals showed. Nor did its essentially negative doctrine of National Security indicate any clear path to real authoritarian rule. Given this lack of a direct move toward a Spanish- and Portuguese-style dictatorship, he called the Medici regime an authoritarian "situation" rather than a full-fledged authoritarian regime.[68] It is also evident that the state terror unleashed by the Medici regime had the unexpected consequence of forcing a profound rethinking of basic human rights on the part of the intellectual and political elite, which created a new sense of what made for a civil society. In short it awakened a new and far more coherent opposition than had existed before, especially after the defeat of all guerrilla movements had shown that violence was useless and only provoked more state terrorism, against which the usual restraints of family and class no longer offered any protection.[69]

All this makes the transition from Medici to Geisel even more of a profound shift, especially in terms of political institutions. Despite the relative success of the hard-liners, General Medici accepted as early as 1971 that General Ernesto Geisel, then head of the state oil company Petrobrás, would be his successor, even though Geisel represented the moderate group of the Castelo Branco era and would be the first non-Catholic president.[70] When Geisel took office, he quickly declared his support for an eventual return to democratic rule. His administration continued the technocratic group that led the various ministries, though Delfim Netto was removed from the government and given an Ambassadorship to France; he was replaced by Mario Henrique

Simonsen, another leading economist. In turn Golbery, who had been head of Dow Chemicals in Brazil after his earlier retirement, became chief of the civilian presidential staff, and General João Figueiredo became head of the SNI.[71] The aim of Geisel was to slowly modify the repression system by reducing the power of the military hard-liners and redemocratizing the country. But how to do this was a difficult question. After much discussion and debate he eventually rejected as possible solutions the corporatist models suggested by some Medici supporters and the idea of using ARENA to turn Brazil into a one-party authoritarian system like the PRI in Mexico, a suggestion offered by Professor Samuel Huntington of Harvard when he advised both the Medici and the Geisel governments on the process of transition.[72] But Geisel firmly believed that when the transition occurred, the government party should be in power. He also was totally committed to a very slow "decompression" with very careful control over who would participate and their level of participation in the process of redemocratization. But even for this limited opening to occur, he needed the same high growth rates that the Medici regime had maintained, despite the first world petroleum crisis of 1973, and even more he needed to control the army and the security forces.[73]

But the new government quickly ran into problems. It soon discovered that it could not easily control the security apparatus and was constantly embarrassed by well-planned acts of violence that it could not, or would not, control. Despite the absence of any armed opposition, journalists, academics, lawyers, and even an American Methodist minister were deliberately seized by the security apparatus, tortured, and then released in the first months of the new regime, publicly showing that the president was not in control of the repression. Moreover, the initial "disappearance" and subsequent torture of the U.S. citizen was meant to provoke a direct confrontation between Geisel and the United States. In fact, in this anti-Geisel campaign, more prisoners "disappeared" in the first six months of his regime than had gone missing in the previous regimes.[74] There were even periods of greater censorship than during earlier regimes, despite the slow decline of formal censorship. Thus the important weekly journal *Veja*, which was only lightly censored between 1968 and 1973, especially compared with the regular newspapers, was severely pre-censored in the Geisel period, even though it supported him in general terms. This censorship usually came from the Ministry of Justice, which was under the control of hard-line military officers.[75] But at the same time the press and the opposition became more vocal and bold now that the government had indicated its willingness to leave power at some future date. Public discussion and open protest became the norm, and even former leaders of the Escola Superior de Guerra like Juarez Távora and former hard-liners like General Albuquerque Lima demanded a return to democracy and an end to the police state.[76]

The first test of this commitment to an "opening," or abertura, came with the elections to the federal legislature in November 1974. These would be direct elections, and the key issue for the regime was maintaining the power of the government party. In the October 1974 indirect gubernatorial elections, the state legislatures voted in a complete set of ARENA governors. The strength of the official party depended on the intimidation of voters, changes in election rules, and the silencing of the opposition leadership, which suggested to many that the regime was heading toward a one-party solution. But the situation changed in 1974 when the opposition won large majorities in the elections for the federal congress and the state assemblies. The outcome of the elections, the most democratic held by the military to that date, was a surprise, since the government believed its party would win. The results demonstrated the unqualified popular opposition to the regime, and they made Geisel's "opening" policy even more difficult among the voters who counted—that is, the army generals. Although Geisel did not contest the results, he allowed the justice minister to increase censorship of the press and was adamant in his support of AI-5, the most dictatorial of the famous Institutional Acts.[77] But as former president Kubitschek declared afterward, the "monster" of public opinion had been unleashed by the elections, and it ultimately could not be muzzled again as it had in the period up to October 1974.[78]

This in fact is what later political scientists would argue as well. The election turned out to be a plebiscite on the regime, and not a vote for any charismatic leader. It showed that all the major urban centers were voting against the continuation of the authoritarian state. In each successive election the opposition kept increasing its advantage, first in the major urban centers and then even in the more traditional periphery areas. The opposition overwhelmed ARENA in the 1978 Senate elections and in 1982 in the election for the Senate and the municipalities. The "monster," despite all the censorship and institutional impediments placed in its way by the generals, could not be silenced. The 1974 vote "established the autonomy of *abertura* as a political process, transforming it into something much less reversible than initially foreseen in the government strategy."[79] In the second half of the decade the political ferment spurred the growth of grassroots movements from neighborhood associations and mothers' clubs to new unions and union leadership and from local religious communities to a popular campaign protesting the cost of living in 1977. All these social movements continued until the end of the military era as civil society became more complex and associations more powerful.[80]

With the hard-line military officers and their security apparatus increasingly aggressive and the civilian opposition more outspoken, the situation was becoming more complicated. The opposition MDB party controlled over a third of the seats in the national legislature and dominated legislatures in several key states. The security forces and hardliners continued to intensify their confrontation with civil society and the Church, and they even challenged the president. In October 1975 came the killing of a leading journalist, Vladimir Herzog, by the Department of Information Operations–Center of Operations for Internal Defense (DOI-CODI), an intelligence and security apparatus under the control of the local army command in São Paulo. The journalist's murder led to a university strike and thirty thousand students marching in protest, forty-two bishops signing a petition against the government action, and Cardinal Dom Paulo Evaristo Arns, archbishop of São Paulo, leading an ecumenical funeral service for Herzog in the Cathedral of São Paulo.[81] This killing broke the silence of the opposition to the whole security apparatus and allowed the Church, the Brazilian Bar Association (OAB), the National Press Association (ABI), and other institutions of the establishment to join forces with the opposition MDB in a public campaign for human rights and the return of legality.

But the army would not stop. In January 1976 came another Second Army "suicide" victim, Manuel Fiel Filho, a major leader of the important metallurgist union. This time Geisel did not defend the action, but directly ordered the dismissal of the general in charge of the Second Army without consulting the High Command. This action finally shifted power in the army to Geisel and his supporters, although there would still be continued rearguard actions of the hard-liners to the end of the administration.[82] Among their many targets now was the Catholic Church. It was the single most powerful and autonomous voice of the opposition, and it was probably the most liberal of the national Catholic Churches in the world. Thus the security apparatus killed and tortured missionaries, lay organization people, and local priests in a systematic way in 1976 and even carried out a destructive invasion of the Catholic University of São Paulo.[83] It was not until the latter half of the next year that Geisel finally got full control over the hard-liners in the army when, in October 1977, he dismissed General Sylvio Frota, the army minister who was then the official leader of the officers fighting against the liberalization of the regime. Again this act of dismissing the army minister, unique to the Geisel period, was done without consulting the High Command.[84]

But the Geisel government itself had difficulty accepting the democratic system and still saw the MDB as the opposition that had to be frustrated if the "opening" was to succeed. The government lost the major cities in the municipal elections of 1976 to this party, and therefore in April 1977 Geisel closed Congress and issued new electoral rules under the dictatorial power of AI-5. Governors would now be elected indirectly, and a third of the Senate would be chosen through the same system. These two measures guaranteed that ARENA would have a majority in Congress and that the election of governors would be controlled by the federal government. In addition, the military modified the representation in the Chamber of Deputies, distorting the proportionality between deputies and their state population. The minimum number of deputies elected by small states was raised and a maximum limit per state imposed, thus reducing the representation of large states. This created a fundamental regional distortion in Congress, which persists to this day, so that the representation of the northern and northeastern states is proportionally much higher than for the more modern and wealthier central and southern states. The new electoral law also restricted the opposition's access to the media. In addition, the mandate of the next presidential term was extended to six years, and other harsher measures were introduced, from censorship of imported publications and repression of student meetings to the expulsion of the leader of the opposition in the Chamber of Deputies.[85]

The revival of an autonomous labor movement is another important development that occurred in the Geisel period. From the first days of the authoritarian regime, the military had maintained the urban and rural unions but put them under tight government control, intervening in most unions, expelling most of their active leadership, and controlling wage negotiations.[86] In the urban area, the trade unions' structure set up in the Vargas period remained rather stable, giving the state great power to manipulate the unions through the use of the *pelegos* (professional trade union leaders linked to the government). In the rural area, the very active peasant leagues that existed prior to the military regimes were destroyed but were replaced by formal unions, which again were under the direct control of the Ministry of Labor. But in the Geisel period there was an emergence of new union leadership in both the rural and the urban areas.

The peasant leagues (unions in all but name) had proliferated in the northeast in the late 1950s and early 1960s under the leadership of Francisco Julião. By the late 1950s these and the peasant "associations" organized in the south under Leonel Brizola formed regional confederations.[87] The National Confederation of Agricultural Workers (CONTAG) was established in early 1964 and was recognized in the last days of the Goulart government. After the golpe, the army abolished all these leagues and associations and imprisoned or assassinated 65 of their leaders and lawyers, including one president of CONTAG; another 1,276 rural laborers, lay workers, priests, and Indians were assassinated by gunmen working for the latifundistas. Yet, surprisingly, the national confederation survived and even prospered in the worst years, as the military eased up on its repression and as the Catholic Church became a leading supporter of the movement. Already by 1968 an independent peasant leader had replaced the military interventor as head of CONTAG, and by 1970 the state was using the new local unions for its rural pension scheme, FUNRURAL. In fact many of these unions also set up health clinics as well. Rural workers by the end of the military era had founded 2,700 unions, half of them in the 1970s, representing more than 9 million rural workers. This was the single largest union category in Brazil and one of the largest in Latin America. Clearly the ability of the state to control the unions in the old Estado Novo style along with the expulsion of its radical leadership made the new rural unions more conservative. In turn, given the military government's strong commitment to modernizing Brazilian agriculture, it needed some support from the rural workers to do this. It thus accepted their more moderate unionization, without of course responding to their demand for land reform. These rural unions would in fact be treated to some extent like the urban and industrial unions now under military control.[88]

The response of the military to the urban unions was the same as in the case of the rural ones: preserve their structure, but liquidate the active leaders, intervene in the more aggressive unions, repress strikes, and remove wage issues from their control. The controlled unions in the period 1964–78 concentrated their efforts on health and social services for their members. But in the urban area and in the new heavy industry sector, new independent leadership emerged in the mid-1970s within the trade unions, and after years of immobility there now occurred the first strikes. Just as in the rural areas, one of the crucial intervening institutions was the Catholic Church, which provided a minimum of protection for the new leadership to emerge.[89] Ten years after the violent repression of the Osasco and Contagem strikes, the automobile workers from São Paulo's ABC region went on strike under new leaders elected in 1977 and afterward. The head of the strike movement was Luiz Inácio da Silva (known as "Lula"), at that time a trade union leader, and years later the president of Brazil. The strike began with a spontaneous sit-down strike of the workers at the Scania truck factory on May 12, 1978, which was soon followed in other automotive factories. To avoid violent confrontations, the workers adopted peaceful tactics and negotiated directly with employers. The employees accepted the negotiations and settled the strike.[90] At the same time, the strike and its resolution were seen as a major step in the return to a democratic society and was supported by the MDB and large sectors of civil society, including the Catholic Church, which was very active in the whole process of democratization. By 1979 both spontaneous strikes and union-organized ones had broken out all over Brazil and had gone well beyond metalworkers into banks and sugar plantations involving more than 3 million workers. Most of these strikes were for wages, but many demanded factory-level union representation and job security, issues that directly challenged the corporate union structure then in place. The government was forced to concede the wage increases (readjusting salaries twice a year instead of once and not manipulating the inflation rate), but made no concessions on revising the current union structure.[91] There is little question, however, that the revived union movement had become a major force in the opposition to the military regime.

Another key factor was a change in U.S. foreign policy. Both Democratic and Republican administrations had actively supported the military from 1964 to 1973, but the election of Jimmy Carter brought a major change. Human rights trumped anticommunism for the first time in U.S. foreign policy, and it now became a major theme of the new government. Carter essentially rejected the generals and put increasing pressure on Geisel above all to end the violence and torture and return to a civilian democratic regime. This often led to sharp conflicts and harsh rejections on both sides, but it unqualifiedly changed the comfortable authoritarian atmosphere that had been the norm of the region until that time. The growing unification of the civilian opposition and the support this opposition received from the U.S. government were part of a changed international atmosphere that unquestionably affected the Geisel government.[92]

By 1979 Geisel was finally meeting directly with the leaders of the opposition, from the MDB to the OAB, and representatives of the National Council of Bishops (CNBB). This resulted in the so-called April Pact between the civilians and the military, which led to the modification of the constitution of 1969. This new document effectively repealed AI-5 by allowing for the return of most basic legal rights, from habeas corpus for people accused of political crimes to the guarantees of an independent judiciary. Also the executive power lost the right to close Congress and the state assemblies or to cancel electoral mandates without due process. But Geisel also extracted the right of the executive to declare a state of emergency for ninety days, during which time most of the powers that were in the AI-5 decree could be used. Although all opposed this special arrangement, the civilian opposition was forced to accept it by Geisel as a part of the negotiated package.[93] Modifications also occurred in the National Security Law, making it less encompassing. Finally, Geisel revoked the banishment acts for many of the people who had suffered such arbitrary measures.[94]

Having decided from his earliest days that General João Baptista Figueiredo would be his choice, Geisel had outmaneuvered General Frota as a potential candidate for the hard-liners and raised Figueiredo to a four-star general to make him equal to all the other senior generals.[95] Thus in the transition to a new military president, Geisel was able to maintain the moderate line in the choice of his successor. In 1978 the military leadership accepted the choice of General Figueiredo, then head of the SNI, to be the president. This election represented the ultimate defeat of the hard-liners in the military. In the actual election itself, the MDB ran its own presidential candidate, General Euler Bentes Monteiro, a liberal from the upper echelons of the army. While the indirect vote guaranteed a government victory, Figueiredo was forced to run a public campaign in which he promised to continue the abertura.

On March 15, 1979, President Figueiredo took office and appointed mostly liberal technocrats in the ministries, with Mario Simonsen and Delfim Netto initially having key positions in regard to the economy. The government was also predominantly civilian, with very few generals being appointed to nonmilitary positions. Golbery, the eminence grise of the previous regime, stayed on as head of the civilian presidential staff.[96] Among the government's first acts was a total amnesty decree, which both freed the military from prosecution and allowed the return from exile of the last of the pre-1964 leaders, which included Leonel Brizola, Luis Carlos Prestes, the secretary general of the PCB, and Francisco Julião, leader of the northeastern peasant leagues.[97]

Figueiredo committed his government to continuing the opening process and was determined to transfer his mandate to a civilian successor, but within a complex process of political negotiations and in the context of a period of economic crisis. Starting from the first oil crisis in 1973, the military regimes had chosen a heterodox (or nonrecessionary) economic adjustment, promoting a strong investment program with foreign funding that completed the industrialization process and made the country less dependent on foreign resources. The price to be paid was the public sector's financial exhaustion and an expansion of foreign indebtedness. The second oil crisis in 1979, and the widespread debt crisis of the emerging countries that resulted from this crisis, made such a program no longer viable. Figueiredo's government faced the need to carry out a brutal recessionary adjustment, without foreign support.[98]

In addition to the deterioration of economy, there was a deterioration in the political scene. Nonetheless, the path to democratization was maintained, under the strong and constant political pressure of the civil society. Figueiredo extended the Geisel amnesty program and made other concessions. But the civilian opposition wanted a broad, general, and unrestricted amnesty. This was finally achieved in 1979, with the government restoring political rights to all those affected by previous exclusion acts. In spite of critics who fought the granting of amnesty as well to military personnel for their acts of repression and torture, this amnesty act represented great progress in the democratization process and was considered a major accomplishment for the government. Amnesty allowed the return of traditional politicians, including active members of Goulart's government. The political scene now became more complex. In 1979 Lula, then president of the São Bernardo's metallurgy trade union, promoted a new strike that was violently repressed, with the imprisonment of hundreds of workers, including himself, and led to government intervention in the union. But although the workers were forced to accept limited pay increases, they gave unqualified support to Lula and all the new union leaders. This ended the pelegos control over the metalworkers unions and also brought Lula into national prominence as an unqualifiedly powerful civilian leader. Moreover, direct bargaining was accepted by both Volkswagen and General Motors, which negotiated the end of the strike with the unions themselves without the usual intervention of the government.[99] But this was the last significant victory of the independent leaders under military rule. Metalworkers' strikes in 1980 and 1981 were stopped; the government not only prohibited the companies from directly bargaining with the workers, but it also intervened in the union and eventually eliminated Lula and his supporters from their leadership positions. Numerous activist union leaders were laid off in many of the other industries that had strikes. These developments were a major setback for the unions.[100]

The original strategy of the government had been to create two parties, with the idea that the military could maintain its power base both in the military period and in an ensuing democratic period with free elections. But its party, ARENA, showed little popularity from the beginning. ARENA's majority was made possible only by changing election rules to benefit the government party and systematically eliminating opposition politicians. In direct and free elections, the opposition seemed able to take control. Given this situation, military leaders decided to support a multiparty solution instead, hoping to split the opposition into many smaller parties, which is what actually occurred. Several opposition parties were formed, but the old unified opposition MDB party also survived as the PMDB (Partido do Movimento Democrático Brasileiro). Among the various parties created, was the PT (Partido dos Trabalhadores), or Workers' Party. It was formed by the new authentic trade union leaderships, under its leader Lula, and included left-wing intellectuals and segments of the urban middle class. The PT was an unusual creation since it had a coherent organization, ideology, and leadership. The other parties, including the PMDB, were more like opposition fronts than organically structured parties. ARENA, the government party, remained unified, but it changed its name to the Partido Democrático Social.[101] In 1980 most of the provisions of Geisel's April Pact were overturned, and direct elections were permitted for all senators and all state governors.[102]

All of these changes were opposed by the far-right groups in the military and security apparatus. In 1980, they tried to create a climate of terror, which culminated with an accidental explosion of a bomb placed in a Rio de Janeiro entertainment center. An army captain and a sergeant were involved, and while the government did not arrest anyone for these actions, the resulting inconclusive investigation led to the resignation of Golbery from the government in August 1981. But the extreme nature of this activity found no support outside of a small group of radical officers who wanted to move toward an Argentine-style regime, and massive public pressure finally forced the government to repress these extreme elements in the army.[103] The government, which had appointed some Medici hard-liners, still proclaimed that it was committed to "the process." In September 1981, when Figueiredo had a mild stroke and was forced to leave the presidency for eight weeks, his civilian vice president was allowed to take over the presidency in his absence, though he had no control over the military or security apparatus. This temporary appointment of a civilian president occurred again when Figueiredo had to undergo bypass surgery in the United States in 1983.[104]

The government, for all its support of ARENA, allowed for continued open elections. In 1982 direct elections for state governors took place. Again to the shock of the military, opposition parties achieved a great victory, taking over the governorship of key states and even achieving a majority in the Senate. In addition to the regime's political deterioration, the deep economic crisis—reinforced by the Mexican debt crisis that begain in 1982—further harmed the government, and popular protest became the norm as the government permitted mass demonstrations. The most important of the protest movements was the massive mobilization of civil society and opposition parties begun in 1983 in favor of direct elections to choose the next president of the republic. Congress was presented with a project to change the constitution and establish direct election for the presidency. Great assemblies took place in almost all states, culminating with the São Paulo manifestation that gathered more than a million people. In spite of this massive and continuous demonstration of popular support for direct elections for the presidency, the military, realizing that such a process would cost it the election, refused to back down on the issue, and ARENA barely prevented a constitutional amendment from being enacted by a two-thirds vote of Congress.

But the presidential elections of 1985 proved to be another surprise for the military. The army named a candidate who was a retired colonel and former minister, thus breaking the mold of four-star generals but expecting to continue with a moderate and controlled presidency since the government party was the dominant power in the Electoral College. But in mid-1984 a civilian politician challenged the official nomination and actively campaigned for the government party nomination. This was the former governor of São Paulo, Paulo Maluf. Although the PDS was bitterly split over his campaign, the national committee finally nominated him as its presidential candidate, to the shock of the military. In turn the PMDB chose the governor of Minas Gerais, Tancredo Neves, as its presidential candidate, with José Sarney—former president of ARENA and a northeastern politician—as his vice-presidential running mate. Sarney brought with him the support of dissident PDS leaders who had created a new Liberal Party Alliance, which now aligned itself with the PMDB. With the generals allowing the PDS to make its own decisions on candidates, and with the election campaigns well covered by the media, the fight began over the delegates to the Electoral College. The result was a stunning victory for Tancredo Neves, who aside from getting support from his PMDB electors polled almost as many PDS electors as did Maluf. The civilian opposition had reached the government sooner than had been anticipated, irritating a segment of the military leaders and the president himself. They had expected the slow transition to continue. It had started in Geisel's government and had been extended during the six years of Figueiredo's government;

and they had assumed that the new president would be one of their own, enabling them to remain in power for another six years. Some hard-line military officers showed their dissatisfaction and put at risk the inauguration of the new president. But they were defeated.

This transition would yet show surprises. The day before the inauguration on March 14, 1985, Tancredo Neves fell ill and underwent surgery, impeding his taking office. There was an emergency meeting with the main political leaderships. For some, the appropriate constitutional track would be the installation of the president of the Chamber of Deputies, who would wait for the elected president's recovery or would call for new elections in case the elected president should be unable to take office. But this was fraught with too many risks, especially given the continued importance of the military. Another option was to make the vice president take office temporarily as president, which in fact was the position of Ulisses Guimarães, then the president of the Federal Chamber of Deputies and a leader of the main opposition party, the PMDB. Although Figueiredo refused to take part in the official transfer, Sarney was inaugurated as temporary president, and one month later he took office when president-elect Tancredo Neves died.

José Sarney's presidency represents an irony in history, since it installed in office a traditional pro-government politician rather than the leader of the democratic opposition. But Sarney well understood his rather unusual position, and he kept the ministers Tancredo Neves had already named and decided to base his political support on the PMDB's parliamentary majority. Sarney's government would be marked by this particular political balance. In moments of crisis, the legitimacy of his installation was questioned, and he was forced to manage a country in a deep economic crisis, which only worsened during his administration. However, his administration undoubtedly represented a major development in the final consolidation of the democratic process. One may say that the long transition, started during Geisel's government and continued during Figueiredo's, would be completed in the Sarney period.

As soon as he assumed office, Sarney began to implement new measures to liberalize the regime. Congress voted to impose direct elections for the presidency, all parties were legalized—including communist ones—and illiterates were enfranchised. Relations with Cuba were reestablished, and the government even successfully survived a militant metallurgical workers' strike, making it possible for the two sides to resolve the conflict. In fact a wave of strikes, allowed to freely resolve themselves without government interference for the first time, mostly led to defeats of the more militant unions. Sarney also established close relations with the military, which in the end gave him complete support. But it became obvious that there was a need for fundamental constitutional change to replace the constitutional changes made by the military regimes that had stressed both centralization and extreme authoritarian. There was thus an immediate demand for a new, more democratic constitution. This led to a debate about whether the new constitution should be created by a newly elected constitutional convention—the position of the left-wing parties—or by the current Congress. More conservative groups and the president wanted the Congress that was to be elected at the end of 1986 to write the new constitution. It was believed that a Congress with constituency power would be more conservative than a group that would only elaborate the constitution and then be dissolved, which would be less predictable in its decisions and probably more representative of civil society and more radical. The most conservative position, supported by President Sarney, won. The resulting constitution approved in 1988 has been criticized for various reasons. It is overlong and very meticulous. The pressure of special interest groups led to unusual amendments not relevant to a constitution, which in fact should have been treated in ordinary legislation. But it was unqualifiedly a democratic constitution and a very advanced one in terms of social and political rights.

The new constitution proposed fiscal decentralization. States and municipalities gained income from the government, creating new financial commitments and mandatory resource allocation. Budgets thus became more rigid, and at the same time it became more difficult to balance government accounts. Several public monopolies were enshrined in the constitution, and the document also had a distinctly nationalist tone. On the other hand, the constitution of 1988 was seen as one of the most advanced in terms of social and political rights, including those for minorities. Elections for president were now made by direct voting in a two-stage process if a majority was not obtained on the first vote, the voting age was dropped to sixteen years of age, and the literacy requirement was abolished. The system of government to be established was also one of the most intensely discussed topics at this time. Main opposition leaders preferred a parliamentary system of government, which was reflected in several norms of the approved constitution. But they were defeated when the issue was finally decided, and the presidential system was maintained. They did manage to approve a plebiscite that would be carried out in five years to decide between the parliamentary and presidential options, but when the plebiscite was held in 2003, the presidential system was selected.[105]

Despite the political and economic crises experienced by the democratically elected governments in the thirty years since the end of the military regime, for the first time in republican history, Brazil has an effective democratic regime. The military returned to the barracks, and the political conflicts are resolved within the constitutional rules. The radical left has abandoned the armed struggle and has committed itself to the support of human rights and basic democratic structures, and the far right no longer seeks its aims through military intervention.

But what of the political program of the military? Although it temporarily liquidated the old Vargas labor elite, and numerous left-wing movements and parties, including the communist parties, it ultimately was a failure. All the old leaders who still had some political base, like Leonel Brizola, returned to power after 1985, and all the old communist leaders and their parties returned to the political arena. The student movement and the urban and rural peasant unions survived the dictatorship as well and emerged more autonomous than before. A whole new generation of political leaders came on the scene, and they would have appeared even earlier had the military not intervened. Though the complex manipulation of the parties probably encouraged a new set of parties to be formed, these quickly became the dominant parties of the nation, an unanticipated result that was not what the generals had hoped for. They really did want a conservative PRI-like party to emerge with a small opposition that they could control and continue to guide with their limited democratic model. But if the political project was a failure, the economic and social projects developed under the military proved to have a different outcome. Although the military wanted a powerful modern state, the details were essentially left to the civilian technocrats, and these did in fact profoundly change Brazil, with these changes still influencing the nature of the Brazilian society and economy to this day.

3   Economic Reforms of the Brazilian Military Period

THAT THE MILITARY era would be one of reform as well as repression had much to do with the military's compromise with a civilian elite that cooperated with the officers and was supported by them. Economists, sociologists, urban planners, university professors, and social security administrators would all be incorporated into the military regimes and find support for their reformist ideas, even as other social scientists and older government administrators were being exiled, imprisoned, or even killed. As Rodrigo Patto Sá Motta has noted, the military regime was not a dichotomous one split between repression and reform but more like an ongoing dialogue between repression and negotiation, repression and accommodation, and repression and co-optation. This enabled the generals to bring some of the most advanced social and economic reformers into the regime and allow them to undertake reforms that would outlast the military era. That many of these reformers came from the middle and upper classes made it easier for the generals to negotiate with them.[1]

Among the military officers, the impulse to create a powerful modern economy ultimately outbalanced their more extreme anticommunism. The military government thus arrived with plans, however inchoate initially, to modernize the economy and the basic infrastructure of the country. But not only did it face an immediate economic crisis inherited from the Goulart period, it also encountered, throughout the two decades of its rule, severe international crises that affected all Latin American countries and that had an impact on both political and economic conditions in the country. In contrast to other Latin American nations, however, Brazil responded to these external crises under the military regime by applying a heterodox economic solution when others were administering classic orthodox shocks to their economies to control public debt and inflation. This led to an extraordinary burst of industrial growth and a major increase in agricultural production and exports. But the undoubted successes with this policy in the end led to impaired public accounts, an external debt crisis, and resurgent inflation by the 1980s, forcing the military and the democratic governments that followed the military regime of 1964–85 to practice extreme recessionary policies.

The Brazilian economy for the first seventy years of the twentieth century had experienced a long period of growth. Initially sustained by the exportation of coffee and later by a process of induced industrialization through the substitution of imports, the country was able to create an ample and complex industrial structure without parallel in Latin America. By the late 1970s Brazil had established an industrial structure that included an important capital goods sector. The continental size of the country created a market of a scale sufficient to sustain not only a consumer durable goods industry but also an industrial sector that could produce both basic inputs and finished capital goods.

This long process of growth was broken by a series of external crises that affected Brazil and the majority of the developing countries at the end of the decade of the 1970s. The crisis began to unfold with the first oil shock of 1973, was reinforced by the second one of 1979, and was followed by the Mexican crisis of 1982 and the generalized external debt crisis of the 1980s. These shocks, for both Brazil and the rest of Latin America, broke the region's long trend of growth in the twentieth century. In the case of Brazil, the average rate of growth, which had been 5.7 percent per annum by the last years of the 1970s, dropped to 2.1 percent in the last twenty years of the century. This later rate of growth was insufficient to maintain the well-being of a still poor country with great social and income inequalities and a population growing at 1.7 percent annually. The post-1970s crisis was also accompanied in

Brazil by a seemingly uncontrollable inflation and an ever increasing public debt.

This process of accelerated growth for eighty years followed by stagnation for two decades occurred, as we have seen, in an ambience of political instability. The country began the twentieth century with a new republican government that until the 1920s was controlled by local elites and an oligarchy based on the coffee economy. Beginning with the international crisis of the 1930s, the structure of political power became more complex, with a greater participation of new economic elites who were less tied to the traditional coffee sector. Under Vargas and Kubitscheck, and again under the nationalist military regimes of 1964–85, Brazil developed a complex economic policy that stressed the forced growth of the industrial sector.[2] Along with the systematic development of a major industrial sector, the military also carried out a modernization of both the financial sector and agriculture.[3]

The Goulart period was marked by growing political unrest among the urban unions and rural peasant leagues, as well as radical movements among the students and even within the Catholic Church itself. From a coalition of forces between these left-wing and nationalist groups came proposals for structural reforms known as "reforms of the base" (reformas de base), which called for such basic changes as land reform, and included proposals to reform education and even the chaotically growing cities of the country. There were also demands for granting illiterates, a significant share of the population, the right to vote. In the economy the situation was critical, with low growth and inflation of about 80 percent per year. Aiming to curb the inflationary process and resume growth, the economist Celso Furtado launched a Triennial Plan. The plan pointed to the external and public sectors as the main causes for inflation and proposed to relieve the pressure of the public sector by increasing taxes, reducing expenditures, and raising funds from the private sector through the capital market. Despite these efforts by the Goulart government, there were no objective conditions for its success. In 1963 inflation rose to 82 percent and output stagnated.[4]

When General Castelo Branco assumed power, the country was in a severe economic crisis. The economy was in a deep recession and was experiencing growing inflation. The government analysis of the crisis was laid out in the so-called Government Plan of Economic Action (PAEG).[5] The plan identified a series of what it claimed were distortions in the structure of the economy that were caused by what was called a distributive crisis. This was defined as the excess aggregate demand on the productive sector due to elevated public-sector deficits financed by money creation, by the expansion of excess credit in the private sector, and by strong wage pressures. These three components created a pressure on demand that could not be met by producers, and this "distribution crisis" provoked inflation that was structurally uncontrollable. In the vision of those responsible for the military regimes' economic policy, the recuperation of the economy needed a stabilization program that attacked the three problems by reducing the public deficit, controlling credit of the private sector, and limiting the increase in salaries. They also suggested that the price distortions and other problems in the economy were due to an inadequate fiscal structure and a rudimentary financial system, and that a modernization of these sectors was necessary in order for growth to be reinitiated.

With this policy analysis as a basis for its plans, the military government put into practice a program of stabilization and reforms, which also had the effect of reinforcing the authoritarian regime. The government reforms successfully created new taxes and established a system of monetary correction for inflation. This "indexation" was first put into effect as a correction to taxes collected, and it greatly aided the national treasury in an economy suffering from high inflation. Indexation was next applied to the federal government bonds, which allowed the public sale of these bonds of both short and long term maturity for the first time. Indexation explains how Brazil was able to create a relatively sophisticated capital market from the 1970s onward, even though inflation never completely disappeared. If this was a positive result of the creation of monetary correction, the experience of the 1980s and 1990s showed that indexation ultimately prevented inflation from being controlled. But these fiscal reforms did create a significant government bond market and enabled the regime to reduce public deficit and finance its activities in a new way. Instead of the traditional money creation, which had been the rule until then, it now obtained funds through the sale of these indexed government bonds.[6]

In the labor area the military government also made very significant changes. One of the most important of these reforms was a new wage law, which had an immediate impact on the growth of wages and income distribution. Before this legislation was passed, salaries had been adjusted annually based on the real inflation of the period. The new legislation would correct the wages according to a formula that took into account not only past inflation, but also inflation estimated to occur in the next twelve months.[7] Since future inflation was traditionally underestimated, the new legislation caused systematic wage loss, with negative distributional effects. This deliberate reduction in real wages, the so-called wage squeeze, restricted both aggregate demand and the cost of manpower to the private sector. Given its control over the unions and their leaders, the government was able to force through this significant reduction in real wages. The real annual average minimum salary, for example, indexed at 100 in 1964, fell to 82 in 1977, despite rapid productivity growth that must have occurred in the period since the GDP grew by 190 percent between 1964 and 1977 (figure 3.1). Such a wage repression would have been impossible to implement in a democratic regime with free unions. It would seem that the repression of wages was more intense in the earlier period and that in the last military administrations there was a serious attempt to compensate for the wage squeeze for low-wage workers by granting them above-inflation indexing.[8] Although the rate of poverty in the nation was influenced by inflation and general economic conditions, it appears that this wage policy also influenced the steady increase in poverty rates in the country, which reached 49 percent in 1983 (figure 3.2).[9]

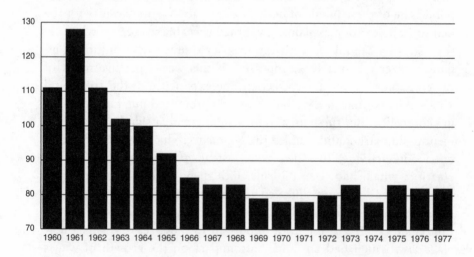

Figure 3.1. Index of Minimum Real Salary (1964 = 100). Source: IPEADATA, _Salário mínimo real—Mensal—R$ valor real—GAC12_SALMINRE12

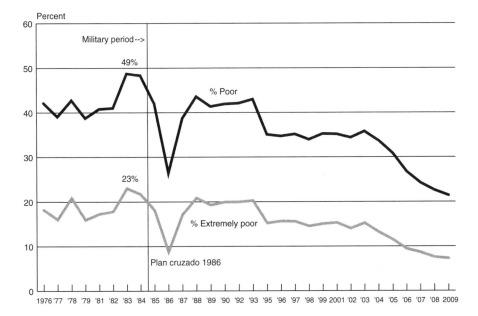

Figure 3.2. Percentage of Poor and Extremely Poor in Brazil, in Select Years 1976/2009. Source: IPEADATA, Pobreza—taxa de pobreza (Po)—% and Pobreza—taxa de extrema pobreza (Po)—(%)

Along with fiscal and monetary control, the government promoted an ample process of correction of prices of goods and public services, including abolishing rent controls. These policies of price liberalization, of course, limited the impact of its policy of monetary, fiscal control and wage reductions on controlling inflation. But even with these counterproductive actions, there is no denying that the government succeeded in reducing inflation. In the city of Rio de Janeiro prices to consumers, which rose 91 percent in 1964, fell 30 percent in 1967. Despite excess industrial capacity, the restrictive credit policies initially led to a fall of industrial activity of 4.7 percent in 1965. The gross national product rose, however, because of the excellent year that agriculture was experiencing, and by the next year the gross national product grew at 6.7 percent because of a strong industrial recuperation, even as there was a severe decline in agriculture in this new year.

When the military seized the government in 1964, the economic authorities also identified limitations in the financial sector that needed to be corrected if the ambitious stability and growth program they wished to develop could be implemented. There was a lack of effective management instruments for an appropriate monetary and credit policy. The legal structure was obsolete; the country lacked a central bank; and, in spite of the growing inflation, the usury laws still limited interest rates. Savers had only a limited supply of financial asset options and rarely obtained effective interest revenues from their applications.

Because of the coexistence of inflation and ceilings on interest rates, the financial market was reduced to short-term bank credits, based on demand deposits. To capture these demand deposits, the major banks overexpanded their branches. Moreover, the public sector was very important in the banking market. Together, the federal and state banks accounted for more than half of the country's banking credits. There were other important public financial entities as well, such as savings banks (called *Caixas Econômicas*) that took deposits through passbook savings accounts and operated housing projects. There was also the National Economic Development Bank, or BNDE, created in 1952 to finance major projects implemented in the postwar period. Private investments, however, depended basically on the entrepreneurs' own resources or short-term loans. There was also no public debt market in the country for medium and long-term bonds.[10]

In 1964 the first military government launched the current financial system. Within a few years Brazil counted on a broad and sophisticated financial structure, despite the return of the inflationary process. The creation of a Central Bank (Banco Central do Brasil) and the establishment of the monetary correction were the fundamental elements of the military reforms that totally modified the financial structure and implemented the capital market. Specialization was the concept adopted for the organization of the financial system. The functions of the commercial banks were redefined to focus on short-term credits, while investment banks were created to operate in the medium- and long-term credit markets. The production of durable goods, such as automobiles and home appliances, would play a fundamental role in the planned growth model, and this needed a major consumer credit market to be operated through new credit and financing organizations. The government also encouraged the establishment of real estate credit societies and created a National Housing Bank (Banco Nacional da Habitação, or BNH) to provide credit for housing and sanitation. The capture of resources through savings accounts and the universal Guaranteed Fund for Time of Service (the Fundo de Garantia por Tempo de Serviço, or FGTS), managed by BNH, represented the main sources of funds for the housing and sanitation projects. The government also organized several other compulsory savings programs for private-sector workers (the Programa de Integração Social, or PIS) and for public-sector employees (the Programa de Formação do Patrimônio do Servidor Público, or PASEP) that counted on compulsory contributions by the companies and public entities. Funds were managed by the public sector and could be withdrawn by beneficiaries in special situations, such as for the purchase of one's own property and for retirement. In the voluntary saving deposit field, several incentives were created, including fiscal incentives for stock acquisition.

In the 1960s and 1970s, important transformations also took place in the stock market. Stock exchanges were reorganized; investment banks and brokerage societies were created; and new sophisticated regulations and market-controlling institutions were established, which included the CVM (Comissão de Valores Mobiliários) founded in 1976 with functions similar to the US Securities and Exchange Commission. In the same year corporation law was also modified and designed more in accordance to capital market demands, particularly in relation to minority stockholder rights. Tax incentives were created for companies and investors operating in the stock market. But except for short periods of euphoria, the stock market had little importance in the mobilization of resources to supply company capital needs. In Brazil, few are the companies that have shared capital control; even when a company issues instruments in the market, it usually uses stock with no voting rights. In Brazil the public took little part in the stock market—individually or through the purchase of stocks by mutual or pension funds. Pension funds appeared in 1977, but few private companies were interested in creating funds or offering complementary retirement plans for their employees. Only state-owned companies and some international corporations built complementary systems, which in the 1980s started becoming major stock-market investors and participating in the governing boards of the largest productive companies.

With government encouragement of specialization in the market, within a few years there appeared a large number of financial entities in the market from investment banks and real estate credit societies to various financing societies and even stock brokerages. This process allowed for the quick expansion of the Brazilian financial market, particularly in the nonbanking segment. Between 1965 and 1973, the total financial assets increased from 24 percent to 43 percent of GDP; loans to the private sector showed a similar increase, exceeding 50 percent in the last year of this time span. The monetary correction allowed the consolidation of this type of market, and in some areas this played a fundamental role in the economy's fast growth. Another important component of nonmonetary assets was the federal public debt, expressed in ORTN instruments or Adjustable Obligations of the National Treasury (Obrigações Reajustáveis do Tesouro Nacional), which were certificates issued with a fixed monetary correction clause, and the Federal Treasury Bills (Letras do Tesouro Nacional, LTN), created in 1970 and negotiated with pre-fixed remuneration and more appropriate as a monetary policy instrument. The public debt market became very important, both enabling deficit financing of the budget and permitting the Central Bank to operate in the monetary market.[11]

The government fostered the formation of large financial groups, created through mergers and acquisitions, usually under the leadership of a commercial bank. Although the legal structure demanded specialization and segregation of each type of operation, the merger process allowed the consolidation of great financial conglomerates. These conglomerates in turn controlled many other financial entities and quickly achieved extensive operations in all segments of the financial market. It was a distortion of the original concept and legal base of the financial laws, but it was believed that the legally isolated and specialized financial entities had little efficacy and that concentration would strengthen the sector and reduce operational costs and thus lead to the reduction of costs for borrowers.

When General Costa e Silva took office in 1967, the economy again showed signs of recession because of the salary squeeze and the restrictive measures to contain inflation that were taken at the end of the Castelo Branco period. Industry, for example, which showed an extraordinary growth of 11.7 percent in 1966, slowed to a growth rate of just 2.2 percent in the following year as a result of these restrictive economic measures.[12] But the authoritarian regime needed political legitimacy and the only practical way to obtain that was through economic growth. This need for growth became the fundamental objective of the Costa e Silva regime and its successor, the government of General

Medici. Although this was the most repressive and authoritarian period of the military era, from 1967 to 1973, it was also the period of the so-called economic miracle because of the high rates of economic growth achieved.

The new government named Antônio Delfim Netto as minister of economy. He directed all his efforts at increasing growth by taking advantage of the process of stabilization and reforms carried out by the previous administration and by combining this with traditional incentives and subsidies to jump-start the economy and take advantage of the enormous idle capacity of the productive sector and of favorable conditions in the international market.[13] The government immediately implemented an expansionist policy, but at the same time it put in place an ample system of control and administration of prices. It created a major system of subsidies for specific areas of the economy, especially the export sector for both industry and agriculture.

In the case of agriculture, along with direct incentives, the government created a sophisticated system of abundant and subsidized credit, which permitted the rapid growth of this sector. The subsidization of agriculture was designed to reduce food costs, since they directly influenced the cost of living for the population, as reflected in both salaries and costs in the productive sector. Thus began an important integration of industry and agriculture, with the latter also representing an important market for national industry.

The modernization of agriculture took place with a still highly concentrated land structure, the legacy of a colonial land ownership system. In contrast to most American countries, Brazil never experienced either a true agrarian land reform in the twentieth century or provided free distribution of land in the nineteenth century. In Brazil the large landed rural estate traditionally represented power and was more of a reserve value than an actual production unit. In these latifundia, the amount of agricultural production was not large in comparison to the size of the property. Unproductive latifundia and archaic labor relations prevailed until the middle of the twentieth century. In the 1950s and 1960s, this poor land structure was one of the main obstacles to the country's sustainable development, because it limited the expansion of productive forces and allowed the survival of a conservative and archaic rural elite. Land concentration, besides its socially perverse and politically conservative effects, hindered the modernization of agriculture and was incapable of providing an appropriate, stable, and low-cost supply of food for the domestic market. In the 1950s and early 1960s an agrarian reform—that is, a breakup of the landholdings of the latifundia—was promoted as a solution to this problem.[14]

But the military governments ended the debate about land reform, and instead they began to systematically promote the modernization of agriculture. Their aim was to create an abundant food supply at low costs, liberate rural labor for urban industry, and create new international markets for agricultural production, thus using agriculture to generate the foreign currency needed for economic growth. Concentration in land ownership was maintained, and the power of conservative rural elites was not challenged. Thus the policy adopted was a conservative modernization one, without changing either land ownership or rural labor relations.

Military support for agricultural modernization involved several different activities. First, there was the supply of very cheap credit. The creation in 1965 of the National Rural Credit System (Sistema Nacional de Crédito Rural, or SNCR) provided significant funds to agricultural producers and represented the principal government instrument used to stimulate agriculture. Next came guarantees of minimum price support for agricultural producers (the so-called Minimum Price Warranty Policy), and allied with this came direct government purchases of buffer stocks of agricultural products, which were used to avoid dramatic price fluctuations for producers and consumers. The Minimum Prices Warranty Policy (Programa de Garantia de Preços Mínimos, PGPM) and the buffer stock operation provided major support for market stability. Before planting, the government fixed minimum prices for the main agricultural products, particularly those destined for the domestic market. It financed the production and commercialization through the Federal Government Acquisitions Program (Aquisições do Governo Federal, AGF) and through the Federal Government Loans (Empréstimos do Governo Federal, EGF). The first was a direct way of buying agricultural products and the second a type of loan, typically signed with an option that provided final sale to the federal government at the minimum price and was put into effect when the minimum price surpassed market prices. Until the 1980s major parts of the cotton, rice, and soybean crops were financed through EGF instruments. Another very important institution that the government created was the

Brazilian Agriculture and Cattle Raising Research Organization (Empresa Brasileira de Pesquisa Agropecuária, or EMBRAPA). Founded in 1973, it provided critical basic research for Brazilian agriculture by testing new seeds and soils and by permitting the expansion of modern agricultural production into new or previously neglected regions.

Along with research and price supports came a complex rural credit system based on two basic sources of capital. The first came from the Banco do Brasil, through its so-called account movement (or Conta Movimento), which enabled the bank to generate an almost unlimited number of loans. The other source of credit came from the commercial banks. These banks were required to apply a part of their demand deposits directly to agricultural credit since they earned high profits by attracting demand deposits that did not pay real interest rates. Credit subsidy came from the fixing of interest rates in nominal terms, usually below inflation rates, and increased when inflation rose. During the 1970s, the credit volume multiplied by four and reached its best year in 1979. The abundance of government credit and its negative costs to farmers provided the needed financing to modernize agriculture in terms of both equipment and supplies. During the seventies, an industrial complex that was built up within Brazil provided agricultural services (machines, equipment, fertilizers, and pesticides); and the demand generated by agricultural modernization represented an important element in explaining the fast industrial growth in that period.

Between 1960 and 1980 the area planted in crops almost doubled, going from 25 million hectares to 47 million hectares, a growth that was accompanied by greatly increased mechanization. The number of hectares per tractor was reduced from 410 hectares to just 99 hectares in the same period. The average consumption of fertilizers per hectare grew from 8.3 kilograms in 1964 to 27.8 kilograms in 1970 and 88 kilograms in 1980.

Thus the government succeeded in creating a modern mechanized agriculture, reducing drastically the need for rural labor and providing a cheap new source of labor for growing urban centers and the new industries being created. An unexpected consequence of both this rural outmigration and agricultural modernization was the profound social and political transformation of the countryside. Much of the old traditional elite, which had been based on land ownership, declined or was replaced by more entrepreneurial farmers, and the old paternalistic political power structure survived only in the more backward regions of the northeast of Brazil. Nevertheless, the transformation was only partially completed. Despite an impressive modernization, a dichotomy emerged in Brazilian agriculture between a modern, competitive, capitalized agriculture and an obsolete one using outdated methods with low productivity, which still absorbed an important share of the poorest segment of the population and was primarily concentrated in subsistence production. Even in the area of modernization, the large size of the most modern and competitive farms was the norm.[15]

Industry represented another basic sector on which the regime concentrated its efforts. Already in the decade of the 1950s, the second Vargas government proposed the industrial import substitution model for Brazil and initiated a more organic process of industrialization with well-defined and well-articulated projects. In 1952 the government presented its principal ideas in a general industrial plan, which called for major investments in infrastructure and in basic and transformation industries. The plan anticipated an active role of the state in this process, and the government created formal institutions and planning processes by which to carry out its new industrial policy. There was also a coherent set of projects proposed for both public and private inputs into the industrial process. A key element in this Vargas plan was the creation of the National Economic Development Bank (Banco Nacional de Desenvolvimento Econômico, BNDE), which proved to be a fundamental institution in this whole process. The Brazilian national oil company, Petrobrás, was created in 1953, with a monopoly over the exploration, refining, and distribution of petroleum. The Vargas administration also created an administrative structure of other institutions and government agencies that effectively carried out the new industrial policies, many of which lasted to almost the end of the century.[16]

The government of Juscelino Kubitschek furthered this import substitution program. His government formulated and implanted a highly successful "Goals Plan" (Plano de Metas), which was a coherent program of public and private investments that profoundly altered the productive structure of the country. In contrast to the Vargas regime, the Kubitschek government encouraged foreign investments in industry. The Brazilian automobile industry was born in this period through investments of multinational companies. The government also favored industry through a currency exchange policy. This multiple exchange system, though simplified in 1957, still maintained distinctions between different types of imports, favoring the primary materials and capital goods essential for national industrial growth. Between 1957 and 1963 the economy grew at an annual rate of 8.2 percent, permitting an annual growth of 5.1 percent per capita.[17]

But growth stopped in 1963 and 1964 and along with the political crises of the first years of the 1960s generated an ample debate with respect to the seeming exhaustion of the import substitution model, particularly in relation to what was called the progressive "external strangulation" of the sector. This referred to the difficulty of the local industry to continue to either replace or increase its machinery with new imports. Local industry could not export to pay for these imports, especially given the crisis in the balance of payments.[18] But the military rejected these arguments, and the strengthening of the centralizing, authoritarian, and interventionist state under its control led to an even greater emphasis on the import substitution model. The military regimes created new mechanisms to control public and private investments, developing a complex system of incentives, which included a generous credit policy and massive investments in state enterprises that controlled the principal segments of the economy, such as production of steel, the chemical industry, mining, the generation and transmission of energy, ports, and railroads. It retained state monopolies over communications and petroleum production. It even began to foster an aviation industry and in 1969 created a mixed state and private company (Embraer) to produce airplanes, first for the Brazilian air force and increasingly for civil aviation. It also provided the only long-term credit available in the country and maintained a majority position in the system of commercial credit. Fiscal and bureaucratic mechanisms regulated the principal international commercial transactions, protecting sectors deemed to be a priority.

The military regimes thus generated a major industrial park dominated by the public sector, totally regulated and protected from international competition. Unlike the contemporary Korean military regime, which devoted all its efforts to fostering an internationally competitive industrial sector, the Brazilian military efforts were designed to transform the internal market and to develop an industrial sector primarily geared to providing all the basic industrial needs of this large country. Moreover, even as the public sector expanded, there developed a strong private national and international participation in Brazil's industrial process, sometimes even in combination with state enterprises in specific branches of industry, such as the petrochemical industry, divided between the public sector and both national and international private capital. Each segment of this tightly controlled industry held a third of the capital invested.

The government did create a system to stimulate manufacturing exports, which until then had little importance in Brazilian foreign trade. Besides offering abundant credit, subsidies, and fiscal advantages, the export sector now counted on a realistic exchange rate, which was maintained at a relatively stable rate through a system of periodic mini-exchange devaluations that accompanied the differentials between the internal and external rates of inflation. While some industries did succeed in exporting to the international market, industry never replaced agriculture as the primary area of Brazilian participation in international trade. But all these policies to promote industry, going back to the early 1950s, finally did succeed in creating the most industrialized nation in Latin America.

The military government subsidized industrial growth through a system of voluntary and forced savings and directed much of these savings into new economic activity. Fiscal incentives for the capital market were granted, since this was seen as a fundamental instrument to mobilize the savings necessary to promote growth. The federal government, besides administering an ample system of credit, incentives, and subsidies to stimulate and direct private investment into high priority areas, also was active in promoting its public enterprises to invest in areas of infrastructure. The relatively comfortable situation of the state finances due to new taxes and the reorganization of government finances permitted the government to participate in a major way in the new investments needed by the expanding economy. Through its control and administration of prices, through its extensive system of incentives and subsidies, and by its direct action through the state enterprises, the government began to exercise an immense control over both public and private decisions in the economic area. Now few private projects were implanted in Brazil without the approval of some public institution, either for obtaining credit, authorization to import goods, or some type of subsidy. Also, few products escaped formal price controls. Finally, the state was the grand producer of energy, steel, minerals, fuels, fertilizers, and chemicals, among other products, and it controlled port services, telecommunications, and railroads, along with exercising a fundamental role in the system of credit.

Although there was rapid growth in the mass of salaries through the expansion of employment, the maintenance of the salary squeeze and the repression of organized labor kept labor costs low for the developing industrial sector. The real value of the minimum wage actually declined by 34 percent between April 1964 and April 1973.[19] Unfortunately, there are no reliable statistics by which to calculate the actual median salaries in the formal sector of the economy. But if we take employment in just the industrial sector, for which we do have reliable data and utilize a reliable deflator, we find either stability or even a fall of median real salaries in this sector, despite the exceptional growth of productivity. There was, of course, some serious growth in the income of specialized workers and managers if not of the skilled and semi-skilled workers.

The gross domestic product (GDP) grew at an average annual rate of 10 percent between 1967 and 1973, and the industrial sector showed an ever higher rate of growth.[20] The economy was modernized, and this explosive growth led to the incorporation of new workers into the formal labor market and the consolidation of a middle class of consumers. Aside from the success of the economic policy adopted internally, the country also benefited from a period of strong international growth, which saw most of the countries of Latin America expanding at very high average rates as well (figure 3.3).

Nevertheless, there were two fundamental criticisms of the economic policies carried out by the government in this period. Growth was accompanied by a process of income concentration that occurred for a variety of reasons, most particularly because of the restrictive salary policy adopted by the government, which prevented the gains in productivity obtained by the new economy from being transferred to the workers. Most of the gains were appropriated in the form of profits, which furthered the profound unequal distribution of income in Brazil, one of the world's most unequal societies. The very system of subsidies reinforced this pattern of concentration. The question of income concentration was even much debated at the time. The government affirmed that the high levels of income inequality were a transitory phenomenon caused by the growth process. But most scholars argued

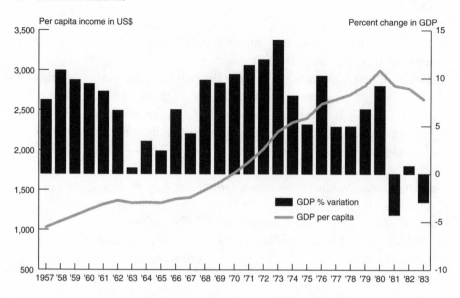

Figure 3.3. Variation in GDP and GDP per Capita, 1958–1983. Source: IPEADATA, PIB—var. real anual—Anual—(% a.a.)—IBGE SCN/Anual—Scn_ PIBG; PIB per capita (preços 2004)—Anual—U.S.$ valor real—IPEA—GAC_ PIBCAP

that there were structural reasons for this distorted distribution. They correctly contended that it would not be eliminated with growth, since there were larger structural impediments involving issues beyond industrial policy, but the obstacles did include the very model of industrialization adopted, fiscal policies and incentives, and even special support for a new middle class. The critics also blamed the government's repressive salary policy as one of the major causes for the increase in this concentration.[21]

The process of increasing external debt represented the other negative aspect of the growth policy of the military regime of this period. Brazilian economic crises have traditionally begun with problems in the external area. At the beginning of the Costa e Silva government, the country was vulnerable to such a crisis due to the low level of existing reserves. This explains why the military government greatly stimulated exports and opened the country to foreign capital, in terms of both direct investments and loans. Because of their lower costs and longer repayment schedules compared to the local lending market, foreign loans were sought from international banks and investors, and this led to a great increase in private financing from abroad. This policy of relying on private international credit fundamentally changed the structure of Brazil's external debt. Until then this debt had been based on international institutional sources of credit such as the World Bank and were obtained at fixed rates. The new debt modality, which included the financing of the state industries, was based on private international banking, with fluctuating interest rates and relatively elevated costs compared to those charged by the previously dominant international agencies. The increase of the external debt, its greater costs, and its floating interest rates made the country more vulnerable to future changes in the international scene. Already by the 1970s, despite the accelerated growth of the advanced economies, there were signs of deterioration in the international economy, with growing inflation and currency-exchange fluctuations that affected even the richest countries. The first petroleum shock in 1973 was a very clear signal of the next crisis, which would manifest itself most emphatically in the decade of the 1980s.

But from 1968 to 1973 all of these economic reforms created the era of the "economic miracle." At a time when it was gagging the political opposition and the press, and controlling the unions, the government's only aim was to show growth at any cost, without consideration of the means or the instruments. Criticism was unacceptable, even impartial criticism that pointed to errors in economic policies. Academic debate was muted and kept out of the media by the regime. Authoritarianism permeated all levels of government just as the regime put into place a major ISI (import substitution industrialization) policy and state capitalism program. This activity included a wide range of public investments in the productive sector, along with incentives and subsidies given to the private sector, the manipulation of major sources of long- and short-term credit, the control over prices and wages, and the administration of the exchange rate. The authoritarianism of the economic policy can be seen in the manipulation that occurred in the index of inflation in the crisis year of 1973, when the government estimated a totally unrealistic inflation rate of just 12.6 percent. Subsequent studies estimated the actual rate at 22.5 percent.[22]

In 1974, General Ernesto Geisel assumed control of the government, and as we have noted, he represented a new, more liberal wing of the military. His fundamental objective was to open the political system, and to legitimate this opening he also needed to show his policies were promoting growth. Plans of recessionary economic stabilization therefore were not politically acceptable. The petroleum shock of 1973 profoundly affected the country, which essentially depended on this form of fuel and imported 73 percent of its consumption. The trade balance, relatively stable until 1973, in the following year showed a deficit of just under $5 billion (U.S.), with exports on the order of only $8 billion. Obviously, this was an exceptional deficit given the size of Brazilian overseas trade and was explained in large part by the importation of around $3 billion in petroleum and derivatives, generating a deficit in the external accounts of over 6 percent of GDP. Inflation meanwhile reached 30 percent, clearly retaking its ascendant trajectory (figure 3.4).

The majority of countries affected by the oil crisis adopted recessionary programs, trying to restrain internal demand and adjust their economies to a new situation of costly energy. These importing countries also had to transfer an important part of their income to the petroleum-exporting countries. The Brazilian government, however, given its basic policy aims as well as its political constraints, followed an alternative route by energizing the economy and developing an ambitious

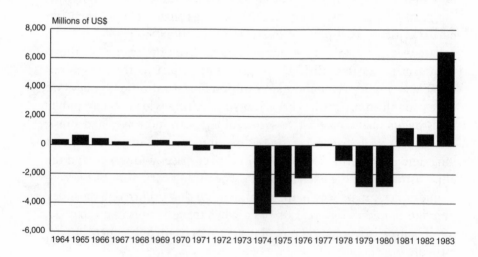

Figure 3.4. Balance of Trade of Brazil, 1964–1983. Source: IPEADATA Balança comercial—(FOB)—saldo—Anual—U.S.$(milhões)—BCB Boletim/BP—Bpn_SBC

program of investments aimed at increasing the internal offer of capital goods and basic consumption items, thus reducing dependency on imports. The abundance of external capital generated by the recycling of resources created by the petroleum-exporting countries permitted Brazil to follow such a trajectory through an ample system of international loans, but at the cost of a growing internal and external debt, accelerating inflation, and a progressive liquidation of the financial capacity of the state (figure 3.5).

The military government's defense against the external crisis was an aggressive policy of state investments, which essentially completed the government's massive intervention in industry with new funding of everything from basic consumables to complex capital goods industries. There was an ample integration of the productive sector, which in fact made the country practically self-sufficient from the industrial point of view. By the end of this long process, Brazil had one of the more extensive industrial structures in the world. But it was a totally regulated economic sector that was both self-sufficient and strongly protected from external competition. In fact, local industry was even protected somewhat from internal competition through the state-defined "market reserves" in many areas of production, and through quotas, incentives, and monopolies.

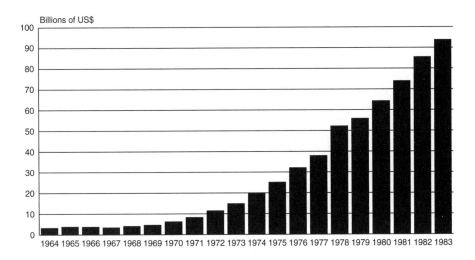

Figure 3.5. Foreign Debt of Brazil, 1964–1983. Source: IPEADATA Dívida externa—Anual—U.S.$(milhões)—BCB Boletim/BP—Bm_DEXTEI

The Second National Development Plan (Segundo Plano Nacional de Desenvolvimento, or II PND) of 1974, which set out these investment programs, led to major advances in the productive base of the country, which was to create a complex capital goods sector and a large basic inputs sector, permitting the country not only to substitute imports but also to export surplus production in many areas. The Second National Plan estimated a very optimistic economic trajectory of growth, despite the international economic scene. Some sectors in fact did well, such as paper and cellulose, which became important items in the gamut of Brazilian exports. However, in many cases there was a delay in the establishment of the more grandiose projects, and there were errors of evaluation of both the internal economy and the future comportment of the international economy. Typical of the disasters were the costly and inefficient nuclear energy program, railroad construction, and new steel mills. Without public criticism or opposition, there was no critical voice to challenge these badly conceived projects.[23]

But despite the elevated costs in macroeconomic terms, these post–oil crisis policies of massive state intervention had a major impact on the economic structure of the country. The industrial sector expanded, the country was far less dependent on imports, and it was able to continue its trajectory of growth. Government support effectively completed the process of import substitution, giving the Brazilian industrial core a totally integrated structure, even with an important new capital goods sector. The country now contained one of the largest, most integrated and complex industrial sectors of any developing country. But this "anti-crisis" program heavily indebted Brazil to foreign capital and made it far more dependent on the international financial market, which was still open to Brazil in the process of adjustment to the first oil shock. It also had a negative impact on internal public accounts by increasing fiscal indebtedness and severely reducing the state capacity for investments.

The second oil crisis of 1979 and the subsequent external debt crisis beginning in the next decade profoundly altered the international economic scene, with serious consequences for the Brazilian economy, as the international resources were no longer made available to Brazil. These twin crises (both internal and external) negatively influenced the state interventionist model, which reached its crisis point at the end of the Geisel administration. Public finances quickly deteriorated and prevented the state from intervening in the economy as it had been accustomed to doing. High inflation and the external debt moratorium were the results of this major spending program designed to compensate for the first oil crisis. While other countries in the same period adopted recessionary economic policies, Brazil had adopted a growth policy, believing it to be the best defense against an external crisis that officials thought would be temporary.

Thus by the end of the Geisel government, the country had become financially vulnerable. Especially after the second oil shock of 1979, the country suffered simultaneously the impact of the increase in prices of oil, a product that it imported in large quantities, the acceleration of international interest rates, and the slow growth of world exports. The world's economies at this time were in the process of readjusting to the new international reality of expensive sources of energy, especially petroleum, and thus reduced their international trade. The Brazilian option of maintaining a level of economic activity that was defined by an annual growth rate greater than 6 percent during this period led to a high deficit in current transactions, which initially were financed by still abundant external resources. But there was an extraordinary increase in the Brazilian external debt, which multiplied itself by four, going from 17 percent of the GNP to accounting for 27 percent of GNP. International interest rates reached more than 10 percent in 1979 and continued to increase in the following years, affecting the larger part of the Brazilian foreign debt, which was built on fluctuating interest rates. For that reason, the costs of interest on the external debt, which was under $1 billion in 1973, surpassed $5 billion in 1979 and doubled again in 1981. In that year, the interest paid on the external debt represented half of the value of all Brazilian exports. The stage was then set for an external Brazilian crisis in the context of a deteriorating international financial market. Furthermore, the deterioration of the internal public accounts and the shock of prices caused by the rise of international oil prices, forced an increase in prices even in the wealthy countries; so national inflation once again tended to increase, surpassing 50 percent per annum in 1979 (figure 3.6).

Unlike the shock of the first oil crisis, when there was an abundance of resources in the international market, after the second oil shock in 1979 there was a decrease in capital available for indebted countries, which increasingly began having problems in renewing their already

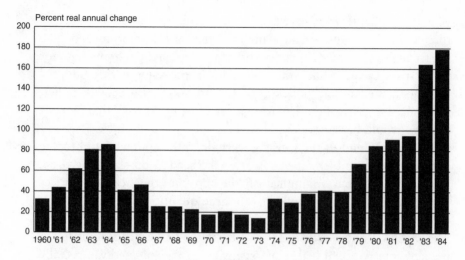

Figure 3.6. Variation in the Cost of Living in the City of São Paulo, 1960–1984.
Source: IPEADATA, PIB—var. real anual—Anual—(% a.a.)—IBGE SCN/
Anual—Scn_PIBG

existing loans. The new administration initially formulated an auster-
ity plan, directed by the economics minister Mario Henrique Simonsen.
The lack of immediate results, especially in relation to the containment
of inflation, and the political difficulties related to the progress of democratization, however, made the new government abandon the auster-
ity plan. Instead, the military brought back Antônio Delfim Netto, the
mastermind behind the "the Brazilian Miracle," who had been outside
the government since the Geisel regime. It was hoped that he could resolve the issue by putting into practice an unorthodox program that ignored the crisis and tried to overcome the inflationary problem through
growth. In December 1979, Delfim Netto promoted a devaluation of
30 percent and immediately preset the exchange rate and monetary
correction for the year of 1980 at 45 percent and 40 percent, respectively, as a way to control inflation. There was quick and important
growth, but inflation soon reached a new level of 100 percent and the
deficit in current accounts surpassed 5 percent of GDP, while reserves
were reduced by $3 billion.

Thus at the end of 1980 the government was forced to make another
radical change in its economic policy, now following the traditional
pattern of reduction of internal consumption as a way to resolve the

balance of payments crisis. Brazil was not the only country to adopt such an orthodox measure. The shock of the second oil crisis and the rise of international interest rates profoundly altered the global situation, affecting not only Brazil but all indebted countries as well. With the Mexican debt crisis beginning in 1982, this situation became clear: a majority of the peripheral countries showed a deterioration of their external accounts and even the economies of the wealthier countries faced serious consequences. Recession began in most countries; trade was diminished between countries; and credit was reduced dramatically in the international financial markets, particularly for these indebted countries. The large private international banks saw their assets affected, since the great majority had significant amounts of credit granted to countries that faced difficulties in honoring their loan agreements. This was the beginning of the world "external debt crisis," which extended through the "lost decade" of the 1980s and affected virtually every Latin American country, obliging all of them to restructure their external debt. It was a long period of low growth, with very high social and political costs for the majority of these countries. In this decade there was a break from a long process of growth that these countries had experienced for most of the second half of the twentieth century.

The International Monetary Fund (IMF) started to take on a fundamental role in this post-1979 adjustment process for the majority of the indebted countries. Those countries that received the IMF's help in restructuring their debt with private banks had to negotiate recessionary adjustment plans with the organization. The logic behind these adjustment programs was alike for all the countries and was based on the principle that their debt crises were provoked by excess internal spending, which fueled the deficit in current transactions and external debt. The plan was to carry out monetary adjustment of the balance of payments through the reduction of internal consumption, especially through reductions in public spending. The fundamental variable was called the Public Sector Borrowing Requirement. Debtor countries needed to obtain a surplus in their balance of trade in order to pay the interest on their external loans and if possible amortize the principal. To make this plan feasible, it was necessary to force a dramatic decrease in internal consumption through recessionary actions carried out via restrictive monetary policy (controlling credit expansion, particularly to the public sector, and the increase of local interest rates), along with cuts in public spending and a reduction in consumer demand, through increased taxes on available income and the control of salaries. This would result in a balance in the public accounts, because of cuts in spending, as well as the elimination of subsidies and incentives of any kind. Finally, a harsh devaluation in the exchange rate would be promoted to stimulate exports. The recession and devaluation of the currency was meant to generate a large commercial surplus, allowing a country to totally or partially meet its international debts.

At the end of 1980, the government tried without the help of the IMF to carry out its own adjustment of the economy through a drastically restrictive policy of reducing internal demand and balancing external accounts, while also containing inflationary pressure. Banking credit was reduced; real interest rates were imposed and public investments restricted. Numerous subsidies were extinguished; more restrictive laws were implemented on salary corrections, reducing even more the real value of wages. These measures created a deep recession, with a decrease of 4.3 percent in the GDP, the first such negative growth rate in the post–World War II period. The commercial balance became positive once more, presenting a surplus of more than a billion dollars, but the balance of payments was still strongly affected by the payment of interest that reached a sum larger than $10 billion, an excessive amount given that the country only exported $23 billion. In 1982 interest payments consumed $12 billion, and exports were reduced to $20 billion, in the face of the global recession and the diminished ability of various countries to import. The deficit in current transactions reached 6 percent of the GDP, and Brazil's available reserves were depleted, making the country in effect insolvent.

The Mexican crisis that began in August 1982 clearly exposed the severity of the situation. The international banks closed their doors to Brazil. They demanded that Brazil sign a formal agreement with the IMF to monitor its economic performance. Brazil signed this deal on November 20, five days after important elections.

Even though the government denied that it was negotiating with the IMF and tried to hide the truth, the crisis was evident, and the opposition obtained important victories in the elections. In February 1983 Brazil signed an agreement with its creditor banks, but the economic situation continued to deteriorate, since the lack of reserves made the country delay its repayments. Furthermore, it was difficult to maintain the agreements signed with the IMF. The program demanded a severe retrenchment for the Brazilian economy, which was already in recession. The strong inflation and indexation made it virtually impossible to fulfill the IMF requirements to limit inflation and the public deficit. There was a succession of letters of intentions, some seven in two years, with the worsening of relations between the economic authorities and the IMF. The government was forced to deepen the recession and even approved a more severely restrictive wage law. In February 1983 a new 30 percent devaluation was undertaken, and in that year production fell 2.9 percent. But thanks to the diminished internal consumption and the devaluation, the commercial balance reached $6 billion of surplus, and the deficit in current transactions was reduced to 3.5 percent of GDP. These restrictive internal measures and the devaluation, along with a fall in the price of oil and the lowering of international interest rates, contributed to the adjustment of the balance of payments that initially helped accomplish the goals agreed to with the IMF. The favorable foreign results repeated themselves in 1984, and the GNP grew by a very substantial 5.4 percent.

But the inflation reached a new high, surpassing 200 percent a year.[24] Thus in the long run this adjustment process had serious consequences for the internal economic structure. The inflation maintained a soaring trajectory, reaching unbearable levels, regardless of the generalized indexation process. In the attempt to contain the inflationary process, salaries were corrected less efficiently, normally causing additional cuts in real wages every time there was an acceleration in the inflation rate. In the attempt to contain the inflation spiral, it was a common practice to contain the readjustments of public tariffs, causing serious problems of financing for the state companies that supplied these services, and it also led to the deterioration of the public accounts. Furthermore, with the difficulty of financing itself in the international market, the Brazilian public sector started to compete for credit in the internal credit market with the private sector, thus increasing even more the internal interest rates and making the financing of the public debt ever more expensive.

Thus this adjustment process, by correcting the external imbalance, provoked an internal one. With the soaring rise of interest rates and the deterioration of public accounts, the productive investment in the country was dramatically reduced. It is also worth remembering that the greater part of the foreign debt was then the responsibility of the public sector. To meet the obligations of the foreign debt, the country started to generate a significant commercial surplus. However, these surpluses were generated by the private sector. The public sector needed to buy foreign currency to attend to its international obligations or increase its reserves, and in this process it generated even greater internal public debt. It was simply exchanging the foreign debt for the internal one. These obligations grew in the internal public sector, normally with short-term financial instruments and high interest rates. The government tried to cut costs and investments, but its public debt rose in an explosive manner.[25]

Thus the military regime bequeathed a severely constrained economy when it handed over the government to an elected democratic administration in 1985. For most of the first decade after the return to civilian government, the Brazilian economy was marked by high and growing inflation, which was little reduced by the several orthodox or heterodox plans attempted by these democratic governments. The industrial sector remained unaltered, without great transformation in either its structure or size, but the public companies were progressively weakened by the government stabilization policies. Given the importance and size of these state companies, many of which provided vital services, the military regimes toward the end had often used them to reduce the impact of inflation by imposing on them unrealistic prices and tariffs, which did not allow them to even cover their costs. The control of state industrial prices did help to control inflation, but represented a subsidy to the private sector that both weakened these state companies and increased state indebtedness. Unable to generate savings from their sales, these state enterprises were forced to resort to the international markets to obtain capital, which initially helped to finance the deficit in the balance of payments, although in the long run it had negative consequences by increasing the public debt. Besides the question of controlled prices, many public enterprises faced serious administrative problems, which were aggravated by their financial conditions. This was the case with the steel industry, which needed strong government support and compulsory extension of its debt payments to the private and public sectors.

Already by the late 1980s, these growing problems led to the first tentative steps to privatize some public companies. But these efforts were unsuccessful. However, fiscal constraints forced the abolition of incentives and subsidies even without the development of a liberal consensus opposed to the import substitution program. The already established industrial structure survived despite the long and profound crisis that affected the country. But there were no improvements in industrial technology or increases in productivity or reductions of costs. The totally regulated system of prices transferred to the consumers the costs of the inefficiencies and lack of competition in the industrial sector. This was the situation at the end of the decade of the 1980s when the liberal philosophy spreading throughout Latin America was finally introduced in Brazil by the second post-military government of Fernando Collor. Although there were some industrial groups and entrepreneurs who supported these measures—largely ignorant of the impact they would have on the productive sectors—the majority of the private sector preferred the status quo.

The other relevant aspect of the crisis of the 1980s was the ongoing inflation. Usually policies that reduced internal consumption were efficient in containing inflationary pressures. However, the Brazilian example appeared to suggest that there was a component of inflationary inertia and that the conventional methods were not effective in an economy that had such a high degree of indexation. In the first half of the 1980s, there appeared the first suggestions of alternative policies to fight the inflation.[26] These studies formed the background for the Plan Cruzado of 1986, which lasted until 1994, when inflation was finally brought under control with the Plan Real. Among the succession of plans tried by the democratic governments after 1985, the great majority had as a base theoretical ideas until then unheard of in the economic literature.

Although inflation affected all areas of the economy and was never effectively controlled by the military governments, other parts of their economic reforms did lead to positive long-term changes. This was especially the case with the financial and agricultural sectors. The financial sector, with the support of the government, thrived in this period of high inflation. During this period the Brazilian finance markets substituted the national currency for an indexed currency in most contracts. Contracts in foreign currency were forbidden, except those with a legitimate foreign link, such as exchange contracts, foreign currency financing, and import or export agreements. The others were usually made in an indexed currency, which was usually defined as a certain number of ORTNs—Adjustable National Treasury Obligations, or the local currency corrected periodically by the ORTN or another index that reflected price variations. This allowed the economy to function even when daily inflation rose above 1 percent. When necessary, daily monetary correction of contracts was used. This system created various types of indexation and price structures. Brazilians lived as if several currencies existed simultaneously, which increased risks, often requiring the creation of a hedge against the lack of balance between two currencies, while allowing arbitration and speculation opportunities. Whoever would take the exchange risk could obtain extraordinary gains, through the difference between dollar costs and the local market remuneration at indexed local currency.[27]

The persistence of inflationary levels, still high by international standards, encouraged commercial banks to continue expanding their branch networks in search of demand deposits and floating funds, without much worry about the cost structure. It was the way in which banks appropriated part of society's high so-called inflationary tax. As most of this borrowing was at less than real costs, the higher the inflation, the higher the potential for earnings by applying these resources at positive real interest rates. This created a major competition among banks over the expansion of their networks. None of this frenzied activity created a long-term private credit market capable of financing productive investments, as industry and commerce still relied exclusively on public credit. In addition, with the creation of the public debt market, the government itself aggressively competed for these private savings using both medium- and long-term instruments characterized by low risk, high liquidity, and total indexation. The market preferred these instruments and despised medium- and long-term credits or securities issued by the private sector.

The high cost for the borrower was another characteristic of this financial system. Interest rates were typically high, remunerating low-risk financial instruments, including bank bonds. The system also operated with extraordinary spreads. Studies conducted by the Central Bank show that there were several reasons for this situation. Besides the uncertainty provoked by inflation, there was a major tax on loans and applications; the system operated with high operational costs; there were risks caused by unsuitable legislation that overprotected the debtor; and the banking system operated with very high levels of profit. A 1983 survey of the profitability of the ten major Brazilian private commercial banks found an annual average rate of 21.4 percent for a period of eighteen years, an exceptional rate for any private company in any economy or sector.[28] An international study completed in 1981 showed that Brazilian banks occupied the first, third, and sixth places in the world ranking of most profitable banks.[29]

Thus the economic deterioration that took place in the 1980s did not affect the Brazilian banking system, which maintained its high profitability. Some large banks did default in this period, but there was no systemic crisis as happened in other Latin American countries, such as Argentina and Mexico.[30] The critical period was during the implementation of the various economic plans when inflation was reduced unexpectedly.[31] High costs along with the loss of the "inflationary tax" affected the profitability of banks that were forced to reduce costs: closing branches, investing in technology, and reducing jobs. A study conducted by the National Census Bureau (the Brazilian Institute of Geography and Statistics, or IBGE) showed that in the early 1980s the financial sector's participation in the GDP remained between 11 percent and 13 percent, and was reduced to 8.4 percent in 1986 in the period of the Plan Cruzado. In 1989 the rate rose to 26 percent, shrinking to approximately 12 percent in the first half of the 1990s. These results show that the financial sector did extremely well in eras of high inflation and less well in periods when inflation was controlled.[32]

In one area the total elimination of support prices and subsidized credit in the post-military era led to a healthy growth of an efficient and quite dynamic sector. This, of course, was Brazilian agriculture. Given the complex markets that had already been established and the dominance of supermarkets in the distribution of food by the decade of the 1980s, it was these commercial enterprises, international trading companies and the producers of farm equipment, that stepped in to offer private agricultural credit to replace the government credit. This plus the expansion into new crops and totally new areas helped by EMBRAPA's research led to an explosion in agricultural exports and the emergence of Brazil as a world agricultural powerhouse in the next quarter century in everything from orange juice and soybeans to chickens and beef. Brazil became the leading world producer of many of these products. Moreover, by the beginning of the twenty-first century, it was this modern agriculture that was driving the Brazil economy and was becoming the major influence on its foreign trade.

Evaluating the military period as a whole, it is evident that there was a significant modernizing transformation in the Brazilian economy. It created a modern tax structure appropriate for an industrialized country. It organized an ample and complex capital markets able to play its role in mobilizing resources to finance the development of the country. It completed the industrial process with the implementation of an industry of basic inputs needed for industrial growth as well as a major capital goods industry. It also modernized agriculture, which was essential in generating foreign exchange and lowering the cost of labor.

However, at the end of the process, the country by the mid-1980s was facing huge economic problems, including rampant inflation, chronic public deficits, and a high internal and external public debt. These problems were passed on to the democratic governments that followed and could only be resolved in the middle of the 1990s. It is difficult to pinpoint the causes for this crisis. Was it errors in the conduct of economic policy during the military era? Was it the inevitable consequences of the major growth spurt that had occurred? Or was it also the result of successive international crises, particularly the international debt crisis? But we must remember that the critical situation in Brazil in the mid-1980s resembled what was occurring in most Latin American countries or other so-called developing countries. In the end the legacy of the military era is a complex amalgam of successes and failures, but it left the country with the largest industrial establishment in Latin America and an agricultural sector that would eventually become a dominant world player.

4 The Social and Institutional Reform Projects of the Brazilian Military

ASIDE FROM ATTEMPTING to reorganize the political system, the military regimes carried out significant reforms in pensions, health, and education. This area of reform, just as with economic policy, had its origins in earlier periods of government, though in this case it was during the authoritarian regime of the first Vargas administration and not during the democratic administrations of Vargas and Kubitschek. The reasons why the Brazilian generals would support such profound changes are many. These social reform measures were extremely popular and gave added support to their regime even in the most violent period of the Medici government. They were also a fundamental part of their "authoritarian developmental" agenda. To prevent the left and radicals from promoting change from below, change had to come from above. They reasoned that only controlled change could create a solid middle class and a "responsible" working class, which would be impervious to the ideologies of the populists and radicals. Finally it was a continuation of the model that had been so successful under the Vargas dictatorship. Although the military hated the Vargas labor politicians, they liked the labor control that was already in place, and they supported and furthered many of the social reforms that Vargas implemented. In fact, the military regimes can be seen as a logical extension of the Vargas period in this specific area. It is now agreed by most scholars that it was the two authoritarian regimes of 1930–45 and 1964–85 that created Brazil's contemporary welfare state. Thus to understand the social reforms, it is important to examine what was done under the Vargas regime and how it relates to what developed under the military. Brazil is one of the classic cases of authoritarian regimes being the initiator of social welfare policies, which was the norm in Latin America, in contrast to the experience of most of the European states.[1]

Until the 1930s, social welfare was of little concern for the governments of Brazil. In the colonial period the royal government maintained pensions for royal officials and the military, and the Church created a host of charitable institutions from hospitals to orphanages. Little changed under the imperial government of the nineteenth century, with some efforts devoted to public education and health and with minimal pensions being granted to select government employees in the last days of the imperial government. But as in most Latin American states, the period up to the Great Depression was one of limited advances in the area of social welfare.[2]

Although the new republican government established in 1889 finally put more emphasis on health and education, carrying out major public health campaigns of vaccination and sanitation and promoting free public schools at the local and state levels, there was little institutional change in terms of health care, pensions, and workman's compensation schemes. It was not until 1919 that the first national workers compensation for job accidents was passed, and it was not until 1923 that the first government-supported pension plan was established under the Eloy Chaves law.[3] This law created a government-sponsored, but employee- and employer-paid, pension fund for railroad workers throughout the nation. Along with employer and employee contributions, railroad tickets were charged a new fee, which was added to the funds of the Retirement and Pension Fund (Caixa de Aposentadorias e Pensões, or CAP). Similar funds were established in 1926 for port workers and in 1928 for telegraph workers. The 1926 decree extended the plans of contributing pensioners to their families and even their heirs. These rights included medical and surgical services, pensions after thirty years of service and fifty years of age, as well as death benefits and even disability pensions after ten years of service. In turn pensions were based on an average of the previous five years of service, with those getting the lowest salaries having 90 percent of their last salaries as pensions and the wealthiest contributors getting just 60 percent. By 1930 there were forty-seven such CAPs in existence, with close to 142,000 contributing members, and there were already 15,000 beneficiaries. But the financing of these funds was precarious, and they would find themselves in financial difficulties within a few years, with benefits exceeding incomes.[4]

These timid responses of the democratically elected republican governments to the increasingly more dramatic "social question," which emerged in the industrial and urban sectors of Brazil and found expression in a series of increasingly larger and more violent strikes and political agitation in the 1910s and 1920s, led to attempts to establish various labor institutes and secretariats to deal both with strikes and with welfare considerations.[5] But those attempts had only limited effect until 1930. Whereas most other countries would slowly move to more universal systems, especially after 1945 with complex negotiations between democratically elected governments, employers, and workers undertaken to establish a modern welfare system, this was not the path followed by Brazil after 1930.[6] From the beginning, social welfare was an authoritarian project in Brazil along the lines of the Bismarckian reforms in Germany, that is, a top-down government-controlled process. Thus Brazil stands as an alternative to the more usual history of the construction of a welfare state based on class and interest-group bargaining under a democratic regime. Instead of the government responding to worker demands and negotiating with employers, in the Brazilian case it was governments that anticipated demands and imposed conditions on both workers and employers. It was a government-initiated approach, with the consumers and payers having little voice in the development of these welfare institutions.

In 1930, Getúlio Vargas seized power and effectively developed a full authoritarian regime with the Estado Novo in 1937. It was this authoritarian regime and the authoritarian governments of the Brazilian military from 1964 to 1985 that established most of the basic infrastructure for the creation of a modern welfare state in Brazil. Although that structure was later modified, universalized, and reformed in the democratic constitution of 1988, the structure itself and many of its basic features are still operative today, when the state spends an impressive 42 percent of its budget on social welfare.[7] The Vargas revolution had as its core aim the adjustment of the state to the new social realities of a more complex society. Vargas began to create a series of basic institutions to deal with labor relations, public health, pensions, and the economy, all designed to move the traditional oligarchic rural-based society into the modern era. This was done with a nondemocratic government that could forge new alliances with the growing industrial sector and harness the evolving labor movement into a permanent support of the regime in exchange for worker protections. Its authoritarian nature allowed it to reduce the power of the old oligarchies, and prevent them from successfully opposing these changes.

Whereas the Old Republic was based on an alliance of regional oligarchies and the coffee elite, the new government had a more complex and heterogeneous structure, which was controlled by groups of military men, technicians, and young politicians.[8] Many of these men, like Vargas himself, had participated in the old regime.[9] Later, the industrialists were incorporated into this new power structure. The old liberalism was replaced by an authoritarian, centralizing, and modernizing regime. But initially none of the newer power groups provided the state with the legitimacy and commitment it required: the middle class because it had no political autonomy from traditional interests; the coffee interests because they were displaced from political power; and the internal market participants because they were not linked to the basic centers of the economy. None of these groups' particular social and economic interests could be used as the basis for the political expression of general interest. As the political scientist Francisco Weffort noted, for Vargas the urban masses were "the only possible source of legitimacy for the new Brazilian government."[10] The style of government inaugurated by Vargas, classified by some as populism or one sensitive to popular pressures, and by others as a regime of mass politics, sought to lead by manipulating popular aspirations. To establish this support from the urban working classes, who were new to national politics, the leaders of the 1930s reform movements believed that only "institutional authoritarianism, or the paternalistic authoritarianism of charismatic leaders," could lead to the industrialization and modernization of Brazil.[11]

On assuming control of the government, Vargas dissolved the national, state, and municipal legislatures and appointed interventors to replace the state governors. He also emphasized the power of the federal government at the cost of the powers of the states.[12] After the approval of a new constitution in 1934, he was elected, via indirect elections, to a constitutional term of office that would last until 1938. In November 1937, when the electoral campaign was in full swing, with Vargas himself competing as a presidential candidate, he decided to carry out a coup d'état, forcing Congress to impose another new constitution and abolish the elections.[13] Thus the Estado Novo was formed. Until his overthrow in 1945, Vargas governed by decree without a national legislature. If in its initial period the Vargas regime was authoritarian, with the creation of the Estado Novo he moved toward a more repressive state, with the suspension of civil liberties, arbitrary imprisonment, total censorship of the press, and the establishment of an extensive propaganda machine.[14]

The pace of structural reform only increased with the Estado Novo. Given that Congress was closed and the opposition was muzzled, Vargas was able to make major changes unopposed. These reforms were consolidated by the early 1940s and led to new state institutions, one of the most important of which was the Public Administration Department (Departamento Administrativo do Serviço Público, or DASP), created in 1938. The DASP trained a new cadre of civil servants able to run all the special institutes and departments that Vargas was establishing and reinforced them, which gave new power to the central state.[15] At the same time, the Vargas regime created numerous executive and advisory organizations to support the executive actions of the federal government. These included the National Institute of Coffee, and numerous institutes for the other major national crops.[16]

The government also spent considerable effort developing programs and created new ministries to deal with the areas of education and health. But the changes to education were mostly ideological and had little serious effect in expanding the slowly evolving system. In fact this was an area where the military regimes of the 1960s to the 1980s had far more of an impact than Vargas. Most of Vargas's changes in education were ideological. As a government influenced by both fascist ideology and the resurgent Catholic Church, it was much concerned with changing the orientation of public and private education. Under the republic there was no longer an official state religion, but the Catholic Church found support in the Vargas regime, which in 1931 decreed the introduction of religious education in public schools. During the term of one of the more pro-fascist and pro-Catholic ideologues of the

Estado Novo, Education Minister Gustavo Capanema, there was much discussion about the need for a new moral and civic culture and there was also a major increase in private and church-controlled secondary education. But under Vargas there was only modest growth in primary education, little growth in secondary education, and none carried out in tertiary education.[17]

As of 1932, only 2.3 million students were attending school in the country, and this represented approximately a quarter of the population twenty years of age and under. Moreover, very few of the students who matriculated were found in post-primary schools. Only 5 percent were enrolled in any form of secondary education, and only 2 percent in superior studies—which included normal schools producing primary and secondary school teachers. In the following twenty-three years, change did occur, but only at a relatively slow pace. Primary education enrollment grew at only 2.1 percent per annum, slightly below the growth of the national population, and tertiary education at just 0.5 percent per annum. Only secondary education expanded faster than population growth, reaching an impressive 5.3 percent per annum.[18]

Even as late as 1940, the number of students matriculated by age cohort was extremely low. In the census of that year, it was reported that only 26 percent of boys aged seven to eighteen were enrolled in school and the figure for girls of these ages was just 25 percent. When broken down by age and level of schooling, primary basic and pre-*colegial* (all together eight years of school), all held about the same ratio of students out of the total population at risk. For the last four years of secondary school, the drop-off was dramatic, with those attending secondary-level schools accounting for just a tenth of the boys and just 8 percent of the girls in this age group. This low level of schooling meant that the illiteracy rate remained extraordinarily high. In the census of 1920 illiterates made up 65 percent of the adult population eighteen years and older, and in the census of 1940 this figure had fallen only to 56 percent of adults, the majority of the nation being still illiterate.[19]

In one area the Vargas regime did carry out a massive new development in education, and interestingly enough, this came not from the reactionary Ministry of Education but from the Ministry of Labor. It was the development of the first serious modern industrial education program. In 1939, when decreeing that large companies with five hundred or more workers had to provide commissary facilities, the government also provided that such companies would be required to maintain "courses of professional development" for workers.[20] This idea of private industry sponsored education was being pushed both by the new Ministry of Labor and by the São Paulo industrial federation (Federação das Indústrias do Estado de São Paulo, FIESP) under the leadership of Roberto Simonsen, largely against the wishes of the Education Ministry.[21] Influenced by German ideas about a modern industrial apprenticeship, the industrialists pushed for control over an area totally neglected by the state until that time. The result was the creation in 1942 of what became one of the world's largest modern privately run industrial education systems: first came SENAI (Serviço Nacional de Aprendizagem Industrial) for industry and then later SENAC (Serviço Nacional de Aprendizagem Comercial) for commerce.[22] The industrialists convinced the federal government to create a payroll tax to develop a school system administered by the private industrial associations in each state. SENAI quickly established training courses and would enroll many thousands of students in short- and long-term programs and would even educate a future president of the republic.[23]

The success of SENAI is in many ways related to one of the more fundamental changes that were undertaken by the Vargas government. In fact, it was in the area of labor relations that the Vargas regime carried out the most profound changes in contrast to the ideology and activities of the governments of the Old Republic. Although it was consistent with previous regimes in violently suppressing movements on the left, the government also carried out a new policy of co-opting urban workers through modern labor legislation. These codes involved the right to unionize, basic worker rights to bargaining, and social security. This creation of modern labor legislation controlled by the state reflected Vargas's perception that urban workers and their organizations, especially in the industrial sector, had become an important part of the national scene. This was a fundamental change from the Old Republic, which thought the labor question was a police issue.[24] While this co-optation diminished the autonomy of labor organization, leading to government-controlled unions and the neutralizing of their leaders, these organizations now became an important part of the Vargas political base.[25] The charismatic figure of Vargas derives in large part from his control and manipulation of the labor movement harnessed to the state.

With the creation of the Ministry of Labor in 1930, the successive legal norms that were developed ordered relations between unions and management in cooperation with the government, and were guaranteed by government approval. Moreover, the government adopted the policy of what is called *unicidade sindical*, which established one single union for each industry or municipality.[26] Such legislation limited the number of foreign workers per enterprise (the law of two-thirds national workers), regularized the workday, guaranteed holidays, and provided for controls and protection of women and child labor. There were also collective work contracts and Boards of Labor Conciliation (Convenções Coletivas de Trabalho and Juntas de Conciliação e Julgamento) composed of representatives of workers and management to deal with labor contracts and disputes. Labor Day (May 1) became a great public event, called the day of the worker. Finally, with much ceremony in the Vasco da Gama stadium in Rio de Janeiro, Vargas signed the first minimum wage decree in Brazilian history. In 1940 he created the union tax, which provided income to the unions that was collected and dispersed by the Ministry of Labor; this tax became a fundamental instrument of the state's co-optation of the unions.[27] The union dues and the single union per industry model were used to cement labor support for the government. The legal framework for all this was the labor law (Consolidação das Leis do Trabalho, or CLT) codified during the period of the Estado Novo (1937–45). It provided that all union elections would be controlled by the Ministry of Labor and that elected union officials could be removed by the labor minister. Strikes were made virtually illegal by forcing all labor disputes to be resolved by a government labor court, thus basically prohibiting collective bargaining between unions and employers.[28]

Vargas also made significant changes and advancements in general health, pension, and welfare legislation. He created an independent Ministry of Education and Health. But in this as in all the other changes, the aim was "a nationalistic social welfarism which had become unequivocally anti-democratic."[29] Although the first modern pension plans began in the 1920s with the creation of the CAPs, which had pension, disability, health, and death benefits, these pension/health plans were extended to all public servants in 1931 and to mine workers in 1932. Slowly but steadily, each economic sector was given its own CAP.[30] In a move to stabilize these early pension funds, or caixas, the

Vargas government rationalized the system by integrating local CAPs into larger institutes, or IAPs—thus reducing the number of pension funds but ensuring pensions for entire sectors of the economy. As many have noted, the move to IAPs represented a significant shift in the social insurance system, from essentially private to primarily public administration and from individual companies to whole classes of workers.[31] The first of these pension sector institutes was the one created for all maritime workers in 1934, and this was followed by one for all commercial and bank workers in 1936. In 1938 it was the turn of transport workers, and by 1939 there were 98 CAPs and five institutes, insuring some 1.8 million workers, all under the control of the Ministry of Labor. By 1945 these institutos and caixas were reduced to just thirty-five, and the number of paying members reached 2.8 million, with 235,000 beneficiaries. This was a major change from the 140,000 enrolled in pension plans before the 1930 Revolution.[32] In 1936 the government took over the surplus funds collected by these CAPs and new IAPs and invested them in government securities of various kinds, to create a capital patrimony for these pension programs.[33] Much of this capital was invested in government-developed industries and in the construction of the new national capital, Brasília. Brazil was like many other Latin American states in applying these surplus funds to national industrial activities, which of course made the industrial elite supportive of their growth.[34]

As part of this new social spending by the state, the government also carried out major initiatives in health policies, though in this case they were far less revolutionary, and more evolutionary, as the imperial and Old Republic governments had always supported health initiatives. From the beginning, public health was a central government concern, first in the ports and the imperial capital, then in the territories, and finally in the states and municipalities. The fact that the early leaders of the sanitation movement were themselves Brazil's leading scientists, with close connections to the political elite, helped in pushing public health issues to the forefront of concerns of the federal government. In the second half of the nineteenth century, Brazil experienced a wave of epidemics that swept through the nation. The epidemics of yellow fever in 1849 and at the end of the century and of cholera in 1855–56 brought a willingness on the part of the imperial and republican governments to deal aggressively with public health and sanitation issues.

By 1902, Oswaldo Cruz, the leading scientist of his day, organized the first campaign against yellow fever, and there soon followed national campaigns against bubonic plague and smallpox and a law forcing obligatory vaccination of the entire population against smallpox. In 1923, another leading scientist, Carlos Chagas, helped found a new National Public Health Department (Departamento Nacional de Saúde Pública). Under his direction the national government promoted maternal and infant health, began work on industrial accidents and rural health, and initiated the registration of medicines and a host of other public health activities. Finally, with the creation of the first pension and retirement groups in the 1920s, there also developed a systematic movement aimed at establishing local clinics for the practice of preventive medicine; these clinics were tied to the new IAPs and CAPs. Many of the pension funds maintained hospitals and clinics and often provided better medical service for their members than was available from the local municipalities or other government agencies.

Vargas strengthened the public health groups in the central government. In 1934 the health section of the Ministry of Education and Health was reorganized into a combined National Directory of Health and Social Medical Assistance (Diretoria Nacional de Saúde e Assistência Médico-Social, DNSAMS), which gathered under its aegis the various programs and administrations dealing with hospitals, ports, and the Federal District as well as the numerous formal campaigns of inoculation and treatment of specific diseases. These campaigns, which seem to have been quiescent in the 1930–34 period, took on a new life once again in the post-1935 period, often with the help of the Rockefeller Foundation. In 1937 the federal public health subministry known as the DNS, or National Department of Health (Departamento Nacional de Saúde), assumed the role of coordinator of all the state health departments, and a special fund for public health was created in all of the municipalities under federal direction. The first systematic attempts to fund and develop rural health clinics occurred at this time, and the government made a major effort to improve child and maternal health.[35] In a Christmas message to the nation in 1932, Vargas directed the state interventors to concern themselves with infant mortality, abandoned children, and juvenile delinquency. In 1932 the government convened a National Conference for the Protection of Children and in 1934 created a directory for this area. In turn, the theme of child protection and health was even mentioned in the Estado Novo charter of 1937, which declared that it was now the state's responsibility to care for the health of children.[36]

The Vargas regime also developed a public housing policy for the first time in Brazilian history. It created special funds known as *carteiras prediais* in the various IAPs and CAPs to subsidize credit for housing construction for workers. These carteiras were later merged into the Fundação da Casa Popular, a federal institution that permitted the state to produce subsidized housing and make home financing easier. Although the later institution was not very successful, the IAPs, CAPs and Housing Foundation constructed some 140,000 houses by the late 1940s. The Vargas government in 1942 froze apartment rents and established government regulation of owners and renters in a special decree law for renters. Given that in 1920 some 81 percent of buildings in the city of São Paulo were inhabited by renters, this was a crucial change in the liberal free-market attitude of previous regimes.[37]

All of these social and economic initiatives of the government created the basis for a modern social welfare state, even though it was still relatively limited in coverage to only a portion of the modern urban sector. Nevertheless, this was a major change from the liberal ideology of previous governments. From the period of Vargas on, it became accepted that the government had some basic responsibilities for the health and welfare of its citizens. All of the governments that followed the Vargas era, whether military or democratic, no longer questioned their right to intervene in the economy to guarantee the health and welfare of citizens. This was now considered part of a citizen's basic rights.

The forty-year period from the overthrow of Vargas's authoritarian state until the return to democratic rule in the post-military era was one in which many of the issues that brought Vargas to power would still be debated and discussed, even if not totally resolved: how to industrialize a late-developing country, how to incorporate the new urban labor force, how to resolve the growing tensions as Brazil changed from a rural to an urban-dominated society, and how to resolve the extraordinary inequalities in the distribution of income and wealth. Both populist post-Vargas democrats and post-Vargas military officers faced these problems. In each case their proposed solutions would differ. But whether adopting a repressive system or an open democratic one, the various regimes were surprisingly similar in what they expected the economy and society to look like after their proposed solutions. Whether it was a top-down military attempt to educate and modernize the society at the cost of workers' wages and rights, or whether it was a democratic regime that sought to extend the modern welfare state and generate a better distribution of income, each had to resolve the questions related to the transformation of Brazil from a predominantly rural and highly stratified society to one that was primarily urban and industrialized.[38]

By the census of 1960, there existed 110,000 industrial establishments in Brazil, employing 1.8 million workers, of whom almost 41 percent were in the areas of textiles, clothing, food processing, and drinks.[39] This sector of light industry, which represented half the value of industrial production in 1949, now accounted for only a third of the value of industrial production. In the same period, metallurgy, equipment manufacturing, the transport material industry, and the chemical industry increased their relative share, reaching about a third of the value of industrial production. From the point of view of the size of productive units, measured by the average number of workers employed, which was sixteen workers per factory overall, some sectors such as textiles, rubber, electrical and communications equipment, pharmaceuticals, paper, and cardboard employed on average more than fifty people. These economic changes between 1930 and 1960 had an impact on the economically active members of the population as well on their productive allocation. Employment in the agricultural sector grew less than employment in industry and services, thus reducing the former's relative importance. A large increase occurred in the services sector, which now employed a third of the population economically active in 1960, compared with 13 percent in industry and 54 percent in agriculture.[40]

Nevertheless, in 1964 the military took over a society that was still primarily rural, poor, and illiterate. In the census of 1960, Brazil exhibited all the classic signs of an underdeveloped society. It had high rates of mortality and fertility and a traditional premodern demographic structure (figure 4.1). The national population was young and the majority illiterate. A high ratio of infants died before their first year of age, and a large number of children died before their fifth birthday, mostly from water-borne infectious diseases, long reduced as killers in the

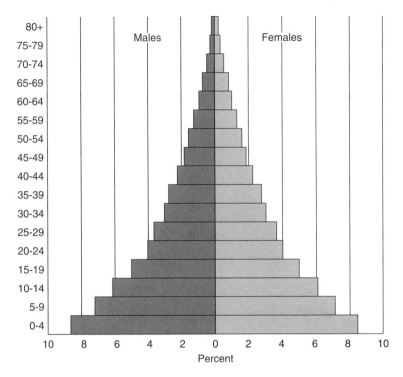

Figure 4.1. Age Pyramid of the Brazilian Population in 1965. Source: CELADE, www.eclac.org/celade/proyecciones/basedatos_BD.htm, accessed 8/14/2014

advanced industrial nations of that time. Although a few large modern urban centers existed, the majority of the population lived in rural areas. Most people were ill-housed and lacked basic access to drinking water and sanitation, and despite Vargas's reforms, most Brazilians still did not have access to modern medical facilities.

In the census of 1960, for example, only 45 percent of the 70 million Brazilians resided in cities, only 43 percent of persons five years of age and older were literate, and the average life expectancy of persons born in that year was only 55.9 years. Fertility was very high in Brazil, with a crude birthrate of forty-two births per thousand resident population and a total fertility rate of 6.2 children per women aged fourteen to forty-nine. Although mortality at fifteen deaths per thousand residents was below fertility, it was still quite high by the standards of the advanced industrial countries. Infant mortality was 109 deaths of children under one year of age to one thousand live births, and an extraordinary 54 percent of all deaths were of persons under fifteen years of age in the period 1960–65. Nevertheless, mortality was much lower than it had been in previous decades, and given the high fertility and this declining mortality, the natural growth rate of the population was high. Population was growing at close to 3 percent per annum in the period just before 1960 and continued in the following decade at this rate, which was one of the highest natural growth rates in the world at this time. This meant that Brazil had one of the youngest populations on the planet, and the median age of the population in the census of 1960 was only 18.7 years.

Although fertility had changed little in the decades preceding 1960, mortality was on a long-term downward trend from the late nineteenth century. Urban campaigns of vaccination and water and sanitation improvements had led to a slow but steady decline in mortality rates beginning early in the century. In fact, this was the case for all of Latin America, which saw an especially pronounced secular decline in mortality everywhere between 1930 and 1950. In Brazil, the crude death rate by the 1940s was in the low twenties per thousand resident population, and, in turn, this rate dropped to just fourteen deaths per thousand population in the next decade and to just six per thousand population by 1980. Infant mortality began to decline, going from well over two hundred deaths per thousand live births in the 1940s to just over one hundred deaths per thousand live births in 1960, although this was still a very high figure.

In contrast to mortality, fertility did not follow this trend. In fact, fertility actually increased slightly until the mid-1960s due to declining rates of both mortality and morbidity. As occurred in many countries in Latin American, sterility rates for women declined, and far higher numbers of women survived into their childbearing years, with the improvements in health thus initially leading to higher rates of fertility. The result of this combination of high fertility and declining mortality led to a process of very rapid population growth in Brazil in the twentieth century. The result was that the Brazilian population, which stood at 52 million in 1950, doubled to 105 million in 1975, just twenty-five years later.

Brazil was a nation not only divided between an advanced urban minority and a backward rural majority, but also profoundly divided by region, class, and race. The second most populous area of the nation was the poverty-stricken northeast, which differed so strikingly in economic and social conditions from the wealthier south-central and southern zones that economists sometimes referred to the nation as "Belindia"—with the south and southeast enjoying a standard of living comparable to that of Belgium, and the northeast having a standard of living on a par with India. Moreover, the elite class took so large a share of national income that Brazil was considered one of the most unequal societies in the world. The richer and better-educated members of the society had the longest life expectancies and the best health, while whites in general socioeconomic terms did better than mulattos, who in turn did better than blacks and Amerindians.

It was this still very traditional society that the military proposed to reform. In this they would have the help of professional civil servants and technicians who were willing to work with an authoritarian government. This administrative and technical elite was primarily trained in the Vargas era and was committed to extending the Vargas reforms. The result was that, by the end of the military period, Brazil was a much-changed society. This was due both to long-term trends in health and education that were instituted before the military takeover and to the forceful changes made by the military in a whole range of social areas. The military regimes that followed the Vargas period extended Vargas policies, yet struggled with the relations he had made with the new popular urban classes. One of the fundamental motives behind the golpe of 1964 was the military's fear of various populist civilian leaders who in the 1950s and early 1960s wanted to emulate Vargas and his ability to generate popular support. But however fearful the military leaders were of the political forces unleashed by Vargas, they also were more than happy to retain the institutions he had created to control the popular movements. Equally, given their tight control over wage increases, the military was forced to provide ever more benefits to the working class in order to prevent a popular mobilization against the regime. At the same time, many of the proposed reforms of the military directly benefited the growing urban middle classes, which became a strong base of support for the authoritarian regime.

The period of military rule was thus an era of unusually profound social changes. Many of these changes were brought about by industrialization and the allied growth of an urban society, processes that preceded military rule but intensified in this period. Others were provoked by policies carried out by the military, and still others were exogenous to the change in political regime. The most important policy changes carried out by the military related to industrialization and the consequent rapid urbanization of the country. The rapid industrialization of this period had both positive and negative aspects. It generated probably the most accelerated period of social mobility in the nation's history, as a new industrial and managerial elite emerged out of a rural and poorly educated population. But it also led to a massive internal migration from poor to rich zones of the country and the consequent growth of metropolitan areas. The lack of housing in these ever expanding centers eventually led to the rise of *favelas*, or squatter settlements, in all the major cities. This all required a response from the government, which led to a massive program of public housing and sanitation through the Banco Nacional da Habitação (National Housing Bank, or BNH). There was also a significant increase in the pace of primary and secondary education, as the military sought to gain the support of the emerging middle class. The military even intensively promoted the expansion of university and technical education. Finally, the government compensated for its wage-squeeze policies with the active expansion of the social welfare system, which included major advances in health delivery and the expansion of a national pension system. In fact, this period of military rule has been defined as the time when Brazil finally established the foundation of a modern welfare state through the universalization of services and creation of powerful federal institutions, although this system was based on authoritarian and technocratic models that were later transformed in the post-military era.[41]

One of the most important areas where government action was fundamental was in education and scientific research. Although there had been slow but steady progress in the development of primary and secondary education before 1964, it was the military regime that gave a great impulse to these two areas of activity. In 1960 only 73 percent of children aged five to nine attended primary school, but this figure rose to 89 percent by 1968. Although comparable figures are unavailable for later years, by 1985 some 79 percent of children aged five to fourteen were in primary school.[42] Moreover, both secondary and university education enrollments were growing faster than the national population in the period from 1960 to 1980.[43]

It was in the secondary school system that the most dramatic changes occurred. Although the primary school system had been on a long trajectory of growth even before the military takeover, this was simply stimulated by continuing investments. But in secondary education there was both an expansion and substantial change. Between 1963 and 1984 the number of secondary school teachers doubled from approximately 121,000 to 215,000, and enrollments increased from 1.7 million to 3 million students. But the big change was the role the government now played in this secondary school area. In 1963 some 60 percent of secondary students were enrolled in private secondary schools, but by 1984 this was reversed, with 65 percent of the students now enrolled in public secondary schools.[44] These approximately 3 million secondary school students now made up 22 percent of all students aged fifteen to nineteen, up from just 12 percent of this age group enrolled in 1972.[45]

The expansions of the secondary schools in turn led to a slow expansion of the number of university students. By 1984 there were sixty-eight universities in Brazil: thirty-five federal ones, ten state universities, two municipal ones, and twenty private institutions. Meanwhile, the university student population had increased from 142,000 in 1964 to 1.3 million in 1984, with women slightly outnumbering men.[46] Also, graduate programs doubled their enrollments to 40,000 students by the mid-1980s.[47] The percentage of youths twenty to twenty-four years of age who were in tertiary educational institutions—universities and technical schools—rose from just 2 percent of all such youths in 1965 to 12 percent in 1985.[48] This was also a period when the government invested heavily in science and technology for the first time in its history.[49] All of this increase in schooling had a major impact on literacy. By 1960, a majority of the adult population was literate. But the pace increased more rapidly as more children were educated. By 1970 literates were two-thirds of the population, and by 1980 they represented 74 percent of the national population. But it would take until the early 1980s for women to become as literate as men, largely as a result of a major increase of women attending primary and secondary schools.[50]

In the traditional areas of social security, the government also began a major effort to modernize and fiscally stabilize the pension system created in the Vargas period. Although the system was still economically viable and was obtaining more funds than it was expending, by the 1960s the relative share of expenditures to income was increasing due to a whole generation of pensioners entering retirement and increasing medical costs. The result seemed to be a potential fiscal crisis that would eventually force the government to intervene, given its control over the financial reserves of these pension institutes. Originally, the social security system was funded by workers and employers, and later with the participation of the government in a tripartite form of funding. But increasing deficits resulted from the insufficiency of government investments in the system and the use of pension reserves by both democratic and military regimes to fund projects and government programs with pension assets. As the military regime extended welfare and social benefits, there was an equally significant impact on the current revenue stream. In the absence of sufficient reserves, welfare became an apportionment, in which current contributors paid for those currently retiring. The funding imbalances were made up by ordinary tax funds.

These funding issues led the military regimes to develop two different approaches. One was to create private pension schemes, and the other was to strengthen and expand the public pension arrangements. Although there were various forms of private supplementary retirement plans in existence, in 1977 the government decided to create the basic regulations of such supplementary pension funds; with modifications, that legal apparatus represents the basis of the private pension market today. Law 6435/77 classified these supplementary plans into two large groups: the Entidades Abertas de Previdência Privada (EAPPs, or Open Entities of Private Insurance), and the Entidades Fechadas de Previdência Privada (EFPPs, or Closed Entities of Private Insurance). The "Open Complementary" plans were created for any individual who wished to join and pay his or her contribution. The "Closed Complementary" plans were based in enterprises in which both employers and employees contributed and, with some modest participation of their employees, the companies administered these plans. In the early years the supplementary plans, especially of the open variety, generated relatively little activity. But the closed plans, which were in existence even prior to the law, became important in all the large state enterprises. Initially there were few such company plans in the private sector. It was the creation of a more stable economy that permitted both open and closed funds to significantly expand, attracting individual investors for the open plans and stimulating the large private companies to create their own closed plans. Although everyone who was formally registered as employed in a company paying its share of the worker's pension contributions was also part of the national social security system, the 1977 law finally offered the possibility for both individuals and companies to obtain supplementary plans on a systematic and secure basis to complement the state system. The state-owned companies and their employee pension funds accumulated significant assets and became ever more important in the national capital market. By 1985 the trust funds of EFPPs held $8.6 billion, which represented 2.6 percent of GDP.[51]

Not only did the government stabilize the market for the open and closed private pension plans, but it also carried out major reforms of the government-sponsored national pension system. The military regime clearly wished to use the social security system both to ease the crisis caused by rapid industrialization and its wage-squeeze policies and to obtain popular support for the regime, especially from the middle class, which would be the first group to massively benefit from these changes in the social security system. To do this the military government sought to consolidate the quite dispersed institutions and agencies and to greatly expand the coverage of the population at risk well beyond employees in the special industries who were previously covered. The resulting basic reform of the pension system would lead to expansion as well as centralization of the pensions under government control. Given that the military centralized all decision making under its control, leaving the local and state administrations with little autonomy, it is no surprise that it consolidated the rather fragmented, limited, dispersed, and poorly financed social security system as one of its major reforms. Or, as one scholar noted, this reform represented one of the characteristics that defined the military regimes: their financial and administrative centralization.[52] But that centralization would create a far more fiscally secure system and enable the regimes to massively expand the state welfare system. What the military governments did not do, as all scholars note, was to use the social welfare program to resolve questions of income distribution. In fact, despite the social mobility in the period of the Brazilian economic "miracle," income inequality changed little.

The origins of a unified system go back to the Kubitschek presidency, which had created the first national social security plan in 1960.[53] Even the revolutionary rural social welfare system enacted by the military had its antecedents in the Goulart administration, which made the first serious gesture to insure rural workers with the creation of the Fund for the Assistance of Rural Workers (Fundo de Assistência ao Trabalhador Rural, or FUNRURAL) in 1963. Initially, however, little was accomplished in this crucial area. But this changed after the seizure of power by the military in April 1964. That these programs were immediately expanded and reformed had a lot to do with the fact that the conservative first labor minister and Castelo Branco's chief of cabinet in the new military regime were well-known social insurance experts.[54]

In 1966 the government overhauled the entire system, and all individual IAPs and CAPs were replaced by the INPS (Instituto Nacional de Previdência Social, or National Institute of Social Welfare). The result was that the scattered pension programs were now unified, and the entire system was placed on a sounder financial basis. Also the government systematically and effectively expanded its coverage to an ever larger ratio of the national population. By 1968, two years after its founding, INPS, which covered both employees and self-employed workers, was insuring 7.8 million persons.[55] In the 1970s INPS expanded its coverage of the work force even further. In 1971 it extended coverage to rural workers, making FUNRURAL an effective institution for the first time through what was called PRORURAL (Programa de Assistência ao Trabalhador Rural), which became part of the FUNRURAL system. This was a profound and original change in the history of Brazilian social welfare. For the first time the government provided both health services and pensions to persons who did not contribute to the social security system. Sales of agricultural products in urban areas were taxed, as were companies. In short, urban workers were taxed to pay for these noncontributory rural workers. The coverage extended to rural workers was thus frankly redistributive. Second, it was designed from the beginning to be a universal program affecting all rural workers regardless of rank or status (though females were not added until 1988). Along with this fundamental redistributive pension plan, the military also promoted rural unionization to replace the peasant leagues. Given that the military rejected any land reform and that it was concerned with providing abundant supplies of cheap food to the urban population, these developments were probably designed to prevent the potential for serious rural violence by offering some welfare support for uninsured rural workers in order to gain rural security.[56]

A second group that made up the population of extremely poor persons both urban and rural included those who were disabled with little support and the very-low-income elderly. In 1974, after much discussion among professionals in the area, the minister of social security decided to adopt the French model of providing benefits for a noncontributory class of persons who were the most vulnerable in the society—those incapable of work because of permanent disabilities or the aged whose family income per capita was equal or inferior to a quarter of the minimum wage.[57] But there were limitations. The government required medical approval to determine the level of disability (of the *inválidos*, as they were called). The very poor who were to receive a pension had to have spent a minimum number of years working at some form of paid labor, or have reached age seventy and lacked significant family support. This system of government support was called the RMV (Renda Mensal Vitalícia) and later became known as the BPC (or Benefício da Prestação Continuada) in the constitution of 1988 and was enabled in the important Organic Social Assistance Law (Lei Orgânica da Assistência Social, or LOAS) of 1993.

By 1977 the program was paying a monthly income to 1.1 million persons, and 1.3 million by 1983, half of whom were disabled and half the elderly poor, and two-thirds of whom were living in urban centers. Initially paid for from social security funds, the program increased so rapidly that by the late 1980s it had to be financed directly by the national treasury. The 1974 program was constantly revised over time and provided increasing benefits, quickly becoming a very significant noncontributory income transfer program, especially after the end of the military era, when the age of eligibility was dropped to sixty-five and the need to have a minimum participation in the labor market was eliminated.[58] By the early 1990s some 1.4 million persons were benefiting from these monthly income transfers, and by the first decade of the new century BPC transfers were more costly than the entire Bolsa Familia program of conditional cash transfers enacted by the Lula government.[59] It is interesting to note that the benefits provided by the programs created under the military were clearly defined as a social right and enshrined in the democratic constitution after the end of the military era, whereas the better known Bolsa Familia, which provides income transfers, is not so based and is only a quasi social right not fully supported in the law.

Along with providing the first noncontributory pensions for the in-firm and some of the aged, the military government systematically ex-panded the participation of new groups of workers in the social secu-rity system. In 1972 it incorporated those working in domestic service, and in 1973 it forced self-employed persons to enter the system. Then in 1977 the INPS incorporated the rural system and integrated it into one National Social Security and Assistance System (Sistema Nacional de Previdência e Assistência Social, or SINPAS). The medical part was moved to an independent National Social Security Institute for Medi-cal Assistance (Instituto Nacional de Assistência Médica e Previdên-cia Social, or INAMPS), while another organization, the Instituto de Administração Financeira da Previdência e Assistência Social (IAPAS), was created to handle the system's finances.[60] Enrollment of insured workers grew rapidly under the new INPS, and by 1980 the social se-curity system had tripled the number of insured participants to almost 26 million Brazilians, three times the number originally insured in its first full year of operation.[61] As scholars have noted, "Even with the maintenance of distinct and disparate benefit plans for urban and rural workers, the fact remains that the beginnings of a single social security system arose with the advent of Sinpas, symbolizing a new stage: uni-versal coverage by social security programmes in Brazil."[62] In the post-military era, there was an expansion and consolidation of this system with the creation in 1990 of the National Institute of Social Security (Instituto Nacional de Seguro Social, or INSS), which integrated INPS and IAPAS. By 2011 this system had 64 million contributors out of a population of 190 million persons.[63]

While the government took the position that economic growth was the primary means to reduce inequality and that its programs were not having an adverse effect during the period of the Brazilian "miracle," it did much to strengthen its antipoverty programs—of which the two major income transfer programs of the 1970s were prime examples—and to promote the steady and solid expansion of the social security system. But its economists and supporters argued that family income was being underestimated. This was one of the reasons the government decided to conduct Brazil's first national household surveys. Known as Pesquisa Nacional por Amostra de Domicílios (PNAD), these were modern household surveys carried out by IBGE beginning in 1966 in the northeast, southeast, and south, which together accounted for almost two-thirds of the national population. By 1971 this became an annual event, and by 1973 the north and center-west regions were incorporated, and the entire nation was covered by the time of the 1981 survey. Although these surveys did not resolve the debate about the increasing inequality under the military regimes, they have become a fundamental source of information on the social and economic condition of Brazilian families. The PNAD surveys have continued to the present day, and they in fact were a fundamental empirical tool enabling both military and post-military democratic governments to successfully target poverty in the country.[64] It has been argued that without the PNAD surveys the government could not have adequately dealt with the income transfer programs that it developed in the post-military period.[65]

In 1966 the military government also created the Fundo de Garantia por Tempo de Serviço, funded by a payroll tax of 8 percent paid by employers. This fund was to be used as a type of unemployment insurance for any workers fired—under the now much looser forms of labor tenure being enacted—or it could be used as a reserve fund for workers going into retirement or making housing purchases. In fact, most of the monies collected went to the national housing bank, the BNH, which promoted a major expansion of home construction.[66] These funds became crucial in developing urban housing as the cities of Brazil massively expanded in this period.

Urban housing had become a vital issue as a result of the profound changes brought about by the industrialization process and the extraordinary regional inequalities in Brazil. Although urban migration was a constant theme in Brazilian history, the process became far more rapid in the second half of the twentieth century. As late as 1960, a majority of the population still resided in rural areas. But, by 1970, more than half of the population was finally listed as urban, and this ratio rose steadily until it reached 71 percent in 1985.[67] It is estimated that in the twenty years from 1960 to 1980 some 27 million rural Brazilians migrated to the cities.[68] Until the 1990s, the states that had the biggest rural to urban migration were the south-central ones, as agriculture modernized faster there and the urban centers in those states grew more rapidly than in most regions. The peak growth of most of the state capital cities was in the twenty-year period from 1950 through 1970, when urban growth often reached well over 5 percent annually. Thus, in the 1950s, Belo Horizonte was growing at 6.8 percent per annum, and was still increasing its population at over 6 percent a year in the next decade. São Paulo was growing at or above 5 percent per annum in these two decades, and even Curitiba reached 7 percent growth in the first decade and almost 6 percent in the 1960s. Only Rio de Janeiro had a slower growth, at only 3 percent annually in these three decades. Brasília, of course, had the most sensational growth, increasing its population by 14 percent per annum in the 1960s. The result was that all these cities—except Rio de Janeiro—more than doubled their populations in this twenty-year period.[69] But urban growth was not evenly spread across all regions of the nation. The northeastern region, for example, reached 50 percent urban population only in 1980, whereas the advanced states of the southeastern region had achieved this percentage twenty years before.[70]

The growth of the cities occurred because of the migration of working-age persons from the rural area, with a significant overrepresentation of women in the migration stream.[71] The increasing market for domestic and factory work drew these women and men to the rapidly expanding cities. The result of this migration was that by 1985 the sex ratio in urban areas was 96 men per 100 women, whereas in rural areas it was 108 men per 100 women.[72] This also led to profound urban-rural differences in total fertility rates, with urban women having 3.8 children per female in their fertile years, compared with 6.4 children in rural areas by 1980.[73]

Not only did the rural population migrate in massive numbers to the cities to better their lives, but this migration also involved large movements across regions. By 1930 the international migrations, which had brought some 4.4 million European and Asian workers to Brazil, was slowing down considerably.[74] Most of that migration came in the period from the 1880s to the 1920s and had gone first to the coffee fields of São Paulo and Paraná, and then to the expanding cities of the region, above all São Paulo. But the continued economic growth of the central and southern states and the end of significant foreign immigration made these south-central regions zones of attraction for the poor of northeastern Brazil. Already in the late 1920s, migration began on a steady basis from the northeast toward the southern regions, and this continued unabated for the next sixty years. By the period 1920–40, São Paulo received more internal immigrants than foreign-born ones.[75] With each decade, the pace increased. Whereas a quarter of the growth of the state of São Paulo in the 1940s was accounted for by migrants coming from other states, this reached 30 percent of total growth in the next two decades and peaked in the 1970–80 period, when 42 percent of the growth of the state population was accounted for by these internal migrants. But this was the peak period for São Paulo native-born immigration. Although internal migration continued, after 1980 the flow of interstate migrants was directed more toward the new agricultural lands of the west and north, which were slowly being opened up for exploitation by the end of the century. In the following decades these interregional migrants accounted for only some 10 percent of the growth of the *paulista* population.[76]

The impact of this out-migration can be seen in the progressive decline of the northeastern region in its importance within the national population. In the first national census of 1872, the northeastern region was the single most populated area of the empire and accounted for 47 percent of the imperial population, with the southeastern states just behind it. By 1920 the southeastern region had 47 percent of the population, and the northeast was down to 37 percent, continuing its steady decline to just 29 percent by the census of 1991.[77] In the 1960s, the northeast lost 1.8 million persons to migration, and in the next decade 2.4 million more left than entered the region.[78] Although the flow of migrants out of the northeast continued without interruption after 1980, the pattern was for a more dispersed migration. This explains why the center-western region increased its share of population from just 3 percent in 1950 to 6 percent in 1991, and the north went from 4 percent to 7 percent in the same period.[79]

From the beginning the caixas and the institutos had provided medical assistance to all members and their families, and this increased even more rapidly when INPS was established. The development of public and private health insurance, and of public and private hospitals and clinics in this period and the great expansion of the pension and health system operated by the government, began to cover significant parts of the Brazilian population. Between 1970 and 1980 those paying into the social security system more than doubled, from 9 percent to 20 percent of the national population, while 30 percent of the urban population was covered. INPS initially covered the health insurance of all those paying into the social security system, but when a separate Ministry of Pensions and Social Assistance was established in 1974, all of these various insurance, pension, and health delivery plans were placed in a new organization directly under the new ministry. This was called the National Healthcare and Social Security Institute (Instituto Nacional de Assistência Médica e Previdência Social, or INAMPS); it was to be the primary government health agency until the end of the military rule.[80] A host of other institutional changes led to a major expansion of the public health system. Between 1970 and 1980 hospital admissions went from 6 million to 13 million—the latter figure being the annual norm even now.[81] Finally in the 1960s came state national and internationally supported programs of infant and child immunization.[82]

At the same time there developed a whole new market in private insurance. Many of these private plans went back to the 1940s and 1950s, and soon there was a complex mixture of public and private health insurance plans, especially related to public hospitals. Starting in 1967, new cooperative medical groups (generically called UNIMEDs) were being created, and by the 1980s they were offering their own private health insurance.[83] By the late 1990s it was estimated that 32 million Brazilians were covered by private health insurance companies, making it the second-largest private insurance market in the world.[84] As of the end of the military period in early 1985, only a third of health institutions were in private hands, but they accounted for two-thirds of the hospital beds and just under half of the professional health workers. In a complex system, however, there was constant overlap between public and private, with many hospitals having both privately insured and publicly insured patients even if they were public institutions.

All of this growth in public and privately insured health had a direct impact on mortality. Already the crude death rate was at fifteen deaths per thousand residents in the 1960s. It began to decline at a more rapid pace in the next few years and was down to eight deaths per thousand residents by the early 1980s. This decline was driven mostly by the steady decline in infant mortality, which fell by nearly half, from one hundred deaths per thousand live births in 1965–70 to just sixty-three per thousand in 1980–85 (figure 4.2). The impact of this improvement in infant mortality can be seen in the decline of infant and child deaths (0–14 years of age) as a share of total Brazilian deaths. Infant and child deaths went from more than half of all deaths recorded in the 1970s to just a third of all deaths by the early 1980s. Finally, these changes had a dramatic impact on life expectancy, which rose eight years for men in the period from 1960–65 to 1985–90 and an extraordinary eleven years for women (figure 4.3)

Although the decline in mortality rates, both total and infant and child mortality, had a great deal to do with government programs, this was not the case with fertility. By the middle of the twentieth century, Brazil was still experiencing quite high birthrates, and the government itself showed little concern with the issue. Although urban elite groups were practicing birth control and had lower fertility than the national average, this group exercised little influence over national trends. In 1960 the total number of children born to women aged 14–49 peaked at 6.3 children. But beginning in the quinquennium of 1965–70, the trend was suddenly and irrevocably reversed. First slowly and then at an ever faster pace, the total fertility rate declined in Brazil, going to 6.2 children in 1960–65, dropping by more than half to 3.0 children in 1980–85, and then fell to just 2.3 children per women by the end of the century.[85]

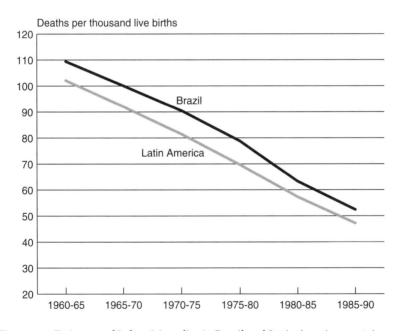

Figure 4.2. Estimates of Infant Mortality in Brazil and Latin America, 1960/ 1965–1995/2000. Source: CELADE, *Observatorio Demografico*, no.4, "Mortali-dade," Oct. 2007, Quadro 6

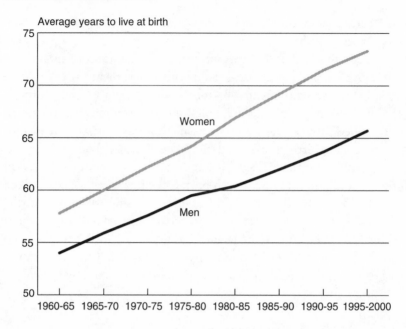

Figure 4.3. Life Expectancy at Birth by Sex, 1960/1965–1995/2000. Source: CEPAL, *Observatorio demográfico*, no. 4, Oct. 2007 "Mortalidad," Cuadro 5

The cause of this fertility decline was not any change in the age of initiation of marriage by women, the percentage of women marrying, or the increase in the number of women who were childless. The age of women marrying for the first time did not change until long after the fertility transition, nor did the number of women ever marrying decline or those remaining childless increase, nor did the ratio of births out of wedlock alter from previous periods. Many of these factors, including the dissolution of unions, did change in succeeding decades, but these transformations came well after the drop in fertility. The only change that did occur at this time was the mass adoption of contraceptives and sterilization, which had their impact in the second half of the 1960s, in a pattern common to all of Latin America.[86] It was older women who most enthusiastically adopted the new contraceptive procedures. But no group of women was exempt, and every age group experienced fertility decline from the high in 1965 to a low in 2000.[87] The biggest drop in fertility occurred among older women as more women terminated their reproductive activity at a far younger age than previously. In fact, the relationship between age and decline in age-specific fertility was almost perfectly inverted, with the rate of decline highest in the older ages and slowing through the younger ages. The age-specific birthrate among women forty-five to forty-nine, for example, declined by 83 percent from 1960 to 1990, and lesser declines were noted for all age groups thirty and older (figure 4.4). This meant that the share of births to mothers fifteen to twenty-nine increased from 53 percent in 1960–65 to 69 percent of all births by 1985–90, with most of the change coming in the under-twenty-five age groups. During the same period, mothers who were thirty and older went from having 47 percent of all births to accounting for just over a third of births.

All of these changes in fertility and mortality had a major impact on the age structure of the population. Whereas in 1965 some 44 percent of the population was under fifteen years of age, by 1985 the percentage fell to 37 percent and continued to fall for the rest of the century. The working-age population in this same period increased to 57 percent, and those who were sixty and older in 1965 rose to 6.4 percent by 1985. The median age of the population climbed from 18.3 years in

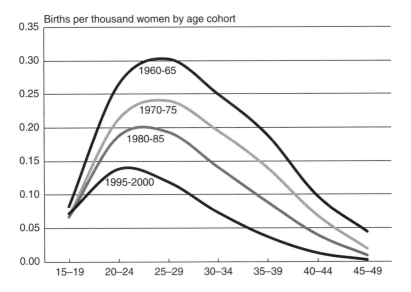

Figure 4.4. Age-Specific Birthrates by Age of Mother in Brazil 1960/1965– 1995/2000. Source: CELADE, *Boletín Demográfico*, no. 68, 2001, p. 57, table 20a

1965 to 21.3 twenty years later.[88] These changes can be seen in the age pyramid for the last year of the military regime (figure 4.5). Compared with the population twenty years earlier (seen above in fig. 4.1), the base is now much smaller and is larger in the working-age cohorts of women and men.

In contrast to the demographic transition in Europe, which began when birthrates were much lower than mid-twentieth-century Latin American figures, the drop in Brazil and most Latin American countries began from quite high rates. In fact, these rates were the highest in the world at midcentury.[89] In the case of Brazil, with its very stratified and partially unarticulated society, the fall was not uniform across all regions and classes. Thus, each region of the country began to decline from different initial levels, but they all moved in the same direction.

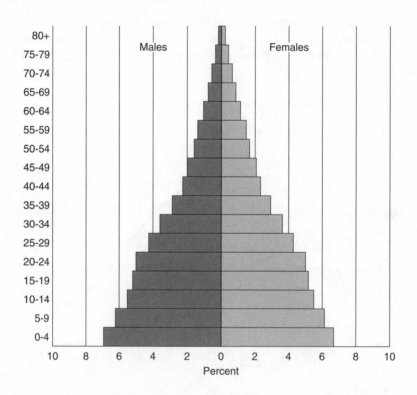

Figure 4.5. Age Pyramid of the Brazilian Population in 1985. Source: Same as figure 4.1

Given these initial rates of decline, the gap between regions did not change over time, and it was only in the twenty-first century with new government aid and health programs that the regional differentiation finally disappeared.

Thus for a host of reasons the military period from 1964 to 1985 was a time of profound social change. Some of these changes were initiated by the generals and their techocratic administrators; others were the result of unanticiapted consequences of their actions; and others occurred because of changes that were unrelated to anything done by the military. The sudden collapse of Brazilian fertility was due to the recent avalability of contraceptives, and the only influence of the military was in not preventing their distribution and consumption—but even in Latin American societies where the Catholic Church blocked their distribution, birthrates fell dramatically in this period. The drop in fertility was also related to urbanization and in turn affected family size, child labor, and a host of other socioeconomic institutions, and these effects were in areas where the government was forced to respond to maintain stability.

Clearly the forced industrialization emphasized by the military regimes and their efforts to modernize and mechanize agriculture had an impact on the massive urbanization that occurred in this period. The government only party resolved the issues of urbanization that resulted. The regime met the educational needs of urban migrants, and incorporated most of them into the social security system, but it was unable to resolve the expansion of the favelas with adequate housing policies and fell behind in providing these urban slums with sanitation and urban services.

But in education, health, and social welfare the military regimes made major advances, largely because they left the relevant ministries to civilian professionals who were intent on modernizing the Brazilian social system. There was none of the hesitation and moralizing of the Vargas regime in relation to basic education. Primary education was fully supported, and there was a major change in public secondary education from previous regimes. Although the small group of elite public high schools was allowed to collapse, the massive expansion of secondary education was impressive. The same can be said of tertiary education, whose foundations were firmly established in this period. This was the period when UNICAMP (Universidade Estadual de Campinas), the second most important research and science university in Brazil, was founded.

Then came the beginnings of noncontributory income transfers from the state to the poorest members of the population, through the FUNRURAL and the income-subsidy programs for the extremely poor and the disabled. This new and innovative idea of providing pensions for those who never entered the social security system was of major importance to post-military regimes and would even be enshrined in the Constitution of 1988. All later governments would expand these income transfer programs. They would also develop new conditional cash transfer programs for keeping children in school or making pregnant women visit clinics, which were folded into the Bolsa Familia program in 2003. Economic growth combined with these fundamental conditional and unconditional income-transfer programs became the most important factors in eliminating extreme poverty in Brazil and in reducing regional differences.

The military government also made a sustained effort to increase the traditional pay-as-you-go social security system by expanding coverage to ever more groups of workers and by reorganizing the system on sound actuarial principles. It also developed a major program for health that began to deliver services to the entire nation. In spite of all the changes initiated by the post-military democratic governments, virtually all commentators agree that the basic foundational structure of Brazil's current welfare state was initiated by Vargas and seriously expanded and institutionalized by the military regimes, and remains essentially intact to this day. Whatever the motivation of the generals and their commitment to public or private initiatives, or to centralized decision making, there is no question that their government significantly moved Brazil toward the universalization of education, pensions, and health care.

Conclusion

THERE IS LITTLE question that the military regimes that ruled Brazil from 1964 to 1985 had a profound impact on the nation. In this it was very similar to the Chilean and Peruvian military government experiences, and unlike the Argentine, Bolivian, and Uruguayan ones. These last three regimes may have adopted some aspects of the neoliberal policies being pushed by the United States and international organizations that proposed free trade, deregulation, and the privatization of many government functions, but they were more interested in repressing the left than in reforming the state. In turn the Chilean reforms were only partially accepted after the return to democracy, and their legacy is still a bitterly fought inheritance even today. In contrast the developmental model and many of the most basic structural changes carried out by the Brazilian military in areas from finance and taxes to welfare and universities became a part of the national system with little debate or opposition. Despite the dismantling of most of the authoritarian and antidemocratic laws and structures after 1985, and the return to federalism and decentralization, most of the social welfare institutions created by the military remained intact. The one area where the military reforms were abandoned was that of the state capitalism model, when in the late 1990s the post-military democratic regimes adopted the so-called Washington Consensus and the government proceeded to privatize most of the state industries.

In its basic commitment to and successful implantation of state-sponsored industrial development, authoritarian Brazil was much like the military regime of South Korea, which from 1961 to 1987 also promoted an authoritarian development model. But in contrast to the South Korean experience, which was a drive to create a competitive export-oriented heavy industry in joint partnership with the state and private capital, in the case of Brazil it was mostly the state that promoted heavy industry and did it largely without private investors. Moreover, despite support for industrial exports, the prime concern of the Brazilian military economic reforms was toward developing a complete industrial sector primarily devoted to the internal market, with a greater stress on agriculture as the primary export sector. Also, whereas in the Korean case it was General Park who was the single most important figure and the prime mover for rapid industrialization, the Brazilian military worked closely with civilian technocrats and both initiated and carried out older development plans that went back to the Vargas era and promoted them as an institution, rather than as the work of a single leader.[1]

In other aspects that we have examined, Brazil differed little from most of the other military regimes in its inability to control the more fascist and violent elements within its ranks. It too saw mass arrests, torture, arbitrary violence meant to create a climate of fear, and rogue officers whose sadism could not be controlled. The Brazilian officers also actively cooperated with the other Southern Cone military regimes, which led to killings and deportations of citizens in all of the nations involved. These were among the worst aspects of the regime and were the norm for most of these Cold War military governments. The only difference in this aspect of the military regime was that in Brazil the total numbers of persons imprisoned, tortured, and killed were proportionally less than in the more violent regimes of Argentina and Chile. But this violence was still significant and has left a bitter memory of this period, which survives today.

What has puzzled many scholars is the inconsistency of the military's repression. The regime destroyed the university student movement, yet it promoted a massive expansion of secondary and tertiary education. It attacked the Universidade de Brasília, one of the more advanced centers in the country, and yet created UNICAMP, which would become one of the nation's best universities. It destroyed the peasant leagues, yet it created the first serious programs of social security for peasant farmers. These more positive initiatives allowed the regime to gather reasonably wide support among the educated elite and apply their skills to the government programs. Although their reforms stressed the hard sciences and engineering over the human sciences and the North American system of departments over the traditional European model, the military did succeed in establishing a modern university system. By the time it was finished, it had created the leading university system in Latin America. Where it failed was in the "massification" of secondary education and the consequent destruction of elite public high schools. While this huge expansion of education led to the nation finally becoming literate, the quality of that education was and remains quite questionable. One could argue that the important need was for coverage of the population, but the cost was quite high in terms of quality.

While the military regime's capital spending led to the creation of Latin America's leading industrial sector, it was a system extremely protected behind high tariff walls. These industries were often unable to compete internationally, though even here it was the military that established the basis for the aerospace manufacturer Embraer, the only significant and long-term industrial export company of Brazil. Given the size of the internal market, the industrial policy of the military was to develop an industrial structure devoted to the internal market. Even though the resulting integrated industrial structure was quite impressive, the protected industries were less able to compete internationally once the tariff walls came down in the 1990s. In this, the Brazilian military's "authoritarian developmentalist" model was far less successful than that of the Korean military regime, which concentrated on building competitive export industries from the beginning and turned South Korea into a significant industrial nation whose industries could compete in the world market.

More complex is the question of why the regime was reformist. Clearly, the pre-coup military had sent its best officers to study with civilians at the Escola Superior de Guerra. These officers were aware of the debates then current about policies needed to develop a modern society in the Brazilian context. But in the end it was the civilian technical advisers who made the basic changes, with a military elite willing to implement their reforms given their more general but rather imprecise concerns about modernization and nationalism. This receptivity is matched only in the Peruvian military, which saw land reform as the only way to modernize the society and committed its officer class to reformist civilian ideas coming out of the United Nations CEPAL agency in Chile. In Chile the military seemed indifferent to these modernizing ideas, and given the dictatorial nature of the regime it was primarily one person, Pinochet, who was willing to accept the arguments of conservative civilian economists who wanted to make Chile the example of a neoliberal state. There is little question that the Chilean model, which initiated many of the fundamental policy ideas contained in the Washington Consensus, had a major international impact, unlike the programs being followed in Brazil.

Finally, the transition to democratic governments in the post-military era was a rather easy one for Brazil. Surprisingly, many of the politicians who were active participants as either supporters or opponents in the military era also participated in the post-military governments and quickly made the transition to democratic rule. But the national experience with military rule left a political legacy in Brazil that was much like that in all the other major Cold War military regime states. This legacy resulted in the successful elimination of the military as a major political actor and the abandonment by the conservative parties of their reliance on military support. Parties that had fought one another bitterly before the military interventions now worked together in the post-military era. Uruguay was a classic case in which this occurred. But in Brazil as well, most of the pro-military elements moved toward accepting the democratic game. Moreover, the "moderating" role of the military in Brazil, which had defined most of the republican era, was eliminated, and the army was successfully subordinated to the civilian state. The unprecedented violence of the Cold War military regimes created a massive reaction from all elements in these Latin American societies and resulted in a major cultural and political shift, in which democratic rule became far more firmly embedded in these societies than at any other time in their history.

Notes

INTRODUCTION

1. In our studies, *The Economic and Social History of Brazil Since 1889* (New York: Cambridge University Press, 2014); "Mudanças Sociais no Período Militar (1964–1985)," and "Mudanças Econômicas no Período Militar (1964–1985)," in *A ditadura que mudou o Brasil,* ed. Daniel Aarão, Marcelo Ridenti and Rodrigo Patto Sá Motta (Rio de Janeiro: Zahar Editora, 2014), pp. 66–91, 92–111; "Creando un estado de bienestar en un régimen autoritario: el caso de Brasil," *Revista Economía y Política* (Santiago de Chile) 1, no. 1 (April 2014), pp. 31–78; "População e Sociedade, 1960–2000," in *História do Brasil Nação: 1808–2010,* ed. Leila Schwarz, 5 vols. (São Paulo: Fundación Mapfre & Editora Objetivo, 2014), 5:31–73; and "The Historical Background to the Rise of MAS, Bolivia 1952–2005," in *Evo Morales and the Movimiento al Socialismo in Bolivia,* ed. Adrian Pearce (London: Institute of the Americas, 2011), pp. 27–61.

CHAPTER 1. NATIONAL SECURITY AND THE DESTRUCTION OF DEMOCRATIC REGIMES IN LATIN AMERICA

1. Lars Schoultz, *Beneath the United States: A History of U.S. Policy Toward Latin America* (Cambridge: Harvard University Press, 1998), p. 334.

2. Quoted in Schoultz, *Beneath the United States,* p. 338.

3. Milton Eisenhower, "Report to the President," *Department of State Bulletin,* vol. 23 (November 1953), p. 698.

4. Quoted in Schoultz, *Beneath the United States,* p. 339.

5. By 1974 the U.S. Army School of the Americas (USARSA) in the Panama Canal had trained 30,000 Latin American officers. The courses were taught in Spanish

and Portuguese and gave "emphasis to Anti-Communism and pro-American in-doctrination." For the senior officers, their training was in the United States at the same advanced military schools that were used by the U.S. officer corps. Overall, from 1950 to 1970 the United States trained some 41,000 Latin American military in Panama or the United States. On the details of U.S. training and military assis-tance in this period, see Alain Rouquié, *The Military and the State in Latin America* (Berkeley: University of California Press, 1982), pp. 128–50, table 5, p. 135.

6. Schoultz, *Beneath the United States,* p. 340.

7. Peter H. Smith, *Talons of the Eagle: Latin America, the United States, and the World,* 4th ed. (New York: Oxford University Press, 2012), p. 129.

8. It is worth noting that the resulting authoritarian regimes that followed the invasion were ferociously anticommunist and antidemocratic; they also perpetu-ated a massive and vicious civil war ("de casi cuatro décadas que causó 250,000 muertos y 50,000 secuestrados-desaparecidos"); *El Pais,* July 2, 2014, found at http://internacional.elpais.com/internacional/2014/07/02/actualidad/1404316341 _759707.html. On this genocidal war by the right and the military in the post-1954 period, see Greg Grandin, *The Last Colonial Massacre: Latin America in the Cold War* (Chicago: University of Chicago Press, 2011).

9. The Carter decision not to actively support military regimes was crucial in allowing democratic forces to organize and take back their governments from the military. But it really had little impact on U.S. aid, which still primarily flowed to the most repressive regimes. See Lars Schoultz, "U.S. Foreign Policy and Human Rights Violations in Latin America: A Comparative Analysis of Foreign Aid Distri-butions," *Comparative Politics* 13, no. 2 (January 1981): 149–70.

10. Michael Grow, *U.S. Presidents and Latin American Interventions: Pursuing Regime Change in the Cold War* (Lawrence: University Press of Kansas, 2008), chap. 3.

11. Smith, *Talons of the Eagle,* pp. 136–37.

12. Timothy Naftali, ed., *The Presidential Recordings of John F. Kennedy,* vol. 1, *July 30–August 1962* (New York: W. W. Norton, 2001), p. 18. Also see James G. Hershberg and Peter Kornbluh, "Brazil Marks 50th Anniversary of Military Coup," (National Security Archive Electronic Briefing, Book No. 465, posted April 2, 2014), 16 pages, found at http://www2.gwu.edu/~nsarchiv/NSAEBB/NSAEBB465/ 1/.

13. Hershberg and Kornbluh, "Brazil Marks 50th Anniversary," pp. 4–5.

14. Hershberg and Kornbluh, "Brazil Marks 50th Anniversary," p. 14.

15. Gaddis Smith, *The Last Years of the Monroe Doctrine, 1945–1993* (New York: Macmillan, 1995), p. 121.

16. There is little doubt that Goulart faced major conflicts over his various re-forms and policies, but it was questionable if he would have been overthrown without major and systematic U.S. interference. This is the conclusion arrived at in the best survey of the Goulart period; see Luiz Alberto Moniz Bandeira, *O governo João Goulart: As lutas sociais no Brasil, 1961–1964,* 7th ed. (Brasília: Editora Uni-versidade de Brasília, 2001), pp. 173–84, 201–5.

17. Hershberg and Kornbluh, "Brazil Marks 50th Anniversary," pp. 16–17.

18. Hershberg and Kornbluh, "Brazil Marks 50th Anniversary," p. 17.

19. Unlike the Brazilian case in which all parts of the U.S. government supported intervention, the Nixon administration, tainted by Watergate and the Vietnam War,

kept most of the CIA and U.S. embassy personnel uninformed of its activities and dealt directly with the coup leaders through its naval mission, which provided strong U.S. support coming directly from Nixon and Kissinger. For the latest survey of this issue, see Jonathan Halam, *The Nixon Administration and the Death of Allende's Chile: A Case of Assisted Suicide* (London: Verso, 2005), chap. 7.

20. A useful survey of the Central American conflicts is found in Smith, *Talons of the Eagle*, pp. 168–75.

21. Michael Reid, *Forgotten Continent: The Battle for Latin America's Soul* (New Haven: Yale University Press, 2007), pp. 120–21.

22. On the transformation of left-wing ideology in this period, see, for example, Vania Markarian, *Left in Transformation: Uruguayan Exiles and the Latin American Human Rights Network, 1967–1984* (London: Routledge, 2013).

23. In his analysis of bureaucratic-authoritarian regimes, O'Donnell dates the founding of this authoritarian regime in Argentina with the golpe of Onganía in 1966. See Guillermo O'Donnell, "Reflections on the Patterns of Change in the Bureaucratic-Authoritarian State," *Latin American Research Review* 13, no. 1 (1978): 7.

24. The truth commission documented 9,000 "disappeared" and the current estimate from the human rights organizations is 30,000. Detailed analysis of this systematic state organized killing and torture machine is found in Luis Alberto Romero, *A History of Argentina in the Twentieth Century* (University Park: Pennsylvania State University Press, 2011), chap. 7, and in Marcos Navarro and Vicente Palmero, *La dictadura militar, 1976–1983: Del golpe de estado a la restauración democrática*, Colección Historia Argentina, 9 (Buenos Aires: Paidos, 2003), chap. 2. Even General Videla has finally admitted to some 9,000 "disappeared" in his latest defense from jail. See Reuters report at www.reuters.com/article/2012/04/14/us-argentina-dictator-idUSBRE83D0CK20120414.

25. On the extraordinary ideology of the military in this period, see the classic study by Marguerite Feitlowitz, *A Lexicon of Terror: Argentina and the Legacies of Torture*, revised ed. (New York: Oxford University Press, 2011).

26. On the destruction of the Exact Sciences Faculty, see Sergio Morero, *La noche de los bastones largos* (Buenos Aires: Grupo Editor Latinamericano, 2002).

27. Roberto Cortés Conde, *The Political Economy of Argentina in the Twentieth Century* (New York: Cambridge University Press, 2009), pp. 244–72.

28. It was the war, an economy in tatters, and a negotiated agreement that offered amnesty and security of the military budget. A rather interesting economic model proposes that such military regimes are inherently unstable, given that they usually generate little loyalty and at the same time increase the cost of repression by increasing military expenditures, and thus they tend to peacefully hand the government back to civilians once they receive amnesty and guarantees that their inflated military budgets will not be cut. See Ronald Wintrobe, *The Political Economy of Dictatorship* (New York: Cambridge University Press, 1998), pp. 56–58.

29. Carlos Huneeus, *The Pinochet Regime* (Boulder, Colo.: Lynne Rienner, 2007), pp. 4–5.

30. These comparative figures come from the dossier organized by the São Paulo newspaper *Folha*, March 23, 2014, found at http://arte.folha.uol.com.br/especiais/2014/03/23/o-golpe-e-a-ditadura-militar/o-acerto-de-contas.html. An

estimated 500 persons were killed or disappeared under the Brazilian military regimes; see www.desaparecidospoliticos.org.br/pagina.php?id=221.

31. The conflicts with foreign nations that might even have been sympathetic to Chile were due to the ruthless hunting of their nationals or the denial of safe conduct to refugees in local embassies. See Heraldo Muñoz, "Las relaciones exteriores del gobierno militar chileno," *Revista Mexicana de Sociología* 44, no. 2 (April–June 1982): 581–83.

32. The standard review of this crisis of the Allende regime and the origins of the military revolt is presented in Arturo Valenzuela, *The Breakdown of Democratic Regimes: Chile* (Baltimore: Johns Hopkins University Press, 1978). Although he says little about the U.S. role in the golpe, he does show military planning for a coup from July to September 1973 with incessant military raids—uncontrolled by the Allende government—looking for supposedly workers' arsenals of weapons and the systematic pressure to force all liberal generals and admirals to retire. Valenzuela, *The Breakdown of Democratic Regimes*, pp. 101–5.

33. If there was coherence to military thinking on the economy, it was a commitment to state control over national industry. This position was in fact supported by the head of the air force, General Gustavo Leigh, who was eventually ousted by Pinochet. See Verónica Valdivia Ortiz de Zárate, "Estatismo y neoliberalismo: Un contrapunto militar, Chile 1973–1979," *Historia* (Santiago) 34 (2001): 167–226. But just how limited Chilean military thinking was in terms of economic or social reforms can be seen in the collection of military planning and ideology documents presented in Augusto Varas and Felipe Agüero, *El proyecto político militar* (Santiago: FLACSO, 1984). But as Valenzuela has noted, "The Chilean experience has shown how easy it is for a professional and 'neutral' military to become a repressive military regime." Valenzuela, *The Breakdown of Democratic Regimes*, p. 109.

34. On the social origins of this group, see Carlos Huneeus, "Technocrats and Politicians in an Authoritarian Regime: The 'ODEPLAN Boys' and the 'Gremialists' in Pinochet's Chile," *Journal of Latin American Studies* 32, no. 2 (May 2000): 461–501.

35. Alejandro Foxley, "The Neoconservative Economic Experiment in Chile," in *Military Rule in Chile*, ed. J. Samuel Valenzuela and Arturo Valenzuela (Baltimore: Johns Hopkins University Press, 1986), p. 13.

36. For the latest survey of this period, see Ricardo Ffrench-Davis, *Entre el neoliberalismo y el crecimiento con equidad: Tres décadas de política económica en Chile* (Santiago de Chile: JC Sáez Editor, 2003).

37. "The Pinochet Money Trail," *New York Times*, December 12, 2004.

38. Huneeus, *The Pinochet Regime*, pp. 15, 338.

39. Huneeus, *The Pinochet Regime*, p. 282.

40. World Bank, *Averting the Old Age Crisis: Policies to Protect the Old and Promote Growth* (Oxford: Oxford University Press, 1994), p. 18.

41. On the reform of the pension scheme, see Sarah Marie Brooks, *Social Protection and the Market in Latin America: The Transformation of Social Security Institutions* (New York: Cambridge University Press), 2009. And for the Chilean reform, its influence, and its results, see Carmelo Mesa-Lago, *Reassembling Social Security: A Survey of Pensions and Health Care Reforms in Latin America* (Ox-

ford: Oxford University Press, 2007). Even the World Bank, which in 1994 pushed the Chilean reform, has greatly modified its approach, especially after the 2008 world crisis. It now accepts both traditional "pay as you go" and hybrid "defined benefits" systems and also the development of conditional cash transfers in the majority of developing nations in which regular pensions cover only a minority of the population. See Robert Holzmann, David A. Robalino, and Noriyuki Takayama, eds., *Closing the Coverage Gap: The Role of Social Pensions and Other Retirement Income Transfers* Washington, D.C.: World Bank, 2009).

42. The plebiscite had a voter participation rate of 92 percent, the highest in Chilean history. See Patricio Navia, "Participación electoral en Chile, 1988–2001," *Revista de Ciencia Política* (Santiago de Chile) 24, no. 1 (2004): 91. For the results of the vote, see Huneeus, *The Pinochet Regime*, p. 420. Much of this popular support finally ended with the disclosures in 2004 about Pinochet's illegal millions in the Riggs Bank of Washington, D.C., and elsewhere. See "The Pinochet Money Trail," *New York Times*, December 12, 2004.

43. Huneeus, *The Pinochet Regime*, pp. 80–83; and Genaro Arriagada Herrera, "The Legal and Institutional Framework of the Armed Forces in Chile," in *Military Rule in Chile*, ed. Valenzuela and Valenzuela, pp. 117–43. Nor were military pensions privatized by the Chicago Boys, so in fact by the end of the regime these pensions cost a very significant 1.5 percent of GDP annually. Huneeus, *The Pinochet Regime*, p. 333.

44. Huneeus, *The Pinochet Regime*, p. 153.

45. Most of the immediate changes that needed to be dealt with were the so-called twenty-nine transitory dispositions, which determined how the post-plebiscite government would be established. One of these would have required a plebiscite to change the constitution. Key among the basic constitutional provisions that remained in existence for some time was the establishment of appointed rather than elected representatives in a partially nonelected Senate. See Robert Barros, *Constitutionalism and Dictatorship: Pinochet, the Junta, and the 1980 Constitution* (New York: Cambridge University Press, 2004), chaps. 7 and 8.

46. This long and tense period of the efforts of the Pinochet army and the civilian right to limit the democratic opening is discussed in Felipe Agüero, "30 años después: La ciencia política y las relaciones Fuerzas Armadas, Estado y sociedad," *Revista de Ciencia Política* (Santiago) 23, no. 2 (2003): 251–72.

47. See Rouquié, *The Military and the State in Latin America*, pp. 312–13.

48. Smith, *Talons of the Eagle*, p. 176. The other exception was the seizure of power in Bolivia in the Revolution of 1952 by the MNR. Defined by the State Department as a pro-fascist and pro-Peronist movement, the MNR government was initially ignored by the United States, which eventually supported the reformist regime with massive aid. In turn the United States had little influence on the military regimes that followed on the downfall of the MNR. In fact some of the most left-wing officers who came to power were participants in the capture and killing of Che Guevara in 1967. See Herbert S. Klein, *A Concise History of Bolivia*, 2nd ed. (Cambridge: Cambridge University Press, 2011), chap. 8.

49. For a survey of the political conflicts of the first Belaúnde regime, see Henry Pease Garcia, *El ocaso del poder oligárquico, lucha política en la escena official*

1968–1975 (Lima: DESCO, 1977), chap. 1; and Carlos Contreras and Marcos Cueto, *Historia del Peru contemparáneo* (Lima: Instituto de Estudios Peruanos, 1999), chap. 8.

50. Lisa L. North, "Ideological Orientations of Peru's Military Rulers," in *The Peruvian Experiment Reconsidered,* ed. Cynthia McClintock and Abraham L. Lowenthal (Princeton: Princeton University Press, 1983), pp. 245–74.

51. The initial APRA model was that agrarian reform and industrialization supported by foreign capital could be carried out by a pluralist democratic state. Julio Cotler, "Crisis política y populismo militar en el Perú," *Revista Mexicana de Sociología* 32, nos. 3–4 (May–June 1970): 746.

52. The standard survey of the school and its teachings is by Jorge Rodriguez Beruff, *Los militares y el poder: Un ensayo sobre la doctrina militar en el Perú 1948–1968* (Caracas: Mosca Azul editores, 1993). Also see Luigi R. Einaudi, "Revolution from Within?: Military Rule in Peru Since 1968," *Studies in Comparative International Development* 8, no. 1 (1973): 71–87. The data on attendance is found in Rodriguez Beruff, *Los militares y el poder,* p. 51, table 10.

53. Einaudi, "Revolution from Within," p. 76.

54. Carlos A. Astiz and José Z. García, "The Peruvian Military: Achievement Orientation, Training, and Political Tendencies," *Western Political Quarterly* 25, no. 4 (December 1972), p. 677.

55. Luigi R. Einaudi, and Alfred C. Stepan, *Latin American Institutional Development: Changing Military Perspectives in Peru and Brazil,* R-586-DOS (Santa Monica: Rand Corporation, April 1971), p. 37.

56. Rodriguez Beruff, *Los militares y el poder,* p. 101. As Rodriguez noted, "The military arrived at their reformist position principally through their formulation of a military doctrine (first of a doctrine of 'total war' and then of a 'revolutionary war') and from its diagnosis of the military implications of . . . 'the relative backwardness' of Peru." Rodriguez Beruff, *Los militares y el poder,* p. 128.

57. Declaration of CAEM in 1963 cited in Einaudi, "Revolution from Within," p. 78.

58. Einaudi, "Revolution from Within," pp. 80–83. The importance of the guerrilla campaigns of 1965–66 in convincing the officers to seriously concern themselves with national social and economic issues is also stressed by Astiz and García, "The Peruvian Military," pp. 677–78. As the then colonel and subdirector for intelligence of the Army General Staff and later a member of the first Velasco government Fernandez Maldonado recalled, the "guerilla movements served to form us. All those who surrounded Velasco in that period had worked in Intelligence," and it was the intelligence groups that infiltrated and destroyed these guerilla movements of Hugo Blanco and others. Interview cited in Dirk Kruijt, "Perú: Relaciones entre civiles y militares, 1950–1990," in *América Latina: Militares y sociedad,* ed. Dirk Kruijt and Edelberto Torres-Rivas (San José: FLACSO, 1991), 2:45–46.

59. Kruijt, "Perú: relaciones entre civiles y militares," p. 34.

60. George D. E. Philip, *The Rise and Fall of the Peruvian Military Radicals, 1968–1976* (London: Athlone, 1978), pp. 77–78.

61. As Julio Cotler has noted, the government of the armed forces would realize many of the demands made by all the progressive parties of the post–World War II era. Cotler, "Crisis política y populismo militar en el Perú," p. 763.

62. See, for example, the declaration of Perón on June 25, 1960, to the "Compañeros de las 62" in Hoover Archives, Stanford University, Perón Collection, box 5, folder 5.24.

63. On the ideology of the military regime, see Julio Cotler, "Democracy and National Integration in Peru," in McClintock and Lowenthal, *The Peruvian Experiment*, pp. 3–38.

64. E. V. K. Fitzgerald, *The Political Economy of Peru, 1956–78: Economic Development and the Restructuring of Capital* (Cambridge: Cambridge University Press, 1979), chap. 6; Augusto Alvarez Rodrich, "Del estado empresario al estado regulador," in *Perú 1964–1994: Economía, sociedad y política*, ed. Julio Cotler (Lima: IEP, 1995), pp. 72–75.

65. The ISI model was timidly introduced by the first Belaúnde presidential regime, but came to full development only with the Velasco military government. The industrial sector peaked at 27 percent of GDP in 1975 when it accounted for 17 percent of the economically active population in the country. In this period, the growth of industry reached as high as 7 percent per annum, but industry suffered negative annual growth rates in the 1980s due to internal shocks and various government policies under the first Alan García presidency. Luis Abugattás, *Estabilización macroeconómica, reforma estructural y comportamiento industrial: La experiencia peruana*, Serie Reformas Económicas no. 48 (Santiago de Chile: CEPAL, 1999), pp. 6–8.

66. Fitzgerald, *The Political Economy of Peru*, pp. 124–25. On the complex debates and issues related to the enactment of this major legislative act, see Philip, *The Rise and Fall of the Peruvian Military Radicals*, pp. 123–27.

67. Fitzgerald, *The Political Economy of Peru*, p. 188.

68. On these reforms, see Cynthia McClintock, *Peasant Cooperatives and Political Change in Peru* (Princeton: Princeton University Press, 1981), chap. 2.

69. Taking a more neutral position on the debates of whether this was a participatory democracy or a corporatist state, McClintock stresses a shifting pattern of reforms over time among different ideological groups of the military; in her view, ultimately this was a process controlled by the military, which thought these associations would replace political parties. See McClintock, *Peasant Cooperatives and Political Change*, pp. 39–63.

70. José Matos Mar and José Manuel Mejía, *La reforma agraria en el Perú* (Lima: Instituto de Estudios Peruanos, 1980), p. 171.

71. A good discussion of this decree is found in Harvey Condori Luque, "Las leyes de agua en el Perú: Planes hidrológicos de cuencas," found at www.monografias .com/trabajos19/ley-de-aguas/ley-de-aguas.shtml#ixzz37UhLq4mI. Also see the report by CERES found at www.cepes.org.pe/legisla/Legislacion%20anterior.htm.

72. Formed in 1960, the MNL consisted of a mixed grouping of socialists and anarchists, but was rejected by the official communist party. At various times it consisted of the Movimiento de Izquierda Revolucionaria (MIR), the Movimiento de Acción Popular Uruguayo (MAPU), the Federación Anarquista Uruguaya (FAU), the Movimiento Revolucionario Oriental (MRO), and the Movimiento de Apoyo al Campesino (MAC). Alfonso Lessa, *La revolución imposible: Los tupamaros y el fracaso de la vía armada en el Uruguay del siglo XX* (Montevideo: Fin de Siglo, 2003), p. 24.

73. Lessa, *La revolución imposible*, p. 21.

74. But despite the imprisonment, torture, killings, and solitary confinement of its leaders in different prisons throughout the country, the MNL survived. In the post-authoritarian period it changed its ideology and joined the Frente Amplia, and in 2010 one of its founding guerrilla leaders, José Mujica, was elected president. On the changes made by the party in the post-authoriarian era, see Adolfo Garcé, "Ideologías políticas y adaptación partidaria: El caso del MLN-Tupamaros (1985–2009)," *Revista de Ciencia Política* (Santiago) 31, no. 1 (2011): 117–37.

75. Charles Guy Gillespie, *Negotiating Democracy: Politicians and Generals in Uruguay* (Cambridge: Cambridge University Press, 1991), pp. 40–42. On the history of the Tupamaros and the MLN, which finally elected José Mujica, one of its key leaders, as president of the republic in 2010, see Alain Labrousse, *Una historia de los Tupamaros: De Sendic a Mujica* (Montevideo: Editorial Fin de Siglo, 2009). Both Gillespie and Labrousse talk about the 1962–70 actions of the Tupamaros as "the Robin Hood" period when it was most popular, but after 1970 it lost its appeal to most Uruguayans.

76. Ananda Simões Fernandes, "Quando o inimigo ultrapassa a fronteira: As conexões repressivas entre a ditadura civil-militar brasileira e o Uruguai (1964–1973)" (M.A. thesis, História Universidade Federal do Rio Grande do Sul, 2009), p. 222. It was reported that the Brazilian military leaders were especially hostile to the new Frente Amplio and became significantly involved with the Uruguayan police and military in attempting to sabotage the electoral campaign of the new party.

77. As Gillespie notes, "Whereas Bordaberry wanted an institutionalized authoritarian regime, the military preferred the ambiguity of an authoritarian solution." Gillespie, *Negotiating Democracy*, p. 54.

78. Virginia Martínez, *Tiempos de dictadura 1973/1985* (Montevideo: Ediciones de la Banda Oriental, 2005), pp. 13–14, 31, 61. On the Plan Condor, see J. Patrice McSherry, *Predatory States: Operation Condor and Covert War in Latin America* (Lanham, Md.: Rowman & Littlefield, 2005). On the various national and international guerrilla movements in this period operating in these nations, see Alberto Aldo Marchesi, "Geographies of Armed Protest: Transnational Cold War, Latin Americanism and the New Left in the Southern Cone, 1964–1976" (Ph.D. diss., New York University, Department of History, 2013), also forthcoming from Cambridge University Press.

79. Gillespie, *Negotiating Democracy*, p. 30.

80. On the progresive expansion of military power in the complex evolution of the regime, see Carlos Demasi, "La evolución del campo político en la dictadura," in *La dictadura cívico militar: Uruguay, 1973–1985*, ed. Carlos Demasi et al. (Montevideo: Ediciones de la Banda Oriental, 2009), pp. 15–116; and Martínez, *Tiempos de dictadura*, p. 87.

81. Gillespie, *Negotiating Democracy*, pp. 56–57.

82. Jaime Yaffe, "Proceso económico y politica economica durante la ditadura (1973–1984)," in Demasi et al., *La dictadura cívico militar*, p. 168.

83. Martínez, *Tiempos de dictadura*, pp. 132, 167, 181–82, 205–6. On the military during the transition, see Demasi, "La evolución del campo político," p. 112. Sanguinette won 31 percent of the vote, and won in both the urban and the rural ar-

eas. Miguel Alcántara Sáez and Ismael Crespo Martínez, *Partidos politicos y procesos electorales en Uruguay (1971–1990)* (Madrid: CEDEAL, 1992), pp. 119–57.

84. On the origins and evolution of the National Revolution of 1952 and its reforms, see Herbert S. Klein, *Parties and Political Change in Bolivia, 1880–1952* (Cambridge: Cambridge University Press, 1969). A useful evaluation of the National Revolution is found in Merilee S. Grindle and Pilar Domingo, *Proclaiming Revolution: Bolivia in Comparative Perspective* (Cambridge, Mass.: David Rockefeller Center for Latin American Studies, Harvard University, 2003), and for the evolution of the ideology of the party from promoting state socialism to supporting neoliberalism, see Eduardo Arze Cuadros, *Bolivia, el programa del MNR y la revolución nacional: Del movimiento de reforma universitaria al ocaso del model neoliberal* (1928–2002) (La Paz: Plural, 2002).

85. A useful survey of this period is found in James Dunkerley, *Rebellion in the Veins: Political Struggle in Bolivia, 1952–82* (London: Verso, 1984). Also see Klein, *A Concise History of Bolivia*, chaps. 8 and 9.

86. Valenzuela, *The Breakdown of Democratic Regimes*, p. 109.

CHAPTER 2. THE BRAZILIAN MILITARY INTERREGNUM

1. As Lars Schoultz has pointed out, underlying U.S. policy toward Latin America from the beginning is a systematic belief that Latin Americans are inferior and cannot be expected to embrace development or properly participate in democratic government on their own. Schoultz, *Beneath the United States*, chap. 19.

2. As Brazilian president Dilma Rousseff, herself a torture victim of the military regime, recently declared, "Torture is like a cancer. It begins in a cell, but compromises all of society. It compromises the system of the torturer and obviously of the tortured, because it affects the most human condition of all of us, which is pain, and destroys the civilizing bonds of a society." *Folha*, July 25, 2014.

3. José Murilo de Carvalho, *Forças armadas e política no Brasil* (Rio de Janeiro: Zahar, 2005), pp. 13–29.

4. Murilo de Carvalho, *Forças armadas*, pp. 48–50.

5. Murilo de Carvalho, *Forças armadas*, p. 51.

6. Murilo de Carvalho, *Forças armadas*, pp. 73–75.

7. Murilo de Carvalho, *Forças armadas*, pp. 78–83. Between 1931 and 1936, some 624 officers were expelled from the army, of whom at least seven were generals. Murilo de Carvalho, *Forças armadas*, p. 83, quadro 3, and p. 85, quadro 5.

8. A survey of this ideology is provided in Bolivar Lamounier, "Formação de um pensamento político autoritário na Primeira República: Uma interpretação," in *História geral da civilização brasileira*, vol. 3, *O Brasil republicano*, ed. Sérgio Buarque de Holanda and Boris Fausto (São Paulo: Difusão Européia do Livro, 1977), pp. 343–74.

9. On the fascist movement, see Hélio Henrique C. Trindade, "El fascismo brasileño en la década del 30: Orígenes históricos y base social del integralismo," *Desarrollo Económico* 12, no. 48 (January–March 1973): 687–723.

10. Conservative Catholic intellectuals both supported their own movements and gave tacit support to the Brazilian fascist party known as the integralistas. See

Margaret Todaro Williams, "Integralism and the Brazilian Catholic Church," *Hispanic American Historical Review* 54, no. 3 (August 1974): 431–52.

11. As Boris Fausto noted in his excellent survey of these intellectuals, "It is possible to find on the right, an authoritarian nationalist ideology, distinct from other aspects, among which are included fascism and Catholic traditionalists." Boris Fausto, *O pensamento nacionalista autoritário* (Rio de Janeiro: Jorge Zahar, 2001), pp. 16–17. It is argued by Sérgio Miceli that the majority of these authoritarian intellectuals were from the old oligarchic elites. Sérgio Miceli, *Intelectuais e classe dirigente no Brasil (1920–1945)* (São Paulo: Difel, 1979), p. 167. He also claims that the dominant modernist group of writers and intellectuals in São Paulo remained democratic and liberal, especially given the fact that Vargas appointed military interventors in the state government who were neither connected to the oligarchic families of the state nor associated with the local elite parties. Miceli, *Intelectuais e classe dirigente,* chap. 1.

12. Though late by European standards, the Italian liberal state had put into place a far more extensive program of social welfare than had Brazil before 1920. It even passed an unemployed act in 1919. It was this late liberal welfare regime that the fascist state expanded and made into a seemingly more modern organization, though without any direct funding from the state, and putting most of the costs on the working class. See Maria Sophia Quine, *Italy's Social Revolution: Charity and Welfare from Liberalism to Fascism* (New York: Palgrave, 2002), chap. 4; and Vera Zamagni, ed. *Povertà e innovazioni istituzionali in Italia* (Bologna: Il mulino, 2000), pp. 671–750.

13. All authors stress Campos's commitment to the cult of the dictator, his imitation of the fascist constitution of Poland in that period, and finally his declared support for both Mussolini and Hitler and the fascist states up until 1945. It would also appear that he was influenced by the strange authoritarian Rio Grande do Sul state constitution written by the governor Júlio de Castilhos in 1891 as well as the German fascist jurist Carl Schmitt. It was these decrees that Campos used in turn to model the "constitutional" *Atos Institucionais* written for the post-1964 military regimes. The preamble to the first of these famous AI decrees stressed that their legitimacy came from the revolutionary act itself, which he held was as legitimate as a popular vote. Pádua Fernandes, "Setenta anos após 1937: Francisco Campos, o Estado Novo e o pensamento jurídico autoritário," *Prisma Jurídico* (São Paulo) 6 (2007): 351–70; Rogério Dultra dos Santos,"Francisco Campos e os fundamentos do constitucionalismo antiliberal no Brasil," *DADOS, Revista de Ciências Sociais* 50, no. 2 (2007): 281–323; and Fausto, *O pensamento nacionalista autoritário,* p. 29.

14. As Bello has noted, Vargas moved the social question from a police issue to one of incorporation of the working class: "Social rights of citizenship were incorporated into the Brazilian legal system 'from above.' Thus, it can be argued that they were obtained not as popular conquest or through the efforts of the working class—as in the European countries that had already adopted them—but as a gift granted by the populist ruler, as in the case of President Vargas, known at the time as 'the father of the poor.'" Enzo Bello, "Cidadania e direitos sociais no Brasil: Um enfoque político e social," *Revista Espaço Jurídico* (Joaçaba) 8, no. 2 (July/December 2007): 139.

15. Fausto stresses their constant reference to "exotic" ideologies and how they thought their authoritarian solutions were more "Brazilian" than these so-called imported ideas. Fausto, *O pensamento nacionalista autoritário*, pp. 52–53.

16. The first quote is from a speech made in August 18, 1933, and the second from his manifesto to the nation, read on May 14, 1932. Getúlio Vargas, *As diretrizes da nova política do Brasil* (Rio de Janeiro: José Olympio Editôra, 1943), p. 233.

17. As Boris Fausto has noted, "A common element of these authoritarian nationalists was the role which they attributed to the so-called racial question"; Fausto, *O pensamento nacionalista autoritário*, p. 38. Many of them were enthusiastic supporters of the eugenics movement, and almost all of them stressed the need to whiten the Brazilian population.

18. This was well expressed in the ideology of General Góes Monteiro, a leading figure in the Vargas government as well as a leader in the revolt against Vargas in 1945. Fausto, *O pensamento nacionalista autoritário*, pp. 63–64.

19. On the theme of anticommunism in Brazilian thought, see Rodrigo Patto Sá Motta, *Em guarda contra o "perigo vermelho": O anticomunismo no Brasil, 1917–1964* (São Paulo: Editora Perspectiva/Fapesp, 2002).

20. Murilo de Carvalho, *Forças armadas*, p. 114.

21. This "moderating" power was actively used to control the government in the period from 1945 to 1964. See Alfred C. Stepan, *The Military in Politics: Changing Patterns in Brazil* (Princeton: Princeton University Press, 1971), chap. 5; Thomas E. Skidmore, *Politics in Brazil, 1930–1964: An Experiment in Democracy* (New York: Oxford University Press, 1967); and Thomas E. Skidmore, *The Politics of Military Rule in Brazil, 1964–85* (New York: Oxford University Press, 1988), chap. 1. On the different factions and their ideologies that emerged among the military leaders in this period, see José Pedro Kunhavalik, "Os militares e o conceito de nacionalismo: Disputas retóricas na década de 1950 e início dos anos 1960"(Ph.D. thesis, Universidade Federal de Santa Catarina, 2009).

22. In the early stages of the school, a considerable proportion of the didactic materials used were translations of U.S. military documents especially on national security and geopolitics. Eduardo Munhoz Svartman, "Guardiões da Nação: Formação profissional, experiências compartilhadas e engajamento político dos generais de 1964" (Ph.D. diss., Universidade Federal do Rio Grande do Sul, 2006), p. 183. This was all part of a constant interaction between Brazilian officers and the U.S. military establishment, with hundreds of Brazilian officers studying in military schools in North America and hundreds more in the Panama Canal Zone. Moreover, the United States became the single largest source of Brazilian armaments in this period. From the 1950s until the 1980s, the United States supplied the bulk of Brazilian arms imports for all three services. But growing disenchantment with U.S. pressure on nuclear arms and human rights under Carter led Geisel to end the 1952 Military Accord. Since then national production and European suppliers have replaced the dominant position of the United States. Eduardo Munhoz Svartman, "Brazil–United States Military Relations During the Cold War: Political Dynamic and Arms transfers," *Brazilian Political Science Review* 5, no. 2 (2012): 75–93.

23. On IPES, see Norman Blume, "Pressure Groups and Decision-Making in Brazil," *Studies in Comparative International Development* 3, no. 11 (1967): 211; and

Elio Gaspari, *A Ditadura Envergonhada* (São Paulo: Companhia das Letras, 2002), p. 153. Dreifuss has shown the linkages between such businessmen's think tanks as IPES, the ESG, and its alumni organization ADEG. René Armand Dreifuss, *1964, a conquista do estado: Ação política, poder e golpe de Classe,* 5th ed. (Petrópolis: Vozes, 1987), chaps. 3, 5, and 8. But Dreifuss goes further and argues that all of the "think-tanks" created in Brazil in the 1950s and 1960s in the universities, in the government, and in private centers like the Fundação Getúlio Vargas were all part of the same "organic" political structure serving multinational interests and hostile to the popular classes. Dreifuss, *1964, a conquista do estado,* p. 77.

24. Luiz Felipe Cezar Mundim, "Juarez Távora e Golbery do Couto e Silva: Escola Superior de Guerra e a organização do estado brasileiro (1930–1960)" (M.A. thesis, Universidade Federal de Goiás, 2007), pp. 183ff.; and Svartman, "Guardiões da nação, pp. 202–3.

25. On the authoritarian Catholicism of Golbery, see Ana Maria Koch, "Catolicismo ultramontano no ideário de Golbery do Couto e Silva," Paper presented at the XXVI Simpósio Nacional de História, ANPUH, 2011 (São Paulo), found at www.snh2011.anpuh.org/site/anaiscomplementares.

26. On the origin and founding of the school and the history of its founders, see Francisco César Alves Ferraz, *À sombra dos carvalhos: Escola Superior de Guerra e política no Brasil, 1948–1955* (Londrina: Editora Uel, 1997), pp. 21–33; and Stepan, *The Military in Politics,* pp. 174–78.

27. Stepan, *The Military in Politics,* p. 179.

28. On the ideology of the ESG and its implications, see Stepan, *The Military in Politics,* pp. 180–83. Also see Eliézer R. de Oliveira de Oliveira, *As forças armadas: Política e ideologia no Brasil (1964–1969),* 2nd ed. (Petrópolis, R.J.: Vozes, 1978), chap. 1. On the complex interaction of the ESG with its alumni, see Ferraz, *À sombra dos carvalhos,* part 3.

29. Interview in CPDOC archives, cited by Svartman, "Guardiões da nação," p. 210. Equally, it was another of the 1964 conspirators, Colonel Golbery do Couto e Silva, who was one of the leaders behind the military manifesto that forced Vargas to dismiss his labor minister, João Goulart, who was promoting a 100 percent raise in the minimum wage. Murilo de Carvalho, *Forças armadas,* p. 114.

30. Although General Geisel shared all of these traits with the other military leaders, it should be noted that he was a Protestant and in fact encouraged the passage of Brazil's first divorce law during his administration.

31. Stepan, *The Military in Politics,* p. 184.

32. Svartman, "Guardiões da nação," pp. 233–36.

33. Murilo de Carvalho, *Forças armadas,* p. 118.

34. Stepan, *The Military in Politics,* pp. 218–219.

35. On Castelo Branco, see Lira Neto, *Castello: A marcha para a ditadura* (São Paulo: Contexto, 2004).

36. Skidmore, *The Politics of Military Rule,* pp. 19–20.

37. Stepan, *The Military in Politics,* pp. 219–21.

38. Skidmore, *The Politics of Military Rule,* p. 20.

39. See Gaspari, *A ditadura envergonhada,* p. 35.

40. For the press, theater, and other media, there would eventually be both pre-publication and post-publication censorship. Moreover, the government quickly

forced the closure of the leading opposition newspaper, *Correio da Manhã*, which had initially supported the coup, and bombed and destroyed most of the left-wing newspapers. But compared with the actions taken in the late 1960s and 1970s, these were relatively mild censorship regimes. See Gláucio Ary Dillon Soares, "A censura durante o regime autoritário," *Revista Brasileira de Ciências Sociais* 4, no. 10 (1989): 21–43; and Maria Helena Moreira Alves, *State and Opposition in Military Brazil* (Austin: University of Texas Press, 1985), pp. 162–64. Censorship groups were founded throughout the country and were staffed by right-wing journalists, academics, and theater people, along with military officers, and by the 1980s there were more than two hundred of them in the country. Beatriz Kusnir, "Da tesourinha ao sacerdote: Os dois últimos chefes da censura brasileira," in *O golpe de 1964 e O regime Militar: Novas Perspectivas*, ed. João Roberto Martins Filho (São Carlos: Editora da Universidade Federal de São Carlos, 2006), pp. 47–65.

41. Skidmore, *The Politics of Military Rule*, pp. 24–25.

42. Reis, *Ditadura e democracia no Brasil*, pp. 49–51.

43. Among these "were three former presidents; six state governors; fifty-five members of the federal Congress." Skidmore, *The Politics of Military Rule*, p. 25. Gaspari gives a higher figure for the total number of "cassados" than Skidmore does in his earlier study.

44. Gaspari, *A ditadura envergonhada*, pp. 130–31, 136.

45. Gaspari, *A ditadura envergonhada*, pp. 135–36.

46. On the origins and development of these Comunidades Eclesiais de Base (CEB), see Scott Mainwaring, *The Catholic Church and Politics in Brazil, 1916–1985* (Stanford: Stanford University Press, 1986), part 3; and his essay "Grassroots Catholic Groups and Politics in Brazil, 1964–1985," Working Paper 98 (South Bend, Ind.: Kellogg Institute, University of Notre Dame, August 1987); Skidmore, *The Politics of Military Rule*, p. 24.

47. Gaspari, *A ditadura envergonhada*, pp. 138–39; and Skidmore, *The Politics of Military Rule*, p. 48.

48. Gaspari, *A ditadura envergonhada*, pp. 153–74; and Alfred Stepan, *Rethinking Military Politics: Brazil and the Southern Cone* (Princeton: Princeton University Press, 1988), chap. 2. For the complex security organization of which SNI was at the top directly under the National Security Council and the president, see Alves, *State and Opposition in Military Brazil*, pp. 128–31.

49. Reis, *Ditadura e democracia no Brasil*, pp. 62–63.

50. Skidmore, *The Politics of Military Rule*, pp. 42–47; and Reis, *Ditadura e democracia no Brasil*, pp. 61–62; Gaspari, *A ditadura envergonhada*, pp. 254–60. Speaking of the judicial changes enacted in AI-2, Gaspari noted, "The militarization of the judicial process inevitably led to the militarization of the political repression, or more precisely, to the politicalization of the military institution." Gaspari, *A ditadura envergonhada*, p. 260.

51. Skidmore, *The Politics of Military Rule*, p. 49.

52. Skidmore, *The Politics of Military Rule*, pp. 56–57.

53. The strikes of the metallurgical workers at Osasco, São Paulo, and at Contagem, Minas Gerais, both in 1968, were the last ones after the military coup of 1964. See Francisco C. Weffort, "Participação e conflito industrial: Contagem

e Osasco, 1968," Caderno 5 (São Paulo: Centro Brasileiro de Análise e Planejamento, 1972).

54. See, for example, Gissele Cassol, "Prisão e tortura em terra estrangeira: A
colaboração repressiva entre Brasil e Uruguai (1964–1985)" (M.A. thesis, Universidade Federal de Santa Maria 2008).

55. Starting in late 1967, the army began invading convents and imprisoning
priests, and from then on the Church—still quite conservative—and the army began to distance themselves from each other. Initially, the Church fully supported
the '64 coup and even dismantled some of its base communities and reduced the
work of its worker priests to satisfy the military. But these Church attacks began
to create ever greater confrontations and eventually led to the open hostility of
the hierarchy to the regime. For the complex evolution of this distancing, see Elio
Gaspari, A ditadura escancarada (São Paulo: Companhia das Letras, 2002), part 3.
On the changing positions of the bishops themselves, see Paulo César Gomes, Os
bispos católicos e a ditadura militar brasileira (São Paulo: Editora Record, 2014).

56. Among these urban guerrillas was the future president of the country, Dilma
Rousseff, who was active in Belo Horizonte in 1969. On the history of these move-
ments, see Jean Rodrigues Sales, A luta armada contra a ditadura militar: A es-
querda brasileira e a influência da revolução cubana (São Paulo: Editora Fundação
Perseu Abramo, 2007). For reflections on these developments, see Jacob Gorender,
Combate nas trevas: A esquerda brasileira: Das ilusões perdidas à luta armada (São
Paulo: Editora Ática, 1987).

57. This violence is well documented in Gaspari, A ditadura envergonhada,
part 3. On the growing opposition to the regime, see Maria Helena Moreira Alves,
State and Opposition in Military Brazil (Austin: University of Texas Press, 1985).

58. For the Institutional Act 5 terms and consequences, see Alves, State and
Opposition, pp. 95–98; for the background to its implantation, see Gaspari, A
ditadura envergonhada, pp. 333–40. For the expulsion of professors, see Gaspari,
A ditadura envergonhada, pp. 329–30; and for the new censorship law and the Operation Bandeirantes, see Skidmore, The Politics of Military Rule, pp. 82, 88, 128.

59. This complex episode is discussed in Gaspari, A ditadura escancarada,
pp. 87–97.

60. Skidmore, The Politics of Military Rule, pp. 95–101.

61. Skidmore, The Politics of Military Rule, p. 108.

62. See José Pastore, Inequality and Social Mobility in Brazil (Madison: University of Wisconsin Press, 1982).

63. Skidmore, The Politics of Military Rule, p. 125.

64. On the complex repressive structure that was created, see Alves, State and
Opposition, pp. 128–31; also Martha K. Huggins, "Murderers' Reformulation of
Memory Legacies of Authoritarianism: Brazilian Torturers," Latin American Per-
spectives 27, no. 2 (March 2000): 57–78. On the background to these decisions, see
Gaspari, A ditadura escancarada, pp. 176–83.

65. On the progressive alienation of the Church, see Scott Mainwaring, The
Catholic Church and Politics in Brazil, 1916–1985 (Stanford: Stanford University
Press, 1986), chaps. 5–6. The role of the Brazilian Church was the opposite of what
would occur under the Argentine military regime. There the Church, as mobilized

with a popular base as the Brazilian Church, was wholeheartedly allied with the military and gave it unconditional support, a policy fully supported by Rome. See Horacio Verbitsky, *La mano izquierda de Dios: La última dictadura (1976–1983),* vol. 4 of *Historia política de la Iglesia Católica* (Buenos Aires: Editora Sudamericana, 2010).

66. The propaganda was organized and run by the military through an organ of the government called the AERP (Assessoria Especial de Relações Públicas), which was conceived in the Costa e Silva period, but only formally launched in the Medici government. The aim was to stress that the military leaders were just ordinary Brazilians working for a moral rejuvenation of the country, and that Brazil itself was on the road to becoming an advanced society. See Laura Maria Naves, "O papel da Aerp na construção da identidade nacional: Análise das propagandas políticas durante o Governo Médici," Anais VIII Conferência Brasileira de Mídia 2012 (Brasília), found at www.unicentro.br/redemc/2012/sumario.asp.

67. Philip Schmitter, "The 'Portugalization' of Brazil?" in *Authoritarian Brazil: Origin, Policies, and Future,* ed. Alfred Stepan (New Haven: Yale University Press, 1973), pp. 170–232.

68. Juan Linz, "The Future of an Authoritarian Situation or the Institutionalization of an Authoritarian Regime: The Case of Brazil," in *Authoritarian Brazil,* ed. Stepan, pp. 233–54.

69. See Francisco Weffort, "Why Democracy?" in *Democratizing Brazil: Problems of Transition and Consolidation,* ed. Alfred Stepan (New York: Oxford University Press, 1989), pp. 327–50.

70. Elio Gaspari, *A ditadura derrotado* (São Paulo: Companhia das Letras, 2003), pp. 108, 185–95.

71. On the ministers appointed and their backgrounds, see Gaspari, *A ditadura derrotada,* part 2, section "O Poder."

72. Skidmore, *The Politics of Military Rule,* pp. 165, 167.

73. Skidmore, *The Politics of Military Rule,* pp. 160–64.

74. Skidmore, *The Politics of Military Rule,* pp. 168–70.

75. Juliana Gazzotti, "A revista Veja e o obstáculo da censura," *Revista Olhar,* ano 3, nos. 5–6 (2001): 1–3.

76. Gaspari, *A ditadura derrotada,* p. 308.

77. Gaspari, *A ditadura derrotada,* part 4, and Skidmore, *The Politics of Military Rule,* pp. 171–74.

78. Elio Gaspari, *A ditadura encurralada* (São Paulo: Companhia das Letras, 2004), p. 13.

79. Bolivar Lamounier, "Authoritarian Brazil Revisited: The Impact of Elections on the Abertura," in *Democratizing Brazil,* ed. Stepan, p. 62, and pp. 64–69 for the results of the subsequent elections.

80. For a survey of many of these developments in the São Paulo region, see Eder Sadee, *Quando novos personagens entraram em Cena: Experiências e lutas dos trabalhadores da Grande São Paulo, 1970–1980* (Rio de Janeiro: Paz e Terra, 1988).

81. For a detailed history of the Herzog crisis and popular mobilization, see Gaspari, *A ditadura encurralada,* pp. 173–201, and Moreira Alves, *State and Opposition,* pp. 156–58.

82. Moreira Alves, *State and Opposition*, p. 159; Skidmore, *The Politics of Military Rule*, pp. 176–78; Gaspari, *A ditadura encurralada*, pp. 219–24.

83. Skidmore, *The Politics of Military Rule*, pp. 183–84.

84. Skidmore, *The Politics of Military Rule*, pp. 197–99.

85. Skidmore, *The Politics of Military Rule*, pp. 190–92.

86. Eduardo Noronha, "A explosão das greves na década de 80," in *O sindicalismo brasileiro nos anos 80*, ed. Armando Boito (Rio de Janeiro: Paz e Terra, 1991), p. 102.

87. On the history and importance of these peasant leagues, see Fernando Antônio Azevedo, "Revisitando as ligas camponesas," in *O golpe de 1964 e o regime militar: Novas perspectivas*, ed. João Roberto Martins Filho (São Carlos: Editora da Universidade Federal de São Carlos, 2006), pp. 27–37.

88. See Regina Reyes Novaes, "Continuidades e rupturas no sindicalismo rural," in *O sindicalismo brasileiro nos anos 80*, ed. Boito, pp. 171–96; and Biorn Maybury-Lewis, *The Politics of the Possible: The Brazilian Rural Workers' Trade Union Movement, 1964–1985* (Philadelphia: Temple University Press, 1994), pp. 6–8, 21–24.

89. Many of the new opposition unionists in the union elections of 1976 and afterward were also members of the Catholic Comunidades Eclesiais de Base, and the Church actively supported the opposition leadership. Margaret E. Keck, *The Workers' Party and Democratization in Brazil* (New Haven: Yale University Press, 1995), pp. 47–49; and Mainwaring, "Grassroots Catholic Groups and Politics in Brazil."

90. For the details of the strike and the role of the new union leaders, see Keck, *The Workers' Party and Democratization in Brazil*, pp. 64–65; and Ricardo Antunes, *A rebeldia do trabalho (O confronto operário no ABC Paulista: As greves de 1978/80)* (Campinas: Editôra da Universidade Estadual de Campinas, 1988), chaps. 1–2.

91. Keck, *The Workers' Party and Democratization in Brazil*, p. 66. There is a lively debate as to whether a new unionism was created after 1978, or if it was simply a modification of the old corporatist structure first established by Vargas in the 1930s. For the latter position, see, for example, Armando Boito Jr., "Reforma e persistência da estrutura sindical," in *O sindicalismo brasileiro nos anos 80*, ed. Boito, pp. 43–91.

92. On the impact of the Carter administration and the visit of Rosalynn Carter to Brazil on the military, see Gaspari, *A ditadura encurralada*, pp. 373–98. It is amazing how little importance most North American scholars have placed on this profound change under the Carter administration. Most cite Jeane Kirkpatrick's articles in *Commentary* that attacked the whole program as naive and dangerous to American interests. See Schoultz, *Beneath the United States*, pp. 362–64, and Smith, *Talons of the Eagle*, pp. 148–49.

93. Moreira Alves, *State and Opposition*, pp. 168–69; Gaspari, *A ditadura encurralada*, pp. 364–66.

94. Skidmore, *The Politics of Military Rule*, p. 203.

95. Gaspari, *A ditadura derrotada*, pp. 333–34.

96. Skidmore, *The Politics of Military Rule*, pp. 211–12.

97. Skidmore, *The Politics of Military Rule,* pp. 215–19.

98. This crisis is discussed in detail in chapter 3.

99. On the strike activity, see Skidmore, *The Politics of Military Rule,* pp. 212–15.

100. On the 1980s defeats, see Antunes, *A rebeldia do trabalho,* chap. 3; Noronha, "A explosão das greves na década de 80," pp. 105–6.

101. On the new party alignments, see Skidmore, *The Politics of Military Rule,* pp. 219–21; and specifically on the founding of PT, see Keck, *The Workers' Party and Democratization in Brazil,* pp. 67–73. On all the new parties formed, see David Maciel, *A argamassa da ordem: Da ditadura militar à Nova República (1974–1985)* (São Paulo: Xamã VM Editora, 2004), pp. 229–61.

102. Skidmore, *The Politics of Military Rule,* p. 227.

103. On the complex internal army debates between the "duros" (hard-liners) and the officers behind the Democratic Military Movement (MDD) in this period, see Maciel, *A argamassa da ordem,* pp. 198–203.

104. Skidmore, *The Politics of Military Rule,* pp. 227–30, 240.

105. Stepan, *Rethinking Military Politics,* chap. 5, and Skidmore, *The Politics of Military Rule,* chap. 8. On the complex demands of the military to retain some residual powers in the pre-Constitutional negotiations, see Eliézer Rizzo de Oliveira, "Constituinte, Forças Armadas e autonomia militar,"in *As Forças Armadas: Política e ideologia no Brasil,* ed. Eliézer Rizzo de Oliveira et al. (Rio de Janeiro: Espaço e Tempo, 1987), pp. 145–85. For their final resolution see Eliézer Rizzo de Oliveira, *De Geisel a Collor: Forças armadas, transição e democracia* (Campinas: Papirus, 1994), part 3.

CHAPTER 3. ECONOMIC REFORMS OF THE BRAZILIAN MILITARY PERIOD

1. See the excellent discussion of why reformers were able to work with the regime provided by Rodrigo Patto Sá Motta, *As universidades e o regime militar* (Rio de Janeiro: Zahar, 2014), p. 18 and chap. 7.

2. Among the numerous studies on the economy of the period prior to the *golpe militar,* see the following: Sonia Draibe, *Rumos e metamorfoses: Estado e industrialização no Brasil: 1930/1960* (Rio de Janeiro: Paz e Terra, 1985); Maria Victoria de Mesquita Benevides, *O governo Kubitschek* (Rio de Janeiro: Paz e Terra, 1976); Maria da Conceição Tavares, "Auge e declínio do processo de substituição," in *Da substituição de importações ao capitalismo financeiro,* ed. Maria da Conceição Tavares (Rio de Janeiro: Zahar, 1972); Albert Hirschmann, "The Political Economy of Import Substitution Industrialization in Latin America," *Quarterly of Economics* 82 (February 1968): 2–32; Albert Fishlow, "Origens e consequências da substituição de importações no Brasil," in *Formação econômica do Brasil: A experiência de industrialização,* ed. Flávio Versiani and José Roberto Mendonça de Barros (São Paulo: Anpec/Saraiva, 1976); Annibal Villanova Villela and Wilson Suzigan, *Política do governo e crescimento da economia brasileira, 1889–1945* (Rio de Janeiro: Ipea, 1973); Pedro Malan, "Relações econômicas internacionais do Brasil, 1945–1964," in *História Geral da Civilização Brasileira,* ed. Boris Fausto (São Paulo: Difel, 1977), tomo 3, vol. 1, pp. 31–106; Antonio Barros

de Castro, *Sete ensaios sobre a economia brasileira* (São Paulo: Forense, 1969); Marcelo de Paiva Abreu, "Inflação, estagnação e ruptura: 1961–1964," in *A ordem do progresso*, ed. Marcelo de Paiva Abreu (Rio de Janeiro: Campus, 1990), pp. 197–231; Luiz Orenstein and Antonio Claudio Sochaczewski, "Democracia com desenvolvimento: 1956–1961," in *A ordem do progresso*, ed. Paiva Abreu, pp. 171–95; José Serra, "Ciclos e mudanças estruturais na economia brasileira do pós-guerra," in *Desenvolvimento Capitalista no Brasil: Ensaios sobre a Crise*, ed. Luiz Gonzaga de Mello Belluzzo and Renata Coutinho (São Paulo: Brasiliense, 1981); Rubens Penha Cysne, "A economia brasileira no período militar," *Estudos Econômicos* 23, no. 2 (1993): 185–226; Salvador Teixeira Werneck Vianna, "Desenvolvimento econômico e reformas institucionais no Brasil: Considerações sobre a construção interrompida" (Ph.D. thesis, Instituto de Economia, UFRJ, 2007); Marly Job de Oliveira, "A política geral do regime militar para construção de suas políticas econômicas" (Ph.D. thesis, FFLCH-USP, São Paulo, 2007); Pedro Malam and Regis Bonelli, "Brazil 1950–1980: Three Decades of Growth-Oriented Economic Policies," Texto para Discussão, no. 187 (Rio de Janeiro: IPEA, 1990); Paul Singer, "O processo econômico," in *História do Brasil Nação: 1808–2010*, 6 vols. (Madrid: Mafre; Rio de Janeiro: Objetiva, 2014), 6:183–231.

3. For a detailed survey of this period, see Francisco Vidal Luna and Herbert S. Klein, *The Economic and Social History of Brazil Since 1899* (New York: Cambridge University Press, 2014).

4. Roberto Macedo, "Plano trienal de desenvolvimento econômico," in *Planejamento no Brasil*, ed. Betty Mindlin Lafer (São Paulo: Perspectiva, 1970); Carlos Lessa, *Quinze anos de política econômica* (Campinas: Cadernos Unicamp, no. 4, 1975).

5. Celso Martone, "O plano de ação econômica," in *Planejamento no Brasil*, ed. Lafer, 29–50.

6. André Lara Resende, "Estabilização e reforma," in *A nova economia brasileira*, ed. Mario Henrique Simonsen and Roberto Campos (Rio de Janeiro: José Olympio, 1979); Celso Furtado, *Um projeto para o Brasil* (Rio de Janeiro: Saga, 1968); Albert Fishlow, "Algumas reflexões sobre a política brasileira após 1964," *Estudos CEBRAP* 6 (January–March 1974): 5–66; Mario Henrique Simonsen, *Inflação: Gradualismo x tratamento de choque* (Rio de Janeiro: Apec, 1970); Albert Fishlow, "A distribuição de renda no Brasil," in *A controvérsia sobre a distribuição de renda e desenvolvimento*, ed. R. Tolipan and A. C. Tinelli (Rio de Janeiro: Zahar, 1975).

7. Simonsen, *Inflação: Gradualismo x tratamento de choque*, pp. 26–27.

8. Unfortunately there is no complete set of average wages for this period. On this theme, see João Saboia, "Salário e produtividade na indústria brasileira: Os efeitos da política salarial no longo prazo," *Pesquisa e Planejamento Econômico* 20, no.3 (December 1990): 581–600; João Saboia, "Política salarial e distribuição de renda: 25 anos de desencontros," in *Distribuição de renda no Brasil*, ed. José Márcio Camargo and Fábio Giambiagi (Rio de Janeiro: Paz e Terra, 2000); Maria Isabel H. da Jornada, "A política salarial: Uma visão panorâmica da Legislação," *Ensaios FEE* (Porto Alegre) 17, no. 2 (1989): 65–78.

9. There was in this period an extensive debate over the question of income concentration. The government affirmed that the high levels of inequality of in-

come distribution were a transitory phenomenon caused by the growth process, while other economists held different opinions. Some argued that there were structural reasons for this distorted distribution and it would not be eliminated with growth, others blamed the government's repressive salary policy as the cause for this concentration. On this theme, see Carlos G. Langoni, *Distribuição de renda e desenvolvimento econômico no Brasil* (Rio de Janeiro: Expressão e Cultura, 1973); Albert Fishlow, "Brazilian Size Distribution of Income," *American Economic Review* 62, no. 1/2 (1972): 391–402; Edmar Bacha and L. Taylor, "Brazilian Income Distribution in the 1960s: 'Facts,' Model Results, and the Controversy," in *Models of Growth and Distribution for Brazil*, ed. Taylor et al. (New York: Oxford University Press, 1980); Ramos and Reis, "Distribuição da renda," pp. 21–45.

10. The BNDES began as a national development bank, but in 1982 the "Social" suffix was added to its title, and it began to work as well in the area of social development.

11. Francisco Vidal Luna and Thomaz de Aquino Nogueira Neto, *Correção monetária e mercado de capitais: A experiência brasileira* (São Paulo: Bolsa de Valores de São Paulo, 1978).

12. Data obtained at Ipeadata. IBGE/SCN: PIB da indústria de transformação, valor adicionado, valor real anual.

13. Angelo Del Vecchio, "A era Delfim: Planejamento estratégico e regime militar" (M.A. thesis, FFLCH-USP, 1992).

14. For the debates on the factors that influenced the evolution of Brazilian agriculture, see José Pastore, Guilherme L. Silva Dias, and Manoel C. Castro, "Condicionantes da produtividade da pesquisa agrícola no Brasil," *Estudos Econômicos*, 6, no. 3 (1976): 147–81; Charles Mueller and George Martine, "Modernização agropecuária, emprego agrícola e êxodo rural no Brasil—a década de 1980," *Revista de Economia Política* 17, no. 3 (July/September 1997): 85–104; Rodolfo Hoffmann, "Evolução da distribuição da posse da terra no Brasil no período 1960–80," *Reforma Agrária* 12, no. 6 (November/December 1982): 17–34; Carlos Nayro Coelho, "70 anos de política agrícola no Brasil, 1931–2001," *Revista de Política Agrícola* 10, no. 3 (July–September 2001); Fernando Homem de Melo, "Agricultura brasileira: Incerteza e disponibilidade tecnológica" (Thesis of Livre Docencia, Universidade de São Paulo, 1978); Fernando Homem de Melo, "Padrões de instabilidade entre culturas da agricultura brasileira," *PPE*, 8, no. 3 (December 1979): 819–44; José Roberto Mendonça de Barros and D. H. Graham, "A agricultura brasileira e o problema da produção de alimentos," *PPE* 8, no. 3 (December 1978): 695–726; Affonso Celso Pastore, "A resposta da produção agrícola aos preços no Brasil" (Ph.D. thesis, Universidade de São Paulo, 1969); Alberto Passos Guimarães, *Quatro séculos de latifúndio* (Rio de Janeiro: Paz e Terra, 1977); and Ruy Muller Paiva, "Reflexões sobre as tendências da produção, da produtividade e dos preços do setor agrícola no Brasil," in *Agricultura subdesenvolvida*, ed. F. Sá (Petrópolis: Vozes, 1968).

15. For a good survey of the transformations that occurred in agriculture in this period and afterward, see Antônio Márcio Buainain, Eliseu Alves, José Maria da Silveira, and Zander Navarro, eds., *O mundo rural no Brasil do século 21: A formação de um novo padrão agrário e agrícola* (Brasília: Embrapa, 2014). The statistics were taken from the websites of the Ministry of Agriculture (www.agricultura

.gov.br); IBGE, twentieth-century statistics (www.ibge.gov.br); Central Bank of
Brasil (www.bcb.gov.br/?RELRURAL); IPEADATA: Temas, Produção (www.ip-
eadata.gov.br/ipeaweb.dll/ipeadata?523053171).

16. For the first phase of industrialization in Brazil, see Wilson Suzigan, *Indústria brasileira, origens e desenvolvimento* (São Paulo: Brasiliense, 1986); Wilson
Cano, *Raíses da concentração industrial em São Paulo* (São Paulo: Difel, 1977);
Warren Dean, *The Industrialization of São Paulo, 1880–1945* (Austin: University
of Texas Press, 1969); Celso Furtado, *Formação econômica do Brasil* (Rio de Janeiro: Fundo de Cultura, 1959); Roberto Simonsen, *A evolução industrial do Brasil
e outros estudos* (São Paulo: Editora Nacional/Edusp, 1973); Sérgio Silva, *A expansão cafeeira e origem da indústria no Brasil* (São Paulo: Alfa Omega, 1976); Pedro
Malan and Regis Bonelli, "Crescimento econômico, industrialização e balanço de
pagamentos: O Brasil dos anos 70 aos anos 80," Texto para Discussão no. 60 (Rio
de Janeiro: Ipea, 1983).

17. Benevides, *O governo Kubitschek;* Orenstein and Sochaczewski, "Democracia com Desenvolvimento, pp. 171–95.

18. Tavares, "Auge e declínio do processo de substituição"; Hirschmann, "The
Political Economy of Import Substitution"; Albert Fishlow, "Origens e consequências da substituição de importações no Brasil," in *Formação econômica do Brasil:
A experiência de industrialização,* ed. Flavio Versiani and José Roberto Mendonça
de Barros (São Paulo: Anpec/Saraiva, 1976); Abreu, "Inflação, estagnação e Ruptura," pp. 197–231.

19. Data obtained at Ipeadata, Salário Mínimo real, mensal, R$ valor real, Veja
também Gráfico 1.

20. Data obtained at Ipeadata, IBGE/SCN. PIB, variação real anual e PIB da
indústria de transformação, valor adicionado, valor real anual.

21. On this theme, see Langoni, *Distribuição de renda;* Fishlow, "Brazilian Size
Distribution of Income"; Bacha and Taylor, "Brazilian Income Distribution in the
1960s"; Lauro R. A. Ramos and José Guilherme Almeida Reis, "Distribuição da
renda: Aspectos teóricos e o debate no Brasil," in *Distribuição de renda no Brasil,*
ed. José Marcio Camargo and Fabio Giambiagi (Rio de Janeiro: Paz e Terra, 2000),
pp. 21–45.

22. There were intense debates both for and against the model of growth that
was adopted and its consequences in this period of the "economic miracle." Some
of the principal works produced at the time on this debate were Antônio Delfim
Netto, "Análise do comportamento recente da economia brasileira: Diagnóstico"
(São Paulo: mimeo, 1967); Simonsen, *Inflação: Gradualismo x tratamento de
choque;* Celso Furtado, *Análise do modelo brasileiro* (Rio de Janeiro: Civilização
Brasileira, 1972); Regis Bonelli and Pedro Malan, "Os limites do possível: Notas
sobre balanço de pagamento e indústria nos ano 70," *Pesquisa e Planejamento
Econômico* 6, no. 2 (August 1976); Maria da Conceição Tavares and José Serra,
"Mais além da estagnação," in *Da substituição de importações ao capitalismo fi-
nanceiro,* ed. Maria da Conceição Tavares (Rio de Janeiro: Zahar, 1972); Maria da
Conceição Tavares, "Sistema financeiro e o ciclo de expansão recente," in *Desen-
volvimento capitalista no Brasil: Ensaios sobre a crise,* ed. Luiz Gonzaga de Mello
Belluzzo and Renata Coutinho (São Paulo: Brasiliense, 1981); Luiz Aranha Correa

do Lago, "A retomada do crescimento e as distorções do 'milagre': 1967–1973," in *A ordem do progresso*, ed. Marcelo de Paiva Abreu (Rio de Janeiro: Campus, 1990), pp. 233–94.

23. On the period of Geisel, see Antonio Barros de Castro and Francisco Eduardo Pires de Souza, *A economia brasileira em marcha forçada* (Rio de Janeiro: Paz e Terra, 1985); Dionísio Dias Carneiro, "Crise e esperança: 1974–1980," in *A ordem do progresso*, ed. Marcelo de Paiva Abreu (Rio de Janeiro: Campus, 1990), pp. 295–322; Rogério Werneck, *Empresas estatais e política macroeconomica* (Rio de Janeiro: Campus, 1987). On the theories behind the II PND, see Pedro Cezar Dutra Fonseca and Sérgio Marley Modesto Monteiro, "O estado e suas razões: o II PND," *Revista de Economia Política* 28, no. 1 (109) (January–March 2007): 28–46.

24. On the crisis and process of adjustment, see Dionísio Dias Carneiro and Eduardo Modiano, "Ajuste externo e desequilíbrio interno: 1980–1994," in *A ordem do progresso*, ed. Marcelo de Paiva Abreu (Rio de Janeiro: Campus, 1990), pp. 323–46; Mario Henrique Simonsen, "Inflação brasileira: Lições e perspectivas," *Revista Brasileira de Economia* 5, no. 4 (October–December 1985): 15–31; Winston Fritsch, "A crise cambial de 1982–83 no Brasil: Origens e respostas," in *A América Latina e a crise Internacional*, ed. C. A. Plastino and R. Bouzas (Rio de Janeiro: Graal, 1988); Rogério Werneck, "Poupança estatal, dívida externa e crise financeira do setor público," *Pesquisa e Planejamento Econômico*, 16, no. 3 (December 1986): 551–74.

25. Werneck. "Poupança estatal."

26. See Pérsio Arida and André Lara Resende, "Inertial Inflation and Monetary Reform in Brazil," in *Inflation and Indexation: Argentina, Brazil, and Israel*, ed. J. Williamson (Cambridge, Mass.: MIT Press, 1985), pp. 27–45; and Francisco L. Lopes, *O choque heterodoxo: Combate à inflação e reforma monetária* (Rio de Janeiro: Campus, 1986).

27. João Sayad and Francisco Vidal Luna, *Política anti-inflacionária e o Plano Cruzado* (São Paulo: Instituto Latino Americano—ILAM, 1987).

28. Almeida, "Concentração de capital nos bancos comerciais brasileiros," p. 174.

29. Felipe Morris, M. Dorfman, J. P. Ortiz, and M. C. Franco, *Latin America's Banking Systems in the 1980s*, World Bank Discussion Papers (Washington: The World Bank, 1990).

30. There was a banking crisis in several countries of Latin America, such as Argentina, Bolívia, Chile, Colombia, Ecuador, México, and Uruguay. See Morris, Dorfman, Ortiz, and Franco, *Latin America's Banking Systems in the 1980s.*

31. Carlos Eduardo Carvalho, "Banco e inflação no Brasil: Da crise dos anos 1980 ao Plano Real," paper given at the Anais do V Congresso Brasileiro de História Econômica (2003) and found at: http://ideas.repec.org/p/abp/he2003/056.html.

32. IBGE-ANDIMA, *Sistema financeiro: Uma análise a partir das Contas Nacionais, 1990–1995* (Rio de Janeiro: Andima, 1997); IBGE, *Contas consolidadas da nação 1980–1993* (Rio de Janeiro: IBGE, 1994)

CHAPTER 4. THE SOCIAL AND INSTITUTIONAL REFORM
PROJECTS OF THE BRAZILIAN MILITARY

1. See Isabela Mares and Matthew E. Carnes, "Social Policy in Developing Countries," *Annual Review of Political Science 2009*, no. 12, their discussion and informative table 1, pp. 96–97. As Esping-Anderson noted in his classic study of modern social welfare, even in Europe where democratic governments played such an important role, "the first major welfare state initiatives occurred prior to democracy and were powerfully motivated by the desire to arrest its realization." Gøsta Esping-Andersen, *The Three Worlds of Welfare Capitalism* (Princeton: Princeton University Press, 1990.), p. 15.

2. A survey of some of these early developments is found in Christopher Abel and Colin M. Lewis, eds., *Welfare, Poverty, and Development in Latin America* (London: Macmillan & St. Antony's College, 1993). See also Carmelo Mesa-Lago, *Modelos de seguridad social en América Latina: Estudio comparativo* (Buenos Aires: Ediciones Siap-Planteos, 1977), chap. 2.

3. For these early laws, see Claudia do Valle Benevides, "Um estado de bem-estar social no Brasil?" (M.A. thesis, Universidade Federal Fluminense, 2011), p. 62.

4. The best single analysis of the CAPS from 1923 to 1930 is found in Jaime A. Oliveira and Sonia Maria Fleury Teixeira, *(Im)previdência social: 60 Anos de história da previdência no Brasil* (Petrópolis: Associação Brasileira Pós-Graduação em Saúde Coletiva, 1986), pp. 20–34 and Table II, p. 342. The law itself is found at www.scribd.com/doc/92369057/Decreto-4682–24janeiro1923-Lei-Eloy-Chaves-Cap.

5. While the most dramatic period of general strikes was 1917–20, the social question remained a major theme in all political debates through the 1910s and 1920s. For a chronology of the strike activity in this period, see Vito Giannotti, *História das lutas dos trabalhadores no Brasil* (Rio de Janeiro: Mauad X, 2007). The standard analyses of these movements are in Boris Fausto, *Trabalho urbano e conflito social* (São Paulo: DIFEL, 1997), and Claudio Batalha, *O movimento operário na Primeira República* (Rio de Janeiro: Jorge Zahar, 2000).

6. The classic review of these political changes and their outcome in democratic states is Esping-Anderson, *The Three Worlds of Welfare Capitalism.*

7. This is the estimated average for central government expenditures in Brazil on social security programs, health, and education for the period 1973–2000. This compares to 45 percent and 46 percent in the United States and Canada, but is below the 50–60 percent range of the Nordic countries. In turn this represents 13.5 percent of GDP. See Alex Segura-Ubiergo, *The Political Economy of the Welfare State in Latin America: Globalization, Democracy, and Development* (Cambridge: Cambridge University Press, 2007), pp. 14–15.

8. The lieutenants, who had a fundamental role in the armed movement that overthrew the established government, as a group had great importance in political leadership and administration in the early years of the new governments. But little by little they were losing strength as an organized group because of their radicalism, their incapacity to question the government, or their being absorbed by the new oligarchic groups that rose to power. Some of the lieutenants individually

maintained an essential role throughout the period Vargas. Fausto, *A Revolução de 1930*, pp. 70–82.

9. Vargas already had been minister of the treasury in the government of Washington Luís and governor of the state of Rio Grande do Sul. On Getúlio Vargas, see Richard Bourn, *Getúlio Vargas of Brazil, 1883–1954: Sphinx of the Pampas* (London: Knight, 1974); John W. F. Dulles, *Vargas of Brazil: A Political Biography* (Austin: University of Texas Press, 1967); Lira Neto, *Getúlio 1882–1930: Dos anos de formação à conquista do poder* (São Paulo: Cia. das Letras, 2012); Lira Neto, *Getúlio 1930–1945: Do governo provisório à ditatura do Estado Novo* (São Paulo: Cia. das Letras, 2013); Lira Neto, *Getúlio 1945–1954: Da volta pela consagração popular ao suicídio* (São Paulo: Cia. das Letras, 2014); and Pedro Paulo Zahluth Bastos and Pedro Cezar Dutra, eds. *A era Vargas: Desenvolvimento, economia e sociadade* (São Paulo: Editora Unesp, 2012).

10. Francisco Weffort, *O populismo na política brasileira* (Rio de Janeiro: Paz e terra S/A. 1980), pp. 49–50.

11. Weffort, *O populismo na política brasileira*, p. 61. Populism in Brazil has been the object of innumerable studies since the 1960s. There recently appeared critical studies on this theme, among them Jorge Ferreira, "O nome e as coisas: o populismo na política brasileira," in *O populismo e sua história*, ed. Jorge Ferreira (Rio de Janeiro: E. Civilização Brasileira, 2000); Angela de Castro Gomes, "O populismo e as ciências sociais no Brasil: Notas sobre a trajetória de um conceito," in *O populismo e sua história*, ed. Ferreira; Angela de Castro Gomes, *A invenção do trabalhismo* (São Paulo: Vértice, 1988); and Boris Fausto, "Populismo in the Past and Its Resurgence," paper presented at the Conference in Honor of Boris Fausto, Stanford, May 21, 2010.

12. There was resistance in many states against the choice of interventors, many of whom were outsiders. The most serious case occurred in São Paulo. The São Paulo society refused to accept the interventor appointed by the central government. In 1932, it led a movement for greater autonomy of the states and a return to the rule of law: "The movement that began . . . has no other intention than to reintegrate the country's legal order and return to the Brazilians their enjoyment of rights and franchises that are the hallmark of our civilization." The movement should have counted on the participation of Minas Gerais and Rio Grande do Sul, but at the last minute these two states remained loyal to the central government, leaving São Paulo to face federal troops with no other allies. Although defeated, the movement served as a warning to the federal government, which appointed as interventor a representative of the bourgeoisie of São Paulo and started to respond with greater attention to the claims of the state. After the so-called Constitutionalist Revolution of 1932, there was also greater federal support for the paulista coffee growers. Edgard Carone, *A Segunda República* (São Paulo: Difusão Européia do Livro, 1973), p. 53.

13. "The Constitution of 1937, . . . left nothing of the old constant of liberalism. It was complete political dictatorship of the president of the republic." Bello, *História da República*, pp. 315–17. On this theme, see Karl Loewenstein, *Brazil Under Vargas* (New York: Macmillan, 1942), chap. 2, and Robert M. Levine, *Father of the Poor?: Vargas and His Era* (Cambridge: Cambridge University Press, 1998).

14. Although the regime then implanted resembled fascism, with several of its members showing great sympathy for that type of government, its political representation in Brazil, *integralismo,* was also placed outside the law in 1938, after the assault on the residence of the president, which was an attempt to overthrow him. The *integralistas,* who hoped to be incorporated into the government itself, were also eliminated from the political process of the Estado Novo. After closing Congress, dissolving political parties, and suppressing the left, the government eliminated the fascist integralistas, the last organized force for political participation. On this theme, see Eli Diniz, "O Estado Novo: Estutura de poder e relações de classe," in *História Geral da Civilização Brasileira,* ed. Boris Fausto (São Paulo: Difel, 1981), tomo 3: O Brasil Republicano, vol. 3: Sociedade e política (1930–1964), pp. 77–119; Lourdes Sola, "O golpe de 37 e o Estado Novo," in *Brasil em perspectiva,* ed. Carlos Guilherme Mota (São Paulo, Difusão Européia do Livro, 1969), pp. 257–84; and Levine, *Father of the Poor.*

15. Lourdes Sola, "O golpe de 37 e o Estado Novo," p. 269. In addition to creating the career civil service with recruitment rules, the DASP (Departamento Administrativo do Serviço Público) established standards to streamline the administrative process. Many of the leading figures in the early pension caixas were also to be key movers in the various ministries and institutes created by Vargas. See James Malloy, *The Politics of Social Security in Brazil* (Pittsburgh: University of Pittsburgh Press, 1979), and Beatriz M. de Souza Wahrlich, *Reforma administrativa da era de Vargas* (Rio de Janeiro: Fundação Getúlio Vargas, 1983).

16. These were called the Instituto do Açúcar e do Álcool, the Instituto do Mate, the Instituto do Pinho, the Instituto Nacional do Sal, and the Instituto do Cacau da Bahia.

17. Simon Schwartzman, Helena M. B. Bomeny, and Vanda M. R. Costa, *Tempos de Capanema* (São Paulo: Editora da Universidade de São Paulo e Ed. Paz e Terra), 1984.

18. See IBGE, *Estatística do Século XX,* Tabela Educação1947aeb-04."

19. See IBGE, *Estatística do Século XX,* Tabela "Educação1947aeb-04."

20. Schwartzman, Bomeny, and Costa, *Tempos de Capanema.*

21. Simonson had also been one of the key persons, along with Júlio de Mesquita Filho, owner of *O Estado de São Paulo,* and the political leader Armando de Sales Oliveira, behind the establishment of the University of São Paulo. Simon Schwartzman, *A Space for Science: The Development of the Scientific Community in Brazil* (University Park: Pennsylvania State University Press, 1991), chap. 5.

22. Federação das Indústrias do Estado de São Paulo (FIESP), Serviço Nacional da Aprendizagem Industrial (SENAI), and the Serviço Nacional da Aprendizagem Comercial (SENAC) were founded in 1946.

23. On the origins of SENAI, see Barbara Weinstein, "The Industrialists, the State, and the Issues of Worker Training and Social Services in Brazil, 1930–50," *Hispanic American Historical Review* 70, no. 3 (August 1990), pp. 379–404, and her book-length study, *For Social Peace in Brazil: Industrialists and the Remaking of the Working Class in São Paulo, 1920–1964* (Chapel Hill: University of North Carolina Press, 1996).

24. Washington Luís affirmed that "the social question is a case for the police." Although always cited, some authors have challenged the veracity of this phrase.

See John D. French, "Proclamando leis, metendo o pau e lutando por direitos," in *Direitos e justiças no Brasil: Ensaios de história social,* ed. Silva Hunold Lara and Joseli M. N. Mendonça (Campinas: Ed. Unicamp, 2006), pp. 379–416.

25. "The state that emerged from the Revolution of 1930 maintained the fundamental policy of politically weakening the working classes, harshly repressing their vanguard and their party organizations, but at the same time sought to establish with the whole working class a new relationship. Politics, pure and simple, carried out by the old ruling classes, no longer had the conditions to be able to sustain itself. In the platform of the Liberal Alliance were already traces of a greater interest in the so-called social problem; worker unrest of the early years of the 1930s ended up effectively "sensitizing" the government to this question." Boris Fausto, *A revolução de 1930,* pp. 107–8.

26. In 1939 the "uniqueness" or monopoly of labor association by territorial unit was established, which represents a ban on more than one union representing the same job category. This rule, which in combination with the union tax represents the harnessing of the power of unions to the state, continues today, although the constitution set the freedom of association for workers. Even the PT, which in the opposition attacked the trade union unity rule and the union tax when it took office, did not bother to amend the legislation.

27. The union tax represented a contribution in the amount of one workday for all workers, unionized or not. The funds raised were distributed to the unions, which could not function without this discretionary contribution. The unions were were thus dependent on the state for their funds and not on the contributions from their union workers. This tax still exists today.

28. Thomas E. Skidmore, *The Politics of Military Rule in Brazil, 1964–85* (New York: Oxford University Press, 1988), pp. 33–34.

29. Thomas E. Skidmore, *Politics in Brazil, 1930–1964: An Experiment in Democracy,* 40th anniversary ed., updated (Oxford: Oxford University Press, 2007), p. 31.

30. James Malloy, *The Politics of Social Security in Brazil* (Pittsburgh: University of Pittsburgh Press, 1979), pp. 40–50; Celso Barroso Leite, "Da lei Elói Chaves ao Sinpas," in *Um século de previdência social: Balanço e perspectivas no Brasil e no mundo,* ed. Celso Barroso Leite (Rio de Janeiro: Zahar, 1983), pp. 39–44.

31. Amélia Cohn, *Previdência social e processo político no Brasil* (São Paulo: Editora Moderna, 1981), p. 8.

32. Francisco Eduardo Barreto de Oliveira, Kaizô Iwakami Beltrão, and Mônica Guerra Ferreira, "Reforma da previdência," Texto para Discussão no. 508 (Rio de Janeiro: IPEA, 1997), p. 7; and Oliveira and Teixeira, *(Im)previdência social: 60 Anos de história da previdência no Brasil,* p. 342, table 2.

33. Eli Iôla Gurgel Andrade, "Estado e previdência no Brasil: Uma breve história," in *A previdência social no Brasil,* ed. Rosa María Marques et al. (São Paulo: Editora Fundação Perseu Abramo, 2003), pp. 71–74.

34. As researchers have noted, "Social security since the 30s was a constant target of political manipulation mainly with regard to the use of the Institutes as savings deposit instruments forced to invest in economic sectors considered strategic by the government, which aimed to promote the process of the country's industrialization and maximize their political support (for example, the construction of Brasília, the

financing of Companhia Vale do Rio Doce, the National Steel Company, etc.)." Francisco Eduardo Barreto de Oliveira, Kaizô Iwakami Beltrão, and Antonio Carlos de Albuquerque David, "Dívida da união com a previdência social: Uma perspectiva histórica," Texto para Discussão no. 638 (Rio de Janeiro: Ipea, 1999). That this was not atypical behavior can be seen in the Mexican experience of establishing a welfare state under Miguel Alemán in the 1940s and of the fascist state under Mussolini during the 1930s. See Rose J. Spalding, "Welfare Policymaking: Theoretical Implications of a Mexican Case Study," *Comparative Politics* 12, no. 4 (July 1980), pp. 419–38; and Maria Sophia Quine, *Italy's Social Revolution: Charity and Welfare from Liberalism to Fascism* (New York: Palgrave, 2002), p. 115.

35. On the health reforms and initiative of this period, see Cristina M. Oliveira Fonseca, *Saúde no Governo Vargas (1930–1945): Dualidade institucional de um bem público* (Rio de Janeiro: Editora Fiocruz, 2007). For the very active international activities in the health field that were supported by Vargas, see André Luiz Vieira de Campos, *Políticas internacionais de saúde na era Vargas: O Serviço Especial de Saúde Pública, 1942–1960* (Rio de Janeiro: Editora Fiocruz; 2006), and Lina Faria, *Saúde e política: A Fundação Rockefeller e seus parceiros em São Paulo* (Rio de Janeiro: Editora Fiocruz; 2007).

36. Cristina M. Oliveira Fonseca, "A saúde da criança na política social do primeiro governo Vargas," *PHYSIS—Revista de Saúde Coletiva* 3, no.2 (1993): 101–2.

37. Nabil Georges Bonduki, "Origens da habitação social no Brasil," *Análise Social* 29, no. 127 (1994): 711–32.

38. For a general review of this period, see the two volumes by Francisco Vidal Luna and Herbert S. Klein, *Brazil Since 1980* (New York: Cambridge University Press, 2006), and *An Economic and Social History of Brazil Since 1889* (New York: Cambridge University Press, 2014).

39. In 1939 and 1949 the same sectors employed 55 percent and 51 percent, respectively.

40. Thomas Merrick and Douglas Graham, *Population and Economic Development in Brazil, 1800 to the Present* (Baltimore: Johns Hopkins University Press, 1979), pp. 64–65.

41. Sonia Draibe defined this period as marking the establishment of a welfare state in Brazil because of the universalization of services and the creation of active government institutions in all areas defined by a modern welfare state. Though this model would be profoundly reformed in the post-military period, the basic structure was elaborated in the decades of the 1960s and 1970s. Sônia Miriam Draibe, "O Welfare State no Brasil: Caracteristicas e Perspectivas," Caderno de Pesquisa, no. 8 (Campinas: UNICAMP, NEPP, 1993), pp. 19–21.

42. Ribeiro, *Estrutura de classe e mobilidade social*, p. 309, table 4.

43. Schwartzman, *A Space for Science*, table 10.

44. These numbers come from *Anuário Estatístico do Brasil, 1964*, pp. 341–42, and *Anuário Estatístico do Brasil, 1986*, pp. 174–75.

45. Ribeiro, *Estrutura de classe e mobilidade social*, p. 309, table 4.

46. Carlos Benedito Martins, "O ensino superior brasileiro nos anos 90," *São Paulo em Perspectiva* 14, no. 1 (2000): 42 (table 1), 43, 48 (table 4); and for the breakdown by sex, see *Anuário Estatístico do Brasil, 1984*, p. 251, table 2.6.

47. Schwartzman, *A Space for Science,* table 10.

48. Ribeiro, *Estrutura de classe e mobilidade social,* p. 309, tables 4 and 5.

49. In 1964 the government's Banco Nacional de Desenvolvimento (BNDES) established a ten-year Fund for Technology with an initial investment of U.S. $100 million. Then in 1974 the small national research council was expanded and more adequately funded and became the National Council for Scientific and Technical Development (Conselho Nacional de Desenvolvimento Científico e Tecnológico (CNPq). Soon the military government was investing heavily in advanced research as well as in basic infrastructure and industrial development, all in the name of a nationalist program. Starting as early as 1953 the government had established a scholarship fund for students primarily training in the sciences. This program was run by Coordenação de Aperfeiçoamento de Pessoal de Nível Superior (CAPES), which had been founded in 1951. By the 1960s several hundred Brazilian scientists had been trained abroad, especially in the United States and England, and on their return they formed a powerful interest group pressing for the creation of modern laboratories and other crucial research tools to allow Brazil to compete in this new postwar world. In 1968 came a new university reform law, which essentially established the North American system of departments, along with three levels of degrees, from undergraduate to master's and doctorate. Recently founded federal universities in Minas Gerais and Brasília were developed along this model, and new publicly supported federal ones were soon established in all the states. Also the state of São Paulo founded a new state university in the city of Campinas two years earlier, with the major participation of foreign scholars; it became known as UNICAMP and quickly competed with the University of São Paulo as the nation's premier university. It was designed from the beginning to be an advanced research center, especially in physics, and several Brazilian scientists working at Bell Labs and U.S. universities returned to work at the new university. The government also created an airplane and computer industry and a nuclear research program both inside and outside the university. All this effort led to Brazil's becoming a significant player in world science; along with India, it was one of the few countries in the less-developed world that could compete in modern science. Schwartzman, *A Space for Science,* chap. 9. But the relationship between the scientific community and the government was not always a peaceful one during the military period. Many scientists were persecuted, forced to retire, or expelled. There was more repression in the humanities and social sciences, but the major centers of scientific research were also affected. The physics department of the University of Brasília was dismantled after an invasion of the university campus. The Sociedade Brasileira para o Progresso da Ciência (SBPC), the principal organ of the scientific community in Brazil, carried out a systematic opposition to the military government and was an important group in the process of re-democratization of the country.

50. IBGE, *Estatísticas do Século XX,* table "População1981aeb-002" found at www.ibge.gov.br/seculoxx/arquivos_xls/populacao.shtm.

51. Oliveira, Beltrão, and Ferreira, "Reforma da previdência," p. 45. It was only in the post-military era that the private for-profit "open" funds began to grow, and it was only in 1995—when private foreign insurance companies could enter the market—that these EAPPs began to have significant assets and contributors. While these open funds have grown rapidly and had assets equivalent to 4.7 percent of

GDP in 2002, the nonprofit EFPPs' trust funds had grown to 14.7 percent of GDP. Kaizô Iwakami Beltrão, Fernanda Paes Leme, João Luís Mendonça, and Sonoe Sugahara, "Análise da estrutura da previdência privada brasileira: Evolução do aparato legal," Texto para Discussão no. 1043 (Rio de Janeiro, IPEA, p. 19; and Francisco E. Barreto de Oliveira, Maria Tereza de Marsillac Pasinato, and Fernanda Paes Leme Peyneau, "Evolução recente do sistema de previdência complementar no Brasil e mercado potencial," p. 11, found at www.abep.nepo.unicamp.br/docs/anais/pdf/2000/Todos/Evolu%C3%A7%C3%A30%20Recente%20do%20Sistema%20de%20Previd%C3%AAncia%20Complementar. . . . pdf.

52. Marta T. S. Arretche, "Políticas sociais no Brasil: Descentralização em um Estado federativo," *Revista Brasileira de Ciências Sociais* 14, no. 40 (June 1999), p. 114. One scholar of the social security system went so far as to argue that the new format was a "hypercentralized mode of organization and decision-making." Sônia Miriam Draibe, "The National Social Policies System in Brazil: Construction and Reform," Caderno de Pesquisa, no. 51 (Campinas: NEPP, UNICAMP, 2002), p. 15. In the post-military period one of the major themes would be the need to decentralize the whole system, especially as related to the medical services.

53. In 1974 all persons over seventy years of age received 60 percent of a minimum salary, but they had to prove that they had contributed to the national pension plan for at least twelve months. In the post-military democratic constitution of 1988, this pension right became universal regardless of whether a person had paid into the social security system or not.

54. Malloy, *The Politics of Social Security*, pp. 124–25.

55. IBGE, *Estatísticas do Século XX* (2003), table "Prev_social19693aeb_02."

56. A good survey of all the debates and issues related to this unusual act can be found in Nicole Régine Garcia, "Prorural: Uma política previdenciária para o campo no governo Medici (1969–1973)" (M.A. thesis, Rio de Janeiro, Casa de Oswaldo Cruz-Fiocruz, 2010). Originally, the FUNRURAL paid a pension of half of a minimum salary for rural workers who had not contributed to any pension plan. Under the post-military democratic governments, this was raised to a full minimum wage, and rural women workers were also included.

57. The most complete analysis of this 1974 program is found Sonia Rocha, *Transferências de renda no Brasil: O fim da pobreza?* (São Paulo: Campus, 2013), chap. 1. Also, for the origin and a background discussion of this unusual law, see Alexandre de Oliveira Alcântara, "O direito fundamental à velhice digna: Limites e possibilidades de sua efetivação" (M.A. thesis, Universidade de Fortaleza, 2007), pp. 75–76.

58. For a survey of the changing requirements of this system, see Ana Amélia Camarano, "Mecanismos de proteção social para a população idosa brasileira," Texto para Discussão, no. 1179 (Rio de Janeiro: IPEA, 2006), pp. 12–13. Rocha notes that these noncontributory income transfers included the original RMV and the PMV or monthly pensions for worker accidents, as well as Amparos Asistencias—sometimes incorrectly listed as BPC grants—which she points out actually include contributor pensions. Rocha, *Transferências de renda no Brasil*, p. 7.

59. In 2005, this program for elderly poor and disabled people benefited 2.7 million persons and cost U.S. $3.4 billion. Of the 1.1 million who were disabled, 40 percent were under twenty-five years of age. Marcelo Medeiros, Debora Diniz,

and Flávia Squinca, "Cash Benefits to Disabled Persons in Brazil: An Analysis of BPC–Continuous Cash Benefit Programme," Texto para Discussão, no. 1179 (Brasília: IPEA, 2006), pp. 24, 31; and Marcelo Medeiros, Tatiana Britto, and Fábio Soares, "Programas focalizados de transferência de renda no Brasil: Contribuições para o debate," Texto para Discussão, no. 1283 (Brasília: IPEA, 2007), p. 9. As of 2015 the estimated cost of the benefício de prestação continuada was R$42 billion, against just R$27 billion for the Bolsa Família. Pedro Fernando Nery, *O programa assistencial mais caro do Brasil: Sobre o benefício de prestação continuada e uma comparação com o bolsa família,* Boletim Legislativo no. 16 (Brasília: Senado Federal, 2014).

60. For a discussion of these changes, see Kaizô Iwakami Beltrão, Sonoe Sugahara Pinheiro, and Francisco Eduardo Barreto de Oliveira, "Rural Population and Social Security in Brazil: An Analysis with Emphasis on Constitutional Changes," *International Social Security Review* 57, no. 4 (2004): 19–49.

61. IBGE, *Estatísticas do Século XX* (2003), table "prev_social1986aeb_01."

62. Betrão, Pinheiro, and Oliveira, "Rural Population and Social Security," p. 24.

63. *Anuário Estatístico da Previdência Social, 2011* (Brasília: MPS, 2012), p. 596.

64. For the history of the IBGE/PNAD surveys, see http://portal.mec.gov.br/index.php?option=com_content&view=article&id=12521:informacoes-gerais-sobre-a-pnad&catid=190:setec. As most recently noted by José Roberto de Toledo in the São Paulo newspaper *Estadão,* "The PNAD is the best thermometer for what is happening in Brazil. Without knowing if there is fever or not, it is difficult to determine a diagnosis or a remedy." Translated from *Estadão,* September 19, 2014.

65. Rocha, *Transferências de renda no Brasil,* p. 3.

66. Malloy, *The Politics of Social Security,* pp. 125–26.

67. The estimates of annual changes in urban population can be found in CELADE, "Brasil: Estimaciones y Proyecciones de Población Urbana y Población Rural según sexo y grupos quinquenales de edad . . . 1950–2050" [revision of 2013]," available at www.eclac.org/celade/proyecciones/basedatos_BD.htm."

68. Ana Amélia Camarano and Ricardo Abramovay, "Êxodo rural, envelhecimento e masculinização no Brasil: Panorama dos últimos 50 anos," Texto para Discussão, no. 621 (Rio de Janeiro: IPEA, 1998), p. 1. The authors point out that Brazil, like several other countries in Latin America, describes urban centers by administrative definition rather than size, which tends to underestimate the rural population. Camarano and Abramovay, "Êxodo rural," p. 6. Based on census materials, it was estimated that net migration of all kinds in this period involved 38 million persons, of which 22 million were interregional migrants. See Manoel Augusto Costa, "Migrações interestaduais no Brasil, 1950/80," Textos para Discussão, no. 144 (Rio de Janeiro: IPEA, 1988), p. 5, table 1.

69. IBGE, *Estatísticas do Século XX* (2003), table pop_S2T04.

70. IBGE, *Estatísticas do Século XX* (2003), table pop_S2T03ab.

71. In the census of 2000, the peak age for migrants to the state of São Paulo was thirty to thirty-four years, and migrants to the state of Rio de Janeiro—which had fewer interstate migrants—were in their forties. IBGE, *Censo Demográfico 2000: Migração e Deslocamento, Resultados da amostra* (Rio de Janeiro, 2003), graph 10.

72. CELADE, "Brasil, "Estimaciones y Proyecciones de Población Urbana y Población Rural según sexo y grupos quinquenales de edad ... 1950–2050" [revision of 2013]," found at www.eclac.org/celade/proyecciones/basedatos_BD.htm.

73. IBGE, *Indicadores sociales: Uma análise da década de 1980* (Rio de Janeiro: IBGE 1995), p. 27.

74. Maria Stella Ferreira Levy, "O papel da migração internacional na evolução da população brasileira (1872 a 1972)," *Revista de Saúde Pública* 8 (suppl.) (1974), pp. 71–73, [São Paulo] table 1; data from 1820 to 1871 from Directoria Geral de Estatistica, *Boletim Commemorativo da Exposição Nacional de 1908* (Rio de Janeiro, 1908), pp. 82–85.

75. Thomas W. Merrick and Douglas H. Graham, *Population and Economic Development in Brazil, 1800 to the Present* (Baltimore: Johns Hopkins University Press, 1979), p. 125, table VI-4.

76. Carlos Américo Pacheco et al., "Análise demográfica do Estado de São Paulo," in *Dinâmica demográfica regional e as novas questões populacionais no Brasil*, ed. Carlos Américo Pacheco and Neide Patarra (Campinas: Instituto de Economia/UNICAMP, 2000), p. 372, table 4.

77. IBGE, *Estatísticas do Século XX*, table "pop_S2T02ab."

78. Neide Patara, Rosana Baeninger, and José Marcos Pinto da Cunha, "Dinâmica demográfica recente e a configuração de novas questões populacionais," in *Dinâmica demográfica regional e as novas questões populacionais no Brasil*, ed. Pacheco and Patarra, p. 30, table 12.

79. IBGE, *Estatísticas do Século XX*, table "pop_S2T02ab."

80. Mauricio C. Coutinho and Cláudio Salm, "Social Welfare," in *Social Change in Brazil, 1945–1985: The Incomplete Transformation*, ed. Edmar L. Bacha and Herbert S. Klein (Albuquerque: University of New Mexico Press, 1989), pp. 233–62.

81. Jairnilson Paim, Claudia Travassos, Celia Almeida, Ligia Bahia, and James Macinko, "The Brazilian Health System: History, Advances, and Challenges," *The Lancet* 377, no. 9779 (2011): 5.

82. The 1970s and early 1980s were also a period when active debate developed among academics and doctors about the nature of the health care system, which would have a profound effect on the creation of SUS and the post-military-period reforms aimed at decentralizing health care. See Hésio Cordeiro, "Instituto de Medicina Social e a luta pela reforma sanitária: Contribuição à história do SUS," *Physis* 14, no.2 (2004): 343–62.

83. Cristina Maria Rabelais Duarte, "UNIMED: História e características da cooperativa de trabalho médico no Brasil," *Cadernos de Saúde Pública* (Rio de Janeiro) 17, no. 4 (July–August 2001): 999–1008.

84. Ligia Bahia, "Planos privados de saúde: Luzes e sombras no debate setorial dos anos 90," *Ciência & Saúde Coletiva* 6, no. 2 (2001): 329–39.

85. CELADE, *Boletín demográfico*, no. 73 (January 2004), p. 18, cuadro 3.

86. José Miguel Guzmán, "Introduction: Social Change and Fertility Decline in Latin America," in *The Fertility Transition in Latin America*, ed. Jose Miguel Guzmán et al. (Oxford: Clarendon Press, 1996), p. xxiii.

87. By the 1980s it was estimated "that approximately 71 per cent of Brazilian women aged 15–54 who are married or have a male partner, use some kind

of contraceptive method. Of these, 44 per cent have been sterilized and 41 per cent use oral contraceptives, while less than 2 per cent use condoms." Vera Paiva, "Sexuality, Condom Use, and Gender Norms Among Brazilian Teenagers," *Reproductive Health Matters* 1, no. 2 (November 1993), p. 99. A study in São Paulo in 1992 found that the most common means of contraception were sterilization, at 43 percent of sexually active women in the sample, and the pill, at 32 percent, with sterilization being inversely related to pill usage by age—younger women overwhelmingly using the pill and women over thirty-five overwhelmingly using sterilization. Néia Schor et al., "Mulher e anticoncepção: Conhecimento e uso de métodos anticoncepcionais," *Cadernos de Saúde Pública* 16, no. 2 (April–June 2000), p. 378, table 2.

88. CELADE, "Brasil: Indicadores del Proceso de Envejecimiento de la Población, Estimados y Proyectados . . . 1950–2100 [revision of 2013]," found at www.eclac.org/celade/proyecciones/basedatos_BD.htm.

89. Juan Chackiel and Susana Schkolnik, "Latin America: Overview of the Fertility Transition, 1950–1990," in *The Fertility Transition in Latin America,* ed. Guzmán et al., p. 4.

CONCLUSION

1. The best single survey of the Korean experience in this period and the role of General Park is the study by John Kie-chiang Oh, *Korean Politics: The Quest for Democratization and Economic Development* (Ithaca: Cornell University Press, 1999). The standard survey of the economy in this period is Byung-Nak Song, *The Rise of the Korean Economy,* 2nd ed. (Hong Kong: Oxford University Press, 1997), which can serve to complement the earlier study by John Lie, *Han Unbound: The Political Economy of South Korea* (Stanford: Stanford University Press, 1998).

Bibliography

Abel, Christopher, and Colin M. Lewis, eds. *Welfare, Poverty, and Development in Latin America.* London: Macmillan & St. Antony's College, 1993.

Abreu, Marcelo de Paiva. "Inflação, estagnação e ruptura: 1961–1964." In *A ordem do progresso,* ed. Abreu, 197–231.

Abreu, Marcelo de Paiva, ed., *A ordem do progresso.* Rio de Janeiro: Campus, 1990.

Abugattás, Luis. *Estabilización macroeconómica, reforma estructural y comportamiento industrial: La experiencia peruana.* Serie Reformas Económicas no. 48. Santiago de Chile: CEPAL, 1999.

Agüero, Felipe. "30 años después: La ciencia política y las relaciones Fuerzas Armadas, Estado y sociedad." *Revista de Ciencia Política* (Santiago) 23, no.2 (2003): 251–72.

Alcântara, Alexandre de Oliveira. "O direito fundamental à velhice digna: Limites e possibilidades de sua efetivação." M.A. thesis in constitutional law, Universidade de Fortaleza, 2007.

Alcántara Sáez, Miguel, and Ismael Crespo Martínez. *Partidos politicos y procesos electorales en Uruguay (1971–1990).* Madrid: CEDEAL, 1992.

Alvarez Rodrich, Augusto. "Del estado empresario al estado regulador." In *Perú 1964–1994: Economía, sociedad y política,* ed. Julio Cutler, 69–91. Lima: IEP, 1995.

Alves, Maria Helena Moreira. *State and Opposition in Military Brazil.* Austin: University of Texas Press, 1985.

Andrade, Eli Iôla Gurgel. "Estado e previdência no Brasil: Uma breve história." In *A previdência social no Brasil,* ed. Rosa María Marques, et al., 69–84. São Paulo: Editora Fundação Perseu Abramo, 2003.

Antunes, Ricardo. *A rebeldia do trabalho (O confronto operário no ABC Paulista: As greves de 1978/80)*. Campinas: Editôra da Universidade Estadual de Campinas, 1988.

Arida, Pérsio, and André Lara Resende. "Inertial Inflation and Monetary Reform in Brazil." In *Inflation and Indexation: Argentina, Brazil, and Israel*, ed. J. Williamson, 27–45. Cambridge, Mass.: MIT Press, 1985.

Arretche, Marta T. S. "Políticas sociais no Brasil: Descentralização em um Estado federativo." *Revista Brasileira de Ciências Sociais* 14, no. 40 (June 1999): 111–41.

Arriagada Herrera, Genaro. "The Legal and Institutional Framework of the Armed Forces in Chile." In *Military Rule in Chile: Dictatorship and Oppositions*, ed. Julio Samuel Valenzuela and Arturo Valenzuela, 117–43. Baltimore: Johns Hopkins University Press, 1986.

Arze Cuadros, Eduardo. *Bolivia, el programa del MNR y la revolución nacional: Del movimiento de reforma universitaria al ocaso del model neoliberal (1928–2002)*. La Paz: Plural, 2002.

Astiz, Carlos A., and José Z. García, "The Peruvian Military: Achievement, Orientation, Training, and Political Tendencies." *Western Political Quarterly* 25, no. 4 (December 1972): 667–85.

Azevedo, Fernando Antônio. "Revisitando as ligas camponesas." In *O golpe de 1964 e o regime militar, novas perspectivas*, ed. João Roberto Martins Filho, 27–37. São Carlos: Editora da Universidade Federal de São Carlos, 2006.

Bacha, Edmar L., and Herbert S. Klein, ed., *Social Change in Brazil, 1945–1985: The Incomplete Transformation*. Albuquerque: University of New Mexico Press, 1989.

Bacha, Edmar L., and L. Taylor. "Brazilian Income Distribution in the 1960s: 'Facts,' Model Results, and the Controversy." In *Models of Growth and Distribution for Brazil*, ed. L. Taylor et al., 296–342. New York: Oxford University Press, 1980.

Bahia, Ligia. "Planos privados de saúde: Luzes e sombras no debate setorial dos anos 90." *Ciência & Saúde Coletiva* 6, no. 2 (2001): 329–39.

Banco Central do Brasil. www.bcb.gov.br/?RELRURAL.

Bandeira, Luiz Alberto Moniz. *O governo João Goulart: As lutas sociais no Brasil, 1961–1964*. 7th ed. Brasília: Editora Universidade de Brasília, 2001.

Barros, José Roberto Mendonça de, and D. H. Graham. "A agricultura brasileira e o problema da produção de alimentos." *PPE* 8, no. 3 (December 1978): 695.

Barros, Robert. *Constitutionalism and Dictatorship: Pinochet, the Junta, and the 1980 Constitution*. New York: Cambridge University Press, 2004.

Bastos, Pedro Paulo Zahluth, and Pedro Cezar Dutra, eds. *A era Vargas: Desenvolvimento, economia e sociadade*. São Paulo: Editora Unesp, 2012.

Batalha, Claudio. *O movimento operário na Primeira República*. Rio de Janeiro: Jorge Zahar, 2000.

Bello, Enzo. "Cidadania e direitos sociais no Brasil: Um enfoque político e social." *Revista Espaço Jurídico* (Joaçaba), 8, no. 2 (July/Dec. 2007): 133–54.

Belluzzo, Luiz Gonzaga de Mello, and Renata Coutinho, eds., *Desenvolvimento capitalista no Brasil: Ensaios sobre a crise*. São Paulo: Brasiliense, 1981.

Beltrão, Kaizô Iwakami, Sonoe Sugahara Pinheiro, and Francisco Eduardo Barreto de Oliveira. "Rural Population and Social Security in Brazil: An Analysis with

Emphasis on Constitutional Changes." *International Social Security Review* 57, no. 4 (2004): 19–49.

Beltrão, Kaizô Iwakami, Fernanda Paes Leme, João Luís Mendonça, and Sonoe Sugahara. "Análise da estrutura da previdência privada brasileira: Evolução do aparato legal." Texto para Discussão no. 1043. Rio de Janeiro: IPEA, 2004.

Benevides, Claudia do Valle. "Um estado de bem-estar social no Brasil?" M.A. thesis in economics, Universidade Federal Fluminense, 2011.

Benevides, Maria Victoria de Mesquita. *O governo Kubitschek*. Rio de Janeiro: Paz e Terra, 1976.

Biglaiser, Glen. *Guardians of the Nation? Economists, Generals, and Economic Reform in Latin America*. Notre Dame: University of Notre Dame Press, 2002.

Blume, Norman. "Pressure Groups and Decision-Making in Brazil." *Studies in Comparative International Development* 3, no. 11 (1967): 205–23.

Boito, Armando, Jr. "Reforma e persistência da estrutura sindical." In *O sindicalismo brasileiro nos anos 80*, ed. Armando Boito, 43–91. Rio de Janeiro: Paz e Terra, 1991.

Bonduki, Nabil Georges. "Origens da habitação social no Brasil," *Análise Social* 39, no. 127 (1994): 711–32.

Bonelli, Regis, and Pedro Malan. "Os limites do possível: Notas sobre balanço de pagamento e indústria nos ano 70." *Pesquisa e Planejamento Econômico* 6, no. 2 (August 1976): 353–406.

Bourn, Richard. *Getúlio Vargas of Brazil, 1883–1954: Sphinx of the Pampas*. London: Knight, 1974.

Brooks, Sarah Marie. *Social Protection and the Market in Latin America: The Transformation of Social Security Institutions*. New York: Cambridge University Press, 2009.

Buainain, Antônio Márcio, Eliseu Alves, José Maria da Silveira, and Zander Navarro, eds. *O mundo rural no Brasil do século 21: A formação de um novo padrão agrário e agrícola*. Brasília: Embrapa, 2014.

Camarano, Ana Amélia. "Mecanismos de proteção social para a população idosa brasileira." Texto para Discussão, no. 1179. Rio de Janeiro: IPEA, 2006.

Camarano, Ana Amélia, and Ricardo Abramovay. "Êxodo rural, envelhecimento e masculinização no Brasil: Panorama dos últimos 50 anos." Texto para Discussão no. 621. Rio de Janeiro: IPEA, 1998.

Camargo, José Marcio, and Fabio Giambiagi, eds. *Distribuição de renda no Brasil* (Rio de Janeiro: Paz e Terra, 2000.

Campos, André Luiz Vieira de. *Políticas internacionais de saúde na era Vargas: O Serviço Especial de Saúde Pública, 1942–1960*. Rio de Janeiro: Editora Fiocruz, 2006.

Cano, Wilson. *Raíses da concentração industrial em São Paulo*. São Paulo: Difel, 1977.

Carneiro, Dionísio Dias. "Crise e Esperança: 1974–1980." In *A ordem do progresso*, ed. Marcelo de Paiva Abreu, 295–322. Rio de Janeiro: Campus, 1990.

Carneiro, Dionísio Dias, and Eduardo Modiano. "Ajuste externo e desequilíbrio interno: 1980–1994." In *A ordem do progresso*, ed. Marcelo de Paiva Abreu, 323–46. Rio de Janeiro: Campus, 1990.

Carone, Edgard. *A segunda República.* São Paulo: Difusão Européia do Livro, 1973.

Carvalho, Carlos Eduardo. "Banco e inflação no Brasil: Da crise dos anos 1980 ao Plano Real." Paper given at the Anais do V Congresso Brasileiro de História Econômica (2003) and found at: http://ideas.repec.org/p/abp/he2003/056.html.

Cassol, Gissele. "Prisão e tortura em terra estrangeira: A colaboração repressiva entre Brasil e Uruguai (1964–1985)." M.A. thesis, Universidade Federal de Santa Maria, 2008.

Castro, Antonio Barros de. *Sete ensaios sobre a economia brasileira.* São Paulo: Forense, 1969.

Castro, Antonio Barros de, and Francisco Eduardo Pires de Souza. *A economia brasileira em marcha forçada.* Rio de Janeiro: Paz e Terra, 1985.

CELADE. "Brasil, Estimaciones y Proyecciones de Población Urbana y Población Rural según sexo y grupos quinquenales de edad . . . 1950–2050" [revision of 2013]." Found at www.eclac.org/celade/proyecciones/basedatos_BD.htm.

CELADE. "Brasil: Indicadores del Proceso de Envejecimiento de la Población, Estimados y Proyectados . . . 1950–2100" [revision of 2013]." Found at www.eclac.org/celade/proyecciones/basedatos_BD.htm.

CELADE. *Boletín demográfico* 37, no. 73 (January 2004).

Chackiel, Juan, and Susana Schkolnik, "Latin America: Overview of the Fertility Transition, 1950–1990." In *The Fertility Transition in Latin America,* ed. Jose Miguel Guzmán et al., 3–26. Oxford: Clarendon Press, 1996.

Coelho, Carlos Nayro. "70 anos de política agrícola no Brasil, 1931–2001." *Revista de Política Agrícola* 10, no. 3 (July–September 2001): 3–58.

Cohn, Amélia. *Previdência social e processo político no Brasil.* São Paulo: Editora Moderna, 1981.

Conde, Roberto Cortés. *The Political Economy of Argentina in the Twentieth Century.* New York: Cambridge University Press, 2009.

Condori Luque, Harvey. "Las leyes de agua en el Perú: Planes hidrológicos de cuencas." Found at www.monografias.com/trabajos19/ley-de-aguas/ley-de-aguas.shtml#ixzz37UhLq4mI.

Contreras, Carlos, and Marcos Cueto. *Historia del Peru contemparáneo* Lima: Instituto de Estudios Peruanos, 1999.

Cordeiro, Hésio. "Instituto de Medicina Social e a luta pela reforma sanitária: Contribuição à história do SUS." *Physis* 14, no. 2 (2004): 343–62.

Costa, Manoel Augusto. "Migrações interestaduais no Brasil, 1950/80." Textos para Discussão, no. 144. Rio de Janeiro: IPEA, 1988.

Cotler, Julio. "Crisis política y populismo militar en el Perú." *Revista Mexicana de Sociología* 32, nos. 3–4 (May–June 1970): 737–84.

Cotler, Julio. "Democracy and National Integration in Peru." In *The Peruvian Experiment Reconsidered,* ed. Cynthia McClintock and Abraham L. Lowenthal, 3–38. Princeton: Princeton University Press, 1983.

Coutinho, Mauricio C., and Cláudio Salm, "Social Welfare." In *Social Change in Brazil 1945–1985: The Incomplete Transformation,* ed. Edmar L. Bacha and Herbert S. Klein, 233–62. Albuquerque: University of New Mexico Press, 1989.

Cysne, Rubens Penha. "A economia brasileira no período militar." *Estudos Econômicos* 23, no. 2 (1993): 185–226.

Dean, Warren. *The Industrialization of São Paulo, 1880–1945.* Austin: University of Texas Press, 1969.

Delfim Netto, Antônio. "Análise do comportamento recente da economia brasileira: Diagnóstico." São Paulo: mimeo, 1967.

Demasi, Carlos. "La evolución del campo político en la dictadura." In *La dictadura cívico militar: Uruguay, 1973–1985,* ed. Aldo Marchesi and Vania Markarian, 15–116. Montevideo: Ediciones de la Banda Oriental, 2009.

Diniz, Eli. "O Estado novo: estrutura de poder e relações de classe." In *História Geral da Civilização Brasileira,* ed. Boris Fausto, tomo 3: O Brasil Republicano, vol. 3: Sociedade e política (1930–1964), pp. 77–119. São Paulo: Difel, 1981.

Directoria Geral de Estatistica. *Boletim Commemorativo da Exposição Nacional de 1908.* Rio de Janeiro, 1908.

Draibe, Sônia Miriam. "The National Social Policies System in Brazil: Construction and Reform." Caderno de Pesquisa, no. 51. Campinas: NEPP, UNICAMP, 2002.

Draibe, Sônia Miriam. "O welfare state no Brasil: Caracteristicas e Perspectivas." Caderno de Pesquisa, no. 8. Campinas: UNICAMP, NEPP, 1993.

Draibe, Sonia. *Rumos e metamorfoses: Estado e industrialização no Brasil: 1930/1960.* Rio de Janeiro: Paz e Terra, 1985.

Dreifuss, René Armand. *1964, a conquista do estado: Ação política, poder e golpe de Classe.* 5a. ed., rev. Petrópolis: Vozes, 1987.

Duarte, Cristina Maria Rabelais. "UNIMED: História e características da cooperativa de trabalho médico no Brasil." *Cadernos de Saúde Pública* (Rio de Janeiro) 17, no. 4 (July–August 2001): 999–1008.

Dulles, John W. F. *Vargas of Brazil: A Political Biography.* Austin: University of Texas Press, 1967.

Dunkerley, James. *Rebellion in the Veins: Political Struggle in Bolivia, 1952–82.* London: Verso, 1984.

Einaudi, Luigi R. "Revolution from Within? Military Rule in Peru Since 1968." *Studies in Comparative International Development* 8, no. 1 (1973): 71–87.

Einaudi, Luigi R., and Alfred C. Stepan. "Latin American Institutional Development: Changing Military Perspectives in Peru and Brazil." R-586-DOS. Santa Monica: Rand Corporation, April 1971.

Eisenhower, Milton "Report to the President." *Department of State Bulletin,* 23 November 1953, pp. 695–717.

Esping-Andersen, Gøsta. *The Three Worlds of Welfare Capitalism.* Princeton, N.J.: Princeton University Press, 1990.

Faria, Lina. *Saúde e política: A Fundação Rockefeller e seus parceiros em São Paulo.* Rio de Janeiro: Editora Fiocruz, 2007.

Fausto, Boris. *O pensamento nacionalista autoritário.* Rio de Janeiro: Jorge Zahar, 2001.

Fausto, Boris. "Populismo in the Past and Its Resurgence." Paper presented at the Conference in Honor of Boris Fausto, Stanford, May 21, 2010.

Fausto, Boris. *Trabalho urbano e conflito social.* São Paulo: DIFEL, 1997.

Feitlowitz, Marguerite. *A Lexicon of Terror: Argentina and the Legacies of Torture*. Revised ed. New York: Oxford University Press, 2011.

Fernandes, Ananda Simões. "Quando o inimigo ultrapassa a fronteira: As conexões repressivas entre a ditadura civil-militar brasileira eo Uruguai (1964–1973)." M.A. thesis, Historia Universidade Federal do Rio Grande do Sul, 2009.

Fernandes, Pádua. "Setenta anos após 1937: Francisco Campos, o Estado Novo e o pensamento jurídico autoritário." *Prisma Jurídico* (São Paulo) 6 (2007): 351–70.

Ferraz, Francisco César Alves. *À sombra dos carvalhos: Escola Superior de Guerra e política no Brasil, 1948–1955*. Londrina: Editora Uel, 1997.

Ferreira, Jorge. "O nome e as coisas: O populismo na política brasileira." In *O populismo e sua história*, ed. Jorge Ferreira. Rio de Janeiro: E. Civilização Brasileira, 2000.

Ffrench-Davis, Ricardo. *Entre el neoliberalismo y el crecimiento con equidad: Tres décadas de política económica en Chile*. Santiago de Chile: JC Sáez Editor, 2003.

Fishlow, Albert. "A distribuição de renda no Brasil." In *A controvérsia sobre a distribuição de renda e desenvolvimento*, ed. R. Tolipan and A. C. Tinelli, 159–89. Rio de Janeiro: Zahar, 1975 .

Fishlow, Albert. "Algumas reflexões sobre a política brasileira após 1964," *Estudos CEBRAP* 6 (January–March 1974): 5–66.

Fishlow, Albert. "Brazilian Size Distribution of Income." *American Economic Review* 62, no. 1/2 (1972): 391–402.

Fishlow, Albert. "Origens e consequências da substituição de importações no Brasil." In *Formação econômica do Brasil: A experiência de industrialização*, ed. Flávio Versiani and José Roberto Mendonça de Barros. São Paulo: Anpec/ Saraiva, 1976.

Fitzgerald, E. V. K. *The Political Economy of Peru, 1956–78: Economic Development and the Restructuring of Capital*. Cambridge: Cambridge University Press, 1979.

Fonseca, Cristina M. Oliveira. "A saúde da criança na política social do primeiro governo Vargas." *PHYSIS—Revista de Saúde Coletiva* 3, no. 2 (1993): 97–116.

Fonseca, Cristina M. Oliveira. *Saúde no Governo Vargas (1930–1945): Dualidade institucional de um bem público*. Rio de Janeiro: Editora Fiocruz, 2007.

Fonseca, Pedro Cezar Dutra, and Sérgio Marley Modesto Monteiro. "O Estado e suas razões: o II PND." *Revista de Economia Política* 28, no. 1 (109) (January–March 2007): 28–46.

Foxley, Alejandro. "The Neoconservative Economic Experiment in Chile." In *Military Rule in Chile*, ed. J. Samuel Valenzuela and Arturo Valenzuela. Baltimore: Johns Hopkins University Press, 1986.

Fritsch, Winston. "A crise cambial de 1982–83 no Brasil: Origens e respostas." In *A América Latina e a crise internacional*, ed. C. A. Plastino and R. Bouzas. Rio de Janeiro: Graal, 1988.

Furtado, Celso. *Análise do "modelo" brasileiro*. Rio de Janeiro: Civilização Brasileira, 1972.

Furtado, Celso. *Formação econômica do Brasil*. Rio de Janeiro: Fundo de Cultura, 1959.

Furtado, Celso. *Um projeto para o Brasil*. Rio de Janeiro: Saga, 1968.

Garcé, Adolfo. "Ideologías políticas y adaptación partidaria: El caso del MLN-Tupamaros (1985–2009)." *Revista de Ciencia Política* (Santiago) 31, no. 1 (2011): 117–37.

Garcia, Nicole Régine. "Prorural: Uma política previdenciária para o campo no governo Medici (1969–1973)." M.A. thesis, Rio de Janeiro, Casa de Oswaldo Cruz-Fiocruz, 2010.

Gaspari, Elio. *A ditadura derrotada*. São Paulo: Companhia das Letras, 2003.

Gaspari, Elio. *A ditadura encurralada* São Paulo: Companhia das Letras, 2004.

Gaspari, Elio. *A ditadura envergonhada*. São Paulo: Companhia das Letras, 2002.

Gaspari, Elio. *A ditadura escancarada* São Paulo: Companhia das Letras, 2002.

Gazzotti, Juliana. "A revista Veja e o obstáculo da censura." *Revista Olhar* 3, nos. 5–6 (2001): 1–9.

Giannotti, Vito. *História das lutas dos trabalhadores no Brasil*. Rio de Janeiro: Mauad X, 2007.

Gillespie, Charles Guy. *Negotiating Democracy: Politicians and Generals in Uruguay*. Cambridge: Cambridge University Press, 1991.

Gomes, Angela de Castro. *A invenção do Trabalhismo*. São Paulo: Vértice, 1988.

Gomes, Angela de Castro. "O populismo e as ciências sociais no Brasil: Notas sobre a trajetória de um conceito." In *O populismo e sua história,* ed. Jorge Ferreira. Rio de Janeiro: Editora Civilização Brasileira, 2000.

Gomes, Paulo César. *Os bispos católicos e a ditadura militar brasileira*. São Paulo: Editora Record, 2014.

Gorender, Jacob. *Combate nas trevas: A esquerda brasileira: Das ilusões perdidas à luta armada*. São Paulo: Editora Atica, 1987.

Grandin, Greg. *The Last Colonial Massacre: Latin America in the Cold War*. Chicago: University of Chicago Press, 2011.

Grindle, Merilee S., and Pilar Domingo, eds. *Proclaiming Revolution: Bolivia in Comparative Perspective*. Cambridge, Mass.: David Rockefeller Center for Latin American Studies, Harvard University, 2003.

Grow, Michael. *U.S. Presidents and Latin American Interventions: Pursuing Regime Change in the Cold War*. Lawrence: University Press of Kansas, 2008.

Guimarães, Alberto Passos. *Quatro séculos de latifúndio*. Rio de Janeiro: Paz e Terra, 1977.

Guzmán, José Miguel. "Introduction: Social Change and Fertility Decline in Latin America." In *The Fertility Transition in Latin America*, ed. Jose Miguel Guzmán et al. Oxford: Clarendon Press, 1996.

Halam, Jonathan. *The Nixon Administration and the Death of Allende's Chile: A Case of Assisted Suicide*. London: Verso, 2005.

Hershberg, James G., and Peter Kornbluh, "Brazil Marks 50th Anniversary of Military Coup." National Security Archive Electronic Briefing, Book No. 465, Posted April 2, 2014, 16 pages. Found at www2.gwu.edu/~nsarchiv/NSAEBB/NSAEBB465/ 1/

Hirschmann, Albert. "The Political Economy of Import Substitution Industrialization in Latin America." *Quarterly of Economics* 82 (February 1968): 2–32.

Hoffmann, Rodolfo. "Evolução da distribuição da posse da terra no Brasil no período 1960–80." *Reforma Agrária* 12, no. 6 (November/December 1982): 17–34.

Holzmann, Robert, David A. Robalino, and Noriyuki Takayama, eds. *Closing the Coverage Gap: The Role of Social Pensions and Other Retirement Income Transfers*. Washington, D.C.: World Bank, 2009.

Huggins, Martha K. "Murderers' Reformulation of Memory Legacies of Authoritarianism: Brazilian Torturers." *Latin American Perspectives* 27, no. 2 (March 2000): 57–78.

Huneeus, Carlos. *The Pinochet Regime*. Boulder, Colo.: Lynne Rienner, 2007.

Huneeus, Carlos. "Technocrats and Politicians in an Authoritarian Regime: The 'ODEPLAN Boys' and the 'Gremialists' in Pinochet's Chile." *Journal of Latin American Studies* 32, no. 2. (May 2000): 461–501.

IBGE. *Censo demográfico 2000: Migração e deslocamento, resultados da amostra.* Rio de Janeiro: IBGE, 2003.

IBGE. *Estatísticas do século XX.* Found at http://seculoxx.ibge.gov.br/populacio nais-sociais-politicas-e-culturais.

IBGE. *Indicadores sociais: Uma análise da década de 1980.* Rio de Janeiro: IBGE, 1995.

IBGE. *Contas consolidadas da nação 1980–1993.* Rio de Janeiro: IBGE, 1994.

IBGE-ANDIMA. *Sistema financeiro: Uma análise a partir das Contas Nacionais, 1990–1995.* Rio de Janeiro: Andima, 1997.

IPEADATA. www.ipeadata.gov.br/.

Jornada, Maria Isabel H. da. "A Política Salarial: Uma visão panorâmica da Legislação." *Ensaios FEE* (Porto Alegre) 17, no. 2 (1989): 65–78.

Keck, Margaret E. *The Workers' Party and Democratization in Brazil.* New Haven: Yale University Press, 1995.

Klein, Herbert S. *A Concise History of Bolivia.* 2nd ed. Cambridge: Cambridge University Press, 2011.

Klein, Herbert S. "The Historical Background to the Rise of MAS, Bolivia, 1952–2005." In *Evo Morales and the Movimiento al Socialismo in Bolivia,* ed. Adrian Pearce, 27–61. London: Institute of the Americas, 2011.

Klein, Herbert S. *Parties and Political Change in Bolivia, 1880–1952.* Cambridge: Cambridge University Press, 1969.

Klein, Herbert S., and Francisco Vidal Luna. "Creando un estado de bienestar en un régimen autoritario: El caso de Brasil." *Revista Economía y Política* (Santiago de Chile) 1, no. 1 (April 2014): 31–78.

Klein, Herbert S., and Francisco Vidal Luna. "População e sociedade, 1960–2000." In *Historia do Brasil Nação: 1808–2010,* ed. Leila Schwarz, 5:31–73. São Paulo: Fundación Mapfre & Editora Objetivo, 2014.

Klein, Herbert S., and Francisco Vidal Luna. "Revisitando o tempo dos militares." In *A ditadura que mudou o Brasil: 50 anos do golpe de 1964,* ed. Daniel Aarão, Marcelo Ridenti, and Rodrigo Patto Sá Motta, 92–111. Rio de Janeiro: Zahar Editora, 2014.

Klein, Herbert S., and Francisco Vidal Luna. "Transformações econômicas no período militar (1964–1985)." In *A ditadura que mudou o Brasil: 50 anos do golpe de 1964,* ed. Daniel Aarão, Marcelo Ridenti, and Rodrigo Patto Sá Motta, 66–91. Rio de Janeiro: Zahar Editora, 2014.

Koch, Ana Maria. "Catolicismo ultramontano no ideário de Golbery do Couto e Silva." Paper presented at the XXVI Simpósio Nacional de História, ANPUH, 2011 (São Paulo). Found at www.snh2011.anpuh.org/site/anaiscomplementares.

Kruijt, Dirk. "Perú: Relaciones entre civiles y militares, 1950–1990." In *América Latina: Militares y sociedad,* ed. Dirk Kruijt and Edelberto Torres-Rivas, 2:29–142. San José: FLACSO, 1991.

Kunhavalik, José Pedro. "Os militares e o conceito de nacionalismo: Disputas retóricas na década de 1950 e início dos anos 1960." Ph.D. thesis, Universidade Federal de Santa Catarina, 2009.

Kusnir, Beatriz. "Da tesourinha ao sacerdote: Os dois últimos chefes da censura brasileira." In *O golpe de 1964 e O regime Militar: Novas perspectivas,* ed. João Roberto Martins Filho, 47–65. São Carlos: Editora da Universidade Federal de São Carlos, 2006.

Labrousse, Alain. *Una historia de los Tupamaros: De Sendic a Mujica.* Montevideo: Editorial Fin de Siglo, 2009.

Lago, Luiz Aranha Correa do. "A retomada do crescimento e as distorções do 'milagre': 1967–1973." In *A ordem do progresso,* ed. Marcelo de Paiva Abreu, 233–94. Rio de Janeiro: Campus, 1990.

Lamounier, Bolivar. "Authoritarian Brazil Revisited: The Impact of Elections on the Abertura." In *Democratizing Brazil: Problems of Transition and Consolidation,* ed. Alfred Stepan, 43–79. New York: Oxford University Press, 1989.

Lamounier, Bolivar. "Formação de um pensamento político autoritário na Primeira República: Uma interpretação." In *História geral da civilização brasileira,* ed. Sérgio Buarque de Holanda and Boris Fausto, tomo 3, vol. 1, pp. 343–74. São Paulo: Difusão Européia do Livro, 1977.

Langoni, Carlos G. *Distribuição de renda e desenvolvimento econômico no Brasil.* Rio de Janeiro: Expressão e Cultura, 1973.

Lara, Silva Hunold, and Joseli M. N. Mendonça. eds., *Direitos e justiças no Brasil: Ensaios de história social.* Campinas: Ed. Unicamp, 2006.

Leite, Celso Barroso. "Da lei Elói Chaves ao Sinpas." In *Um século de previdência social: Balanço e perspectivas no Brasil e no mundo,* ed. Celso Barroso Leite. Rio de Janeiro: Zahar, 1983.

Lessa, Alfonso. *La revolución imposible: Los tupamaros y el fracaso de la vía armada en el Uruguay del siglo XX.* Montevideo: Fin de Siglo, 2003.

Lessa, Carlos. *Quinze anos de política econômica.* Campinas: Cadernos Unicamp, no. 4, 1975.

Levy, Maria Stella Ferreira. "O papel da migração internacional na evolução da população brasileira (1872 a 1972)." *Revista de Saúde Pública* 8 (suppl.) (1974): 49–90.

Lie, John. *Han Unbound: The Political Economy of South Korea.* Stanford: Stanford University Press, 1998.

Linz, Juan. "The Future of an Authoritarian Situation or the Institutionalization of an Authoritarian Regime: The Case of Brazil." In *Authoritarian Brazil, Origin, Policies, and Future,* ed. Alfred Stepan, 233–54. New Haven: Yale University Press, 1973.

Loewenstein, Karl. *Brazil Under Vargas*. New York: Macmillan, 1942.

Lopes, Francisco L. *O choque heterodoxo: Combate à inflação e reforma monetária*. Rio de Janeiro: Campus, 1986.

Luna, Francisco Vidal, and Thomaz de Aquino Nogueira Neto. *Correção monetária e mercado de capitais: A experiência brasileira*. São Paulo: Bolsa de Valores de São Paulo, 1978.

Luna, Francisco Vidal, and Herbert S. Klein. *Brazil Since 1980*. Cambridge: Cambridge University Press, 2006.

Luna, Francisco Vidal, and Herbert S. Klein. *The Economic and Social History of Brazil Since 1899*. New York: Cambridge University Press, 2014.

Macedo, Roberto. "Plano trienal de desenvolvimento económico." In *Planejamento no Brasil*, ed. Betty Mindlin Lafer, 52–67. São Paulo: Perspectiva, 1970.

Maciel, David. *A argamassa da ordem: Da ditadura militar à Nova República (1974–1985)*. São Paulo: Xamã VM Editora, 2004.

Mainwaring, Scott. *The Catholic Church and Politics in Brazil, 1916–1985*. Stanford: Stanford University Press, 1986.

Mainwaring, Scott. "Grassroots Catholic Groups and Politics in Brazil, 1964–1985." Working Paper 98. South Bend, Ind.: Kellogg Institute, University of Notre Dame, August 1987.

Malan, Pedro. "Relações econômicas internacionais do Brasil, 1945–1964." In *História Geral da Civilização Brasileira*, ed. Boris Fausto, tomo 3, vol. 1, pp. 31–106. São Paulo: Difel, 1977.

Malan, Pedro, and Regis Bonelli. "Brazil 1950–1980: Three Decades of Growth-Oriented Economic Policies." Texto para Discussão no. 187. Rio de Janeiro: IPEA, 1990.

Malan, Pedro, and Regis Bonelli, "Crescimento econômico, industrialização e balanço de pagamentos: O Brasil dos anos 70 aos anos 80." Texto para Discussão no. 60. Rio de Janeiro: Ipea, 1983.

Malloy, James. *The Politics of Social Security in Brazil*. Pittsburgh: University of Pittsburgh Press, 1979.

Marchesi, Aldo, and Vania Markarian. *La dictadura cívico militar: Uruguay, 1973–1985*. Montevideo: Ediciones de la Banda Oriental, 2009.

Mares, Isabela, and Matthew E. Carnes. "Social Policy in Developing Countries." *Annual Review of Political Science*, no. 12 (2009): 93–113.

Markarian, Vania. *Left in Transformation: Uruguayan Exiles and the Latin American Human Rights Network, 1967–1984*. London: Routledge, 2013.

Martínez, Virginia. *Tiempos de dictadura 1973/1985*. Montevideo: Ediciones de la Banda Oriental, 2005.

Martins, Carlos Benedito. "O ensino superior brasileiro nos anos 90." *São Paulo em Perspectiva* 14, no. 1 (2000): 41–60.

Martins Filho, João Roberto, ed., *O golpe de 1964 e o regime militar: Novas perspectivas*. São Carlos: Editora da Universidade Federal de São Carlos, 2006.

Martone, Celso. "O plano de ação econômica." In *Planejamento no Brasil*, ed. Betty Mindlin Lafer, 29–50. São Paulo: Perspectiva, 1970.

Matos Mar, José, and José Manuel Mejía, *La reforma agraria en el Perú*. Lima: Instituto de Estudios Peruanos, 1980.

Maybury-Lewis, Biorn. *The Politics of the Possible: The Brazilian Rural Workers' Trade Union Movement, 1964–1985*. Philadelphia: Temple University Press, 1994.

McClintock, Cynthia. *Peasant Cooperatives and Political Change in Peru*. Princeton: Princeton University Press, 1981.

McClintock, Cynthia, and Abraham L. Lowenthal, eds. *The Peruvian Experiment Reconsidered*. Princeton: Princeton University Press, 1983.

McSherry, J. Patrice. *Predatory States: Operation Condor and Covert War in Latin America*. Lanham, Md.: Rowman & Littlefield, 2005.

Medeiros, Marcelo, Tatiana Britto, and Fábio Soares, "Programas focalizados de transferência de renda no Brasil: Contribuições para o debate. Texto para Discussão, no. 1283. Brasília: IPEA, 2007.

Medeiros, Marcelo, Debora Diniz, and Flávia Squinca. "Cash Benefits to Disabled Persons in Brazil: An Analysis of BPC–Continuous Cash Benefit Programme." Texto para Discussão, no. 1179. Brasília: IPEA, 2006.

Melo, Fernando Homem de. "Agricultura brasileira: Incerteza e disponibilidade tecnológica." Thesis of Livre Docência, Universidade de São Paulo, 1978.

Melo, Fernando Homem de. "Padrões de instabilidade entre culturas da agricultura brasileira." *PPE* 8, no. 3 (December 1979): 819–44.

Merrick, Thomas, and Douglas Graham, *Population and Economic Development in Brazil, 1800 to the Present*. Baltimore: Johns Hopkins University Press, 1979.

Mesa-Lago, Carmelo. *Modelos de seguridad social en América Latina: Estudio comparativo*. Buenos Aires: Ediciones Siap-Planteos, 1977.

Mesa-Lago, Carmelo. *Reassembling Social Security: A Survey of Pensions and Health Care Reforms in Latin America*. Oxford: Oxford University Press, 2007.

Miceli, Sérgio. *Intelectuais e classe dirigente no Brasil (1920–1945)*. São Paulo: Difel, 1979.

Ministério da Agricultura. www.agricultura.gov.br/.

Morero, Sergio. *La noche de los bastones largos*. Buenos Aires: Grupo Editor Latinamericano, 2002.

Morris, Felipe, M. Dorfman, J. P. Ortiz, and M. C. Franco. *Latin America's Banking Systems in the 1980s*. World Bank Discussion Papers. Washington: World Bank, 1990.

Motta, Rodrigo Patto Sá. *As universidades e o regime militar*. Rio de Janeiro: Zahar, 2014.

Motta, Rodrigo Patto Sá. *Em guarda contra o "perigo vermelho": O anticomunismo no Brasil, 1917–1964*. São Paulo: Editora Perspectiva/Fapesp, 2002.

Mueller, Charles, and George Martine. "Modernização agropecuária, emprego agrícola e êxodo rural no Brasil—a década de 1980." *Revista de Economia Política* 17, no. 3 (July/September 1997): 85–104.

Mundim, Luiz Felipe Cezar. "Juarez Távora e Golbery do Couto e Silva: Escola Superior de Guerra e a organização do Estado brasileiro (1930–1960)." M.A. thesis, Universidade Federal de Goiás, 2007.

Muñoz, Heraldo. "Las relaciones exteriores del gobierno militar chileno." *Revista Mexicana de Sociología* 44, no. 2 (April–June 1982): 577–97.

Murilo de Carvalho, José. *Forças armadas e política no Brasil*. Rio de Janeiro: Zahar, 2005.

Naftali, Timothy, ed., *The Presidential Recordings of John F. Kennedy*. Vol 1: *July 30–August 1962*. New York: W. W. Norton, 2001.

Navarro, Marcos, and Vicente Palmero. *La dictadura militar, 1976–1983: Del golpe de estado a la restauración democrática*. Colleción Historia Argentina, 9. Buenos Aires: Paidos, 2003.

Naves, Laura Maria. "O papel da Aerp na construção da identidade nacional: Análise das propagandas políticas durante o Governo Médici." Anais VIII Conferência Brasileira de Mídia 2012 (Brasília). Found at www.unicentro.br/redemc/2012/sumario.asp.

Navia, Patricio. "Participación electoral en Chile, 1988–2001." *Revista de Ciencia Política* (Santiago de Chile) 24, no. 1 (2004): 81–103.

Nery, Pedro Fernando. *O programa assistencial mais caro do Brasil: Sobre o benefício de prestação continuada e uma comparação com o bolsa família*. Boletim do Legislativo no. 16. Brasília: Senado Federal, 2014.

Neto, Lira. *Getúlio 1882–1930: Dos anos de formação à conquista do poder*. São Paulo: Cia. das Letras, 2012.

Neto, Lira. *Getúlio 1930–1945: Do governo provisório à ditatura do Estado Novo*. São Paulo, Cia. das Letras, 2013.

Neto, Lira. *Getúlio 1945–1954: Da volta pela consagração popular ao suicídio*. São Paulo, Cia. das Letras, 2014.

Neto, Lira. *Castello: A marcha para a ditadura*. São Paulo, Contexto, 2004.

Noronha, Eduardo. "A explosão das greves na década de 80." In *O sindicalismo brasileiro nos anos 80*, ed. Armando Boito, Rio de Janeiro: Paz e Terra, 1991.

North, Liisa L. "Ideological Orientations of Peru's Military Rulers." In *The Peruvian Experiment Reconsidered*, ed. Cynthia McClintock and Abraham L. Lowenthal, 245–74. Princeton: Princeton University Press, 1983.

Novaes, Regina Reyes. "Continuidades e rupturas no sindicalismo rural." In *O sindicalismo brasileiro nos anos 80*, ed. Armando Boito, 171–96. Rio de Janeiro: Paz e Terra, 1991.

O'Donnell, Guillermo. "Reflections on the Patterns of Change in the Bureaucratic-Authoritarian State." *Latin American Research Review*, 13, no. 1 (1978): 3–38.

Oh, John Kie-chiang. *Korean Politics: The Quest for Democratization and Economic Development*. Ithaca: Cornell University Press, 1999.

Oliveira, Eliézer Rizzo de. *As Forças Armadas: Política e ideologia no Brasil (1964–1969)*. 2nd ed. Petrópolis, R.J.: Vozes, 1978.

Oliveira, Eliézer Rizzo de. *De Geisel a Collor: Forças Armadas, transição e democracia*. Campinas: Papirus, 1994.

Oliveira, Francisco Eduardo Barreto de, Kaizô Iwakami Beltrão, and Antonio Carlos de Albuquerque David. "Dívida da União com a previdência social: Uma perspectiva histórica." Texto para Discussão, no. 638. Rio de Janeiro: Ipea, 1999.

Oliveira, Francisco Eduardo Barreto de, Kaizô Iwakami Beltrão, and Mônica Guerra Ferreira. "Reforma da previdência." Texto para Discussão, no. 508. Rio de Janeiro: IPEA, 1997.

Oliveira, Francisco E. Barreto de, Maria Tereza de Marsillac Pasinato, and Fernanda Paes Leme Peyneau. "Evolução recente do sistema de previdência complementar no Brasil e mercado potencial." Found at www.abep.nepo.unicamp. br/docs/anais/pdf/2000/Todos/Evolu%C3%A7%C3%A3o%20Recente%20 do%20Sistema%20de%20Previd%C3%AAncia%20Complementar.pdf.

Oliveira, Jaime A., and Sonia Maria Fleury Teixeira. *(Im)previdência Social: 60 anos de história da previdência no Brasil.* Petrópolis: Associação Brasileira de Pós-Graduação em Saúde Coletiva, 1986.

Oliveira, Marly Job de. "A política geral do regime militar para construção de suas políticas econômicas." Ph.D. thesis, FFLCH-USP, São Paulo, 2007.

Orenstein, Luiz, and Antonio Claudio Sochaczewski. "Democracia com desenvolvimento: 1956–1961." In *A ordem do progresso,* ed. Marcelo de Paiva Abreu, 171–95. Rio de Janeiro: Campus, 1990.

Ortiz de Zárate, Verónica Valdivia. "Estatismo y neoliberalismo: Un contrapunto militar, Chile 1973–1979." *Historia* (Santiago) 34 (2001): 167–226.

Pacheco, Carlos Américo, et al. "Análise demográfica do Estado de São Paulo." In *Dinâmica demográfica regional e as novas questões populacionais no Brasil,* ed. Carlos Américo Pacheco and Neide Patarra. Campinas: Instituto de Economia UNICAMP, 2000.

Pacheco, Carlos Américo, and Neide Patarra, eds. *Dinâmica demográfica regional e as novas questões populacionais no Brasil.* Campinas: Instituto de Economia, UNICAMP, 2000.

Paim, Jairnilson, Claudia Travassos, Celia Almeida, Ligia Bahia, and James Macinko. "The Brazilian Health System: History, Advances, and Challenges." *The Lancet* 377, no. 9779 (2011): 1778–97.

Paiva, Ruy Muller. "Reflexões sobre as tendências da produção, da produtividade e dos preços do setor agrícola no Brasil." In *Agricultura subdesenvolvida,* ed. F. Sá. Petrópolis: Vozes, 1968.

Paiva, Vera. "Sexuality, Condom Use, and Gender Norms Among Brazilian Teenagers." *Reproductive Health Matters* 1, no. 2 (November 1993), 98–109.

Plastino, C. A., and R. Bouzas, eds. *A América Latina e a crise internacional.* Rio de Janeiro: Graal, 1988.

Pastore, Affonso Celso. "A resposta da produção agrícola aos preços no Brasil." Ph.D. thesis, Universidad de São Paulo, 1969.

Pastore, José, Guilherme L. Silva Dias, and Manoel C. Castro. "Condicionantes da produtividade da pesquisa agrícola no Brasil." *Estudos Econômicos* 6, no. 3 (1976): 147–81.

Pastore, José. *Inequality and Social Mobility in Brazil.* Madison: University of Wisconsin Press, 1982.

Patara, Neide, Rosana Baeninger, and José Marcos Pinto da Cunha. "Dinâmica demográfica recente e a configuração de novas questões populacionais." In *Dinâmica demográfica regional e as novas questões populacionais no Brasil,* ed. Carlos Américo Pacheco and Neide Patarra, 1–44. Campinas: Instituto de Economia, UNICAMP, 2000.

Pease Garcia, Henry. *El ocaso del poder oligárquico, lucha política en la escena oficinal 1968–1975.* Lima: DESCO, 1977.

Philip, George D. E. *The Rise and Fall of the Peruvian Military Radicals, 1968–1976.* London: Athlone, 1978.

Quine, Maria Sophia. *Italy's Social Revolution: Charity and Welfare from Liberalism to Fascism.* New York: Palgrave, 2002.

Ramos, Lauro R. A., and José Guilherme Almeida Reis. "Distribuição da renda: Aspectos teóricos e o debate no Brasil." In *Distribuição de renda no Brasil,* ed. José Márcio Camargo and Fabio Giambiagi, 21–45. Rio de Janeiro: Paz e Terra, 2000.

Reid, Michael. *Forgotten Continent: The Battle for Latin America's Soul.* New Haven: Yale University Press, 2007.

Reis, Daniel Aarão. *Ditadura e democracia no Brasil: Do golpe de 1964 á Constituição de 1988.* Rio de Janeiro: Zahar, 2014.

Resende, André Lara. "Estabilização e reforma." In *A nova economia brasileira,* ed. Mario Henrique Simonsen and Roberto Campos. Rio de Janeiro: José Olympio, 1979.

Rocha, Sonia. *Transferências de renda no Brasil: O fim da pobreza?* São Paulo: Campus, 2013.

Rodriguez Beruff, Jorge. *Los militares y el poder: Un ensayo sobre la doctrina militar en el Perú 1948–1968.* Caracas: Mosca Azul Editores, 1993.

Romero, Luis Alberto. *A History of Argentina in the Twentieth Century.* University Park: Pennsylvania State University Press, 2011.

Rouquié, Alain. *The Military and the State in Latin America.* Berkeley: University of California Press, 1982.

Saboia, João. "Política Salarial e distribuição de renda: 25 anos de desencontros," in José Márcio Camargo and Fábio Giambiagi, eds, *Distribuição de renda no Brasil.* Rio de Janeiro: Paz e Terra, 2000.

Saboia, João. "Salário e produtividade na indústria brasileira: Os efeitos da política salarial no longo prazo." *Pesquisa e Planejamento Econômico* 20, no. 3 (December 1990): 581–600.

Sadee, Eder. *Quando novos personagens entraram em cena: Experiências e lutas dos trabalhadores da Grande São Paulo, 1970–1980.* Rio de Janeiro: Paz e Terra, 1988.

Sales, Rodrigues. *A luta armada contra a ditadura militar: A esquerda brasileira e a influência da revolução cubana.* São Paulo: Editora Fundacao Perseu Abramo, 2007.

Santos, Rogerio Dultra dos. "Francisco Campos e os fundamentos do constitucionalismo antiliberal no Brasil." *DADOS, Revista de Ciências Sociais* 50, no. 2 (2007): 281–323.

Sayad, João, and Francisco Vidal Luna. *Política anti-inflacionária e o Plano Cruzado.* São Paulo: Instituto Latino Americano–ILAM, 1987.

Schmitter, Philip. "The 'Portugalization' of Brazil?" In *Authoritarian Brazil: Origin, Policies, and Future,* ed. Alfred Stepan, 170–232. New Haven: Yale University Press, 1973.

Schor, Néia, et al., "Mulher e anticoncepção: Conhecimento e uso de métodos anticoncepcionais." *Cadernos de Saúde Pública* 16, no. 2 (April–June 2000): 377–84.

Schoultz, Lars. "U.S. Foreign Policy and Human Rights Violations in Latin America: A Comparative Analysis of Foreign Aid Distributions." *Comparative Politics* 13, no. 2 (January 1981): 149–70.

Schoultz, Lars. *Beneath the United States: A History of U.S. Policy Toward Latin America.* Cambridge, Mass.: Harvard University Press, 1998.

Schwartzman, Simon. *A Space for Science: The Development of the Scientific Community in Brazil.* University Park: Pennsylvania State University Press, 1991.

Schwartzman, Simon, Helena M. B. Bomeny, and Vanda M. R. Costa. *Tempos de Capanema.* São Paulo: Editora da Universidade de São Paulo e Ed. Paz e Terra, 1984.

Segura-Ubiergo, Alex. *The Political Economy of the Welfare State in Latin America: Globalization, Democracy, and Development.* Cambridge: Cambridge University Press, 2007.

Serra, José. "Ciclos e mudanças estruturais na economia brasileira do pós-guerra." In *Desenvolvimento capitalista no Brasil: Ensaios sobre a Crise,* ed. Luiz Gonzaga de Mello Belluzzo and Renata Coutinho. São Paulo: Brasiliense, 1981.

Serra, José. *Cinquenta anos esta noite: o golpe, a ditadura e o exílio.* Rio de Janeiro: EditoraRecord, 2014.

Silva, Sérgio *A expansão cafeeira e origem da indústria no Brasil.* São Paulo: Alfa Omega, 1976.

Simonsen, Mario Henrique. "Inflação brasileira: Lições e perspectivas." *Revista Brasileira de Economia* 5, no. 4 (1985): 15–31.

Simonsen, Mario Henrique. *Inflação: Gradualismo x tratamento de choque.* Rio de Janeiro: Apec, 1970.

Simonsen, Roberto. *A evolução industrial do Brasil e outros estudos.* São Paulo: Editora Nacional/Edusp, 1973.

Singer, Paul. "O processo econômico." In *História do Brasil nação: 1808–2010,* 6:183–231. Rio de Janeiro: Objetiva, 2014.

Skidmore, Thomas E. *Politics in Brazil, 1930–1964: An Experiment in Democracy.* New York: Oxford University Press, 1967.

Skidmore, Thomas E. *The Politics of Military Rule in Brazil, 1964–85.* New York: Oxford University Press, 1988.

Smith, Gaddis. *The Last Years of the Monroe Doctrine, 1945–1993.* New York: Macmillan, 1995.

Smith, Peter H. *Talons of the Eagle: Latin America, the United States, and the World.* 4th ed. New York: Oxford University Press, 2012.

Soares, Gláucio Ary Dillon. "A censura durante o regime autoritário." *Revista Brasileira de Ciências Sociais* 4, no. 10 (1989): 21–43.

Sola, Lourdes. "O golpe de 37 e o Estado Novo." In *Brasil em perspectiva,* ed. Carlos Guilherme Mota, 257–84. São Paulo: Difusão Européia do Livro, 1969.

Song, Byung-Nak. *The Rise of the Korean Economy.* 2nd ed. Hong Kong: Oxford University Press, 1997.

Spalding, Rose J. "Welfare Policymaking: Theoretical Implications of a Mexican Case Study." *Comparative Politics* 12, no. 4 (July, 1980): 419–38.

Stepan, Alfred C. *The Military in Politics: Changing Patterns in Brazil.* Princeton: Princeton University Press, 1971.

Stepan, Alfred. *Rethinking Military Politics: Brazil and the Southern Cone.* Princeton: Princeton University Press, 1988.

Stepan, Alfred C., ed. *Democratizing Brazil: Problems of Transition and Consolidation.* New York: Oxford University Press, 1989.

Suzigan, Wilson. *Indústria brasileira: Origem e desenvolvimento.* São Paulo: Brasiliense, 1986.

Svartman, Eduardo Munhoz. "Brazil–United States Military Relations During the Cold War: Political Dynamic and Arms Transfers." *Brazilian Political Science Review* 5, no. 2 (2012): 75–93.

Svartman, Eduardo Munhoz. "Guardiões da nação: Formação profissional, experiências compartilhadas e engajamento político dos generais de 1964." Ph.D. diss., Universidade Federal do Rio Grande do Sul, 2006.

Tavares, Maria da Conceição. "Auge e declínio do processo de substituição." In *Da substituição de importações ao capitalismo financeiro,* ed. Maria da Conceição Tavares. Rio de Janeiro: Zahar, 1972.

Tavares, Maria da Conceição. "Sistema financeiro e o ciclo de expansão recente." In *Desenvolvimento capitalista no Brasil: Ensaios sobre a crise,* ed. Luiz Gonzaga de Mello Belluzzo and Renata Coutinho. São Paulo: Brasiliense, 1981.

Tavares, Maria da Conceição, and José Serra. "Mais além da estagnação." In *Da substituição de importações ao capitalismo financeiro,* ed. Maria da Conceição Tavares. Rio de Janeiro: Zahar, 1972.

Taylor, Lance, Edmar L. Bacha, Eliana A. Cardoso, and Frank J. Lysy. *Models of Growth and Distribution for Brazil.* New York: Oxford University Press, 1980.

Tolipan, Ricardo, and Arthur Carlos Tinelli, eds. *A controvérsia sobre distribuição de renda e desenvolvimento.* Rio de Janeiro: Zahar, 1975.

Trindade, Helio Henrique C. "El fascismo brasileño en la década del 30: Orígenes históricos y base social del integralismo." *Desarrollo Económico* 12, no. 48 (January–March 1973): 687–723.

Valenzuela, Arturo. *The Breakdown of Democratic Regimes: Chile.* Baltimore: Johns Hopkins University Press, 1978.

Valenzuela, Julio Samuel, and Arturo Valenzuela, eds. *Military Rule in Chile: Dictatorship and Oppositions.* Baltimore: Johns Hopkins University Press, 1986.

Varas, Augusto and Felipe Agüero. *El proyecto político militar.* Santiago: FLACSO, 1984.

Vargas, Getúlio. *As diretrizes da nova política do Brasil.* Rio de Janeiro: José Olympio Editora, 1943.

Verbitsky, Horacio. *La mano izquierda de Dios: La última dictadura (1976–1983).* Vol. 4 of *Historia política de la Iglesia Católica.* Buenos Aires: Editora Sudamericana, 2010.

Vecchio, Angelo Del. "A era Delfim: Planejamento estratégico e regime militar." M.A. thesis, FFLCH-USP, São Paulo, 1992.

Versiani, Flávio, and José Roberto Mendonça de Barros, eds. *Formação econômica do Brasil: A experiência de industrialização.* São Paulo: Anpec/Saraiva, 1976.

Vianna, Salvador Teixeira Werneck. "Desenvolvimento econômico e reformas institucionais no Brasil: Considerações sobre a construção interrompida." Ph.D. thesis, Instituto de Economia, UFRJ, 2007.

Villela, Annibal Villanova, and Wilson Suzigan. *Política do governo e crescimento da economia brasileira, 1889–1945.* Rio de Janeiro: Ipea, 1973.

Wahrlich, Beatriz M. de Souza. *Reforma administrativa da era de Vargas.* Rio de Janeiro: Fundação Getúlio Vargas, 1983.

Weffort, Francisco C. "Participação e conflito industrial: Contagem e Osasco, 1968." Caderno 5. São Paulo: Centro Brasileiro de Análise e Planejamento, 1972.

Weffort, Francisco. *O populismo na política brasileira.* Rio de Janeiro: Paz e Terra, 1980.

Weffort, Francisco. "Why Democracy?" In *Democratizing Brazil: Problems of Transition and Consolidation,* ed. Alfred Stepan, 327–50. New York: Oxford University Press, 1989.

Weinstein, Barbara. *For Social Peace in Brazil: Industrialists and the Remaking of the Working Class in São Paulo, 1920–1964.* Chapel Hill: University of North Carolina Press, 1996.

Weinstein, Barbara. "The Industrialists, the State, and the Issues of Worker Training and Social Services in Brazil, 1930–50." *Hispanic American Historical Review* 70, no. 3 (August 1990): 379–404.

Werneck, Rogério. *Empresas estatais e política macroeconomica.* Rio de Janeiro: Campus, 1987.

Werneck, Rogério. "Poupança estatal, dívida externa e crise financeira do setor público." *Pesquisa e Planejamento Econômico* 16, no. 3 (December 1986): 551–74.

Williams, Margaret Todaro. "Integralism and the Brazilian Catholic Church." *Hispanic American Historical Review* 54, no. 3 (August 1974): 431–52.

Wintrobe, Ronald. *The Political Economy of Dictatorship.* New York: Cambridge University Press, 1998.

World Bank. *Averting the Old Age Crisis: Policies to Protect the Old and Promote Growth.* Oxford: Oxford University Press, 1994.

Yaffe, Jaime. "Proceso económico y politica economica durante la dictadura (1973–1984)." In *La dictadura cívico militar: Uruguay, 1973–1985,* ed. Carlos Demasi et al., 117–78. Montevideo: Ediciones de la Banda Oriental, 2009.

Zamagni, Vera, ed. *Povertà e innovazioni istituzionali in Italia.* Bologna: Il mulino, 2000.

Index